THE ART AND SCIENCE OF
FENCING

NICK EVANGELISTA

MASTERS PRESS

NTC/Contemporary Publishing Group

Library of Congress Cataloging-in-Publication Data

Evangelista, Nick.
    The art and science of fencing / by Nick Evangelista.
       p.   cm.
    Includes bibliographical references.
    ISBN 1-57028-075-4
    1. Fencing.   2. Fencing—History.   I. Title.
GV1147.E83
796.8'6—dc20   96-2806
                                  CIP

Cover design by Michael Welch
Cover photograph copyright © Gary Morrison/Tony Stone Images
All interior photographs provided by Nick Evangelista, unless noted otherwise
Edited by Kathleen Prata
Proofread by Pat Brady and Michele Desceglie

Published by Masters Press
A division of NTC/Contemporary Publishing Group, Inc.
4255 West Touhy Avenue, Lincolnwood (Chicago), Illinois 60646-1975 U.S.A.
Copyright © 1996 by Nick Evangelista
Printed in the United States of America
International Standard Book Number: 1-57028-075-4

99 00 01 02 03 04 EB 20 19 18 17 16 15 14 13 12 11 10 9 8 7 6 5 4 3

TABLE OF CONTENTS

Foreword 3
Introduction 7
A Note for the Beginner 10
For the Woman Fencer 11

PART I: HISTORIES 13
Fencing: A Social History 14
Ralph Faulkner: The Old Man and the Sword 23
My Life in Fencing 31

PART II: A FENCING PHILOSOPHY 39
My Fencing Philosophy 40

PART III: THE BEGINNING FENCER 43
The Language of Fencing 44
Why Fencing? 45
Getting Started 49
The First Fencing Lesson 60
Fencing Thought 63
Learning the Weapons of Fencing — Progressively 65
Approaching Your First Bout 67
Conventions: Behavior on the Fencing Strip 70
Some Particulars of Sport Fencing 73
Your First Tournament 76

PART IV: THE FOIL 79
The Foil 81
The Body of the French Foil 84
The Set of the Blade 86
Holding the French Foil 87
On Guard 89
The Lines of the Body 94
Initial Footwork: Advancing and Retreating 98
The Engagement 100
Absence of Blade 102
Point in Line 103
The Lunge 104
The Recovery 110
The Fleche 111
The Running Attack 113
The Simple Attack 114

Preparations 117
Invitations 118
The Parry 119
The Riposte 128
Composed Attacks 131
Feints 135
The Counterattack 136
Continued Attacks 138
The Secondary Intent Attack 140
Attacks on the Blade 144
Taking the Blade 145
Moving in the Low Line 147
Foil Tactics 150
Some Final Thoughts on Strategy 152

PART V: BEYOND METHOD: CONCEPTS 157
Classical Form: Fencing's Yardstick 158
Fencing with the Fingers 160
Timing 161
Distance 163
Speed 165
Strength 166
Balance 168
Honor 170

PART VI: THE ÉPÉE 173
The Épée 174
The Nature of Épée Fencing 175
The French Épée 177
The Épée on Guard 178
General Principles of Épée Fencing 180
Épée Offense 181
Épée Defense 184
The Épée Bout 187
Reminders and Final Thoughts 188

PART VII: THE SABRE 191
The Sabre 193
The Nature of Sabre Fencing 195
The Conventions of Sabre Fencing 196
The Body of the Sabre 198
The Sabre Target Area 199
Sabre Lines 200
Holding the Sabre 202
The Sabre On Guard Position 203
Footwork and Distance in Sabre 205
Cut and Thrust: Sabre Offense 206
The Cut 207

Point Attacks 210
The Sabre Defense 212
The Riposte 215
Composed Attacks 217
Sabre Counterattacks 218
The Sabre Bout 219
Some Final Thoughts on the Sabre 220

PART VIII: ASSORTED ASPECTS OF FENCING 223
Conventional Exercises 224
The Left-handed Fencer 227
Fencing for Kids 230
Warming up 232
Caring for Your Fencing Equipment 234

PART IX: ELECTRICAL FENCING 237
Some Thoughts on Electrical Fencing 238
Pitfalls of Electrical Fencing 241

PART X: FENCING LIVES 243
The Man Who Made Sport of Fencing 244
The Greatest Swordsman in the World 246
Swordswoman, Unexcelled 249
America's Fencing Master 253
The French Connection 255
King of the Swashbucklers 257
Falcon with a Sword 258
A.K.A. Speedy 260
Maestro and Scholar 262
The Modern Musketeer 265

PART XI: THE SECRET OF SUCCESS 267
The Fire 268
A Final Thought 269

APPENDIX I: FENCING TERMS 271
Assorted Fencing Terms 272
Pronunciations 273

APPENDIX II: RESOURCES 275
The United States Fencing Association 276
Fencing Equipment Supply Companies 277
The Swashbuckler Film: Fencing in the Movies 278
Literature of the Sword 280
Books about Fencing: A Selected Reading List 282

APPENDIX III: THEATRICAL FENCING 285
Theatrical Fencing 286
About the Author 288

DEDICATION

This one's for my wife, Anita, who has never let me get bogged down in the silly, fantasy aspects of fencing for any extended periods of time.

CREDITS:

Edited by Kathleen Prata

Cover designed by Suzanne Lincoln

Proofread by Pat Brady and Michele Disceglie

All photos provided by Nick Evangelista, unless noted otherwise

ACKNOWLEDGMENTS

First and foremost, thanks beyond thanks to my late fencing master Ralph Faulkner, without whom I would have never had a chance to develop as a fencer or a teacher. To him I owe my life's path.

As always, thanks and much love, to former women's fencing champion Polly Craus August, for her support of my endeavors.

Thanks to Sewell Shurtz, longtime student of Maestro Ralph Faulkner, and fencing great of the 1950s, for his involvement in this book.

Thanks to Tony De Longis for over 20 years of friendship.

Thanks again to Dr. William Gaugler, of San Jose State University, from whom I always learn new things about fencing. Our discussions are always stimulating.

Also, thanks to Maestro George Ganchev, former professional world fencing champion, who brought unique moments to my fencing experience.

Thanks to all the fencing masters who have come before — from Achille Marozzo to Charles Besnard to Domenico Angelo to Alfred Hutton to Aldo Nadi to Giorgio Santelli to Aladar Kogler — for paving the way, with sweat and blood, for me to write this book. There would not be fencing without you.

SPECIAL THANKS

I'd like to extend a special thanks to all my students, who, over the years, have acted as guinea pigs for my teaching theories and methods.

Those who had faith in my teaching abilities include: Clark Akers, Anita Anderson, Dave Beckham, Michael Bellocchio, Doug Blair, Jason Brown, Nora Cedar, John Coven, Lilly Cross, Dave Crossley, Bobby di Cicco, Doug Blair, Robin Douglas, John Driscoll, Jamie Evangelista, Justin Evangelista, James Garrett, Tom Greene, Allen Hampton, Bob Hays, Edie Ishii, Ken Jacobs, Arnold Jacques, Quinn Kellner, Richard Kim, Kathleen King, Wortham Krimmer, Dan Lesovsky, Frank Martin, Spencer Martin, Virginia Mekkelson, Phil Merlino, Melinda McRae, Peter Muhich, Hardy Muller, Dan Neikes, Bob O'Sullivan, Isabelle Pafford, Kellee Patterson, Sergio Parra, Josie Rachford, Tom Ryan, John Sanderford, Andy Scamman, John Shattuck, Bill Shaw, Patrick Shaw, Nanne

Snow, Melodee Spevack, Andy Smith, Jessica Smith, Sean Smith, Richard Thomas, Tod Thorn, Jim Troyer, Fernando Vazquez, Rik Vig, Jonathan Wallis, Steve White, and Glenn Young .... to name a few.

Without you, there would be no Evangelista School of Fencing.

THE ART AND SCIENCE OF FENCING

"The entire secret of arms consists of only two things: to give, and not to receive."
From Moliere's *Le Bourgeois Gentilhomme (1671)*

"It is the fencing master's strict moral duty towards his artistic ancestors to see to it that centuries-old traditions are respected, honored, and enforced."
Aldo Nadi *(1899-1965)*

FOREWORD

When Nick Evangelista asked me to write the foreword for his new book on fencing, I naturally wanted to rise to the honor. I confess my admiration for style and the spontaneous dramatic gesture. I am an actor, action sequence coordinator and movement teacher. I have labored throughout my career to cultivate a variety of skills to tell my character's story more effectively and dynamically. I'm often called upon to train top actors with a variety of bladed weapons and have developed my own unique style with the bullwhip while achieving proficiency and accuracy in its use.

Nick and I go back a long way. We both had the enormous good fortune to study with one of the truly great teachers of the sword, master Ralph Faulkner, known affectionately to his students as "The Boss." Nick was his assistant, and I was an enthusiastic student and admirer of them both for more than a dozen years. Although separated by distance and time, I am enormously proud to call Nick Evangelista my friend. The stunning proficiency and vision of his first book, *The Encyclopedia of the Sword*, made me eager to contribute to his second effort.

"Just write what fencing means to you," he said.

That shouldn't be too hard, I thought. And then I thought some more. How do you, with a few choice phrases, sum up something that has literally changed your life?

Fencing is intensely personal. It is tough, one-on-one competition and not just with your opponent of the moment. The fiercest battles are the ones you fight within yourself. From that standpoint fencing is a perfect metaphor for life. I'll try to explain.

I was not a physically gifted kid. I was extremely awkward and completely ineffective in sports, especially the team variety. I couldn't seem to find anything I was good at and desperately wanted to effect a change. My senior year in high school I tried lifting weights and was amazed to discover how quickly my body responded to the effort. I even made the wrestling team. I became stronger now but still lacked any awareness of how to make all the parts work as a whole. Around this time I suffered a serious leg injury. The doctors told me that my leg would never be completely sound again and that I would always walk with a limp. I resented the limitations they thought I should accept and went looking for a new sport that would allow me to stay active, despite my injury. I had been performing since high school and fencing seemed just the sort of stylish skill an actor should cultivate. How hard could it be? Ah, the hubris of youth.

Fencing is both the hardest and the easiest thing I've ever attempted. It offers never-ending challenges while rewarding me with a constant companion and ally that manifests itself daily in almost imperceptible ways.

Unlike many things in life, the body repays sustained effort with visible improvements in both appearance and performance. Fencing drills hone and refine the entire body. Big muscles become strong, small muscles become fast and subtle. The whole engine, including the heart, works better and more efficiently. Even the brain gets with the program as confidence grows. Prepare the body and your mind has the tools to better help you accomplish your goals.

Master Faulkner had a four step analysis for fencing an opponent:

1) What is he doing?

2) How is he doing it?

3) What can I do about it?

4) Can I do it?

I've found his formula offers an effective plan of action both on the fencing strip and when facing the many challenges life likes to throw in my path.

Fencing helps to forge a link between the physical and mental powers we all desire. Physical prowess increases as the individual parts of the body combine seamlessly to accomplish each specific task. Strength flows instantly and gracefully from a growing center of balance. Hand/eye coordination sharpens as if by magic.

But aren't all these benefits to be expected? After all, you've worked hard, you deserve success. But something always seems to get in the way. You're facing an opponent on the fencing strip and you know you can beat him, but somehow you always short circuit and lose. Why?

In life and on the fencing piste you are ultimately alone. Alone with your inability to live up to your own expectations. Alone with the doubts you have come to believe reflect unique, unalterable limitation. That's a lot of distractions when demanding the flawless delivery and instantaneous execution of your master plan of the moment. Fencing helps you to shed those confusions and transform terrors into triumphs.

Fencing teaches you to focus on the immediacy of each moment. Instead of confusing yourself with a lot of jumbled thoughts that set the stage for failure, you develop the ability to relax. Alert but calm. At once aware of the big picture and the smallest detail. Your body will be there when you need it. That's what the physical training has been about. Fencing develops the ability to leave yourself alone and just get the job done. And when you find yourself accomplishing what you never thought possible, you realize that, to a great extent, the limitations we accept in ourselves are mostly of our own making.

I admit it. I have a romantic idealism about those who embrace the art of swordplay and make it their lives. I think people who fence want to hang onto admirable traditions like personal honor and individual responsibility. They try, in their own small way, to leave things a little better than they find them. They believe individual actions do make a difference, even small ones. It begins with a personal determination to always do your best. I can live with that.

En garde!
Anthony De Longis

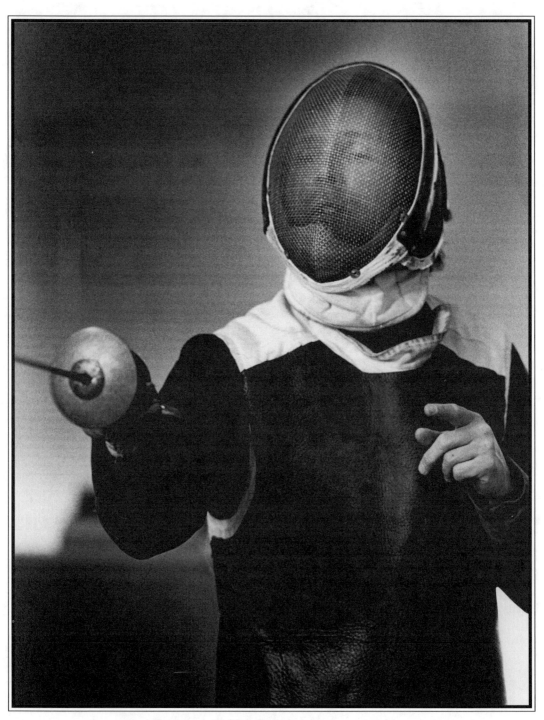

Fencing master Nick Evanglista (photo by Bob McEowen)

INTRODUCTION

This is a book about fencing.

Fencing is the art of sword fighting. It has a proud tradition that stretches back hundreds of years. Kings and commoners both have engaged in fencing, which has been practiced as both a skill for killing and a sport. It survived a societally imposed banishment that has sent lesser activities into anachronistic oblivion. The sword has been termed the "Queen of Weapons," and has been viewed as a symbol of justice, nobility and male sexuality. Fencing has been called a "noble art" and a "science." It has also been likened, most favorably to chess. It is into this world of foils, épées, and sabres that we now plunge.

Over the years, I have been lucky to have been associated with a number of teachers and students of fencing who treat this unique activity with the respect and attention it deserves. But there are many others I've known who have not. Fencing, for them, is just an avenue for personal gain, a set of win/loss records, or a way of venting seriously overblown egos. This is unfortunate, because, when approached honestly, fencing has so much to offer, which will be pointed out in the following pages.

There are a number of good volumes on fencing which have been published over centuries. Domenico Angelo's *The School of Fencing* (1763) speaks of fencing truths we still recognize in the 20th century. During the 19th century there was Alfred Hutton's *The Swordsman* (1892) and Louis Rondelle's *Foil and Sabre* (1892). In modern times, we have Louis and Regis Senac's *The Art of Fencing* (1904), Leon Bertrand's *Cut and Thrust* (1927), Julio Castello's *Theory of Fencing* (1931), and Luigi Barbasetti's *The Art of Foil* (1932). More recently, there is Roger Crosnier's *Know the Game —Fencing* (1952), Julius Alpar's *Sword and Masque* (1967) and Dr. William Gaugler's precise study of the Italian school of fencing, *Fencing Everyone* (1987). Aldo Nadi's excellent *On Fencing*, first published in 1943, made such an impression on the fencing community over the years that it was reissued in 1994 for a whole new generation of fencers.

In point of fact, I wrote the volume you now hold in your hands to be different from all other books on fencing. There was no point in churning out something that would merely restate concepts and approaches in the same old way. Why create a carbon copy of other teachers' views? The best books on fencing don't need to be rehashed. The bad ones shouldn't be.

My idea was to go beyond mere definitions of technique and draw the human element into the equation. It is human beings, after all, who carry out the manipulation of the foils, epees and sabres. We aren't machines on the fencing strip. Fencing is not some cold, impersonal mechanism, but a vigorous, red-blooded, highly personal expression of mind and body.

I have, therefore, filled my text with observations by famous fencing masters, accounts of the lives of successful fencers, details of my own fencing adventures, and so on, to put flesh on fencing. Human experience, after all, is the essence of our art. I wanted to infuse this into the text, have it drip from the pages like honey. It is important for beginning fencers to realize they are part of something deeply rooted in man's existence. Fencing is filled with emotion and physical exertion. It is challenging, sometimes unpredictable, always changing, like life itself. This is part of its lure.

Moreover, once I started writing, I felt compelled to go beyond the simple "do's" of fencing. Explaining the "whys" and "wherefores" of the game has always been part of my approach to teaching, and even on paper I can't escape it. There are valid reasons for what transpires on the fencing strip. To understand these ideas not only makes the learning experience more interesting, but more easily accepted and absorbed. I certainly didn't want to make all the information covered so dogmatic, dry and technically advanced you had to already be an established fencer of many years to understand it.

Explaining the "whys" and "wherefores"

I can still recall the frustrating confusion of my early days in fencing, of the struggle I had to make sense of concepts — now so clear and obvious — that once seemed as obscure to me as Egyptian hieroglyphics. I hope I can help bridge this mental gap for even one beginner.

Of course, I don't believe anyone can learn to fence solely from a book. Yet, if I've accomplished what I set out to do, the following material will be a welcomed supplement for fencers — a source of understanding for novices and, perhaps, a reminder of basic concepts for more advanced students.

Underlying everything in this book is my love of fencing. Fencing has been an integral part of my life for over 25 years, and, amazingly, grows in importance as time goes on. It is my bread and butter, but it is also my life's path. So if I can inspire one person to give fencing a try, if I can impart a bit of enlightenment, answer a question, put someone on the right track, or speak out effectively against those things that I feel diminish fencing, then I have accomplished what I've set out to do. I thank you for reading *The Art and Science of Fencing*, and hope that it in some way touches your mind.

A NOTE FOR THE BEGINNER

If you are just beginning in fencing, read this book initially from start to finish, without skipping around. I have put it together in a way that the later material builds on what has come before — in the exact same manner as I would teach it to a student who has come to me for lessons.

Jumping around the book, before you know what's going on, will tend to confuse you. For instance, if you don't already know what a parry is, then my description of the composed attack will be meaningless. Or if I'm tackling the secondary intent attack, and you haven't first dealt with the lunge, you will more than likely believe that I have written this book while I was heavily medicated.

Once you have a reference point, though, bolstered by some solid experience, it will be easier to make heads and tails of all the information you'll come across within these pages.

This, of course, is just a suggestion.

FOR THE WOMAN FENCER

As with my first book on fencing, *The Encyclopedia of the Sword*, when speaking of the individual fencer in terms of "he," "him," and "his" — and not "she," "her" and "hers" — I am not purposefully excluding the female of the species from the art of fencing.

Rather it is for the sake of brevity and consistency that I limit my vocabulary to one point of view. To be constantly inserting "he/she," "him/her" and "his/hers" into the text would needlessly bog down the flow of information.

Women form an integral part of the fencing process and the exclusion of the pronouns "she," "her" or "hers" is not intended to be an insidious way of omitting the female population from this sport.

PART I
HISTORIES

FENCING: A SOCIAL HISTORY

Fencing cannot be separated from its past. Therefore, to better understand and appreciate what fencing is today — its traditions, attitudes and techniques — and to eventually take on the fencer persona, we must go back to its foundations, to a time when the sword was part of everyday life.

While it is true that men have fought with swords for thousands of years, the sport we call fencing finds its origins not so long ago in human history. And, as fencing historian Edgerton Castle noted in his classic volume, *Schools and Masters of Fence* (1885), it begins with a paradox; that is, a seemingly contradictory statement that is nevertheless true. Fencing, the art of sword fighting, sprang out of the introduction of firearms to warfare during the 16th century.

During the Middle Ages, the sword was used almost exclusively in an offensive capacity. Personal protection, one's defense, was derived from the wearing of heavy metal armor. Broad, cumbersome blades were, therefore, needed to smash through such obstructions. This translated into very little specialized weapon maneuvering, either offensively or defensively. Swords were, in effect, nothing more than giant can openers. To be fair, though, fighting was still no easy proposition. Winning took strength, endurance and determination. Armor, as its continued use for centuries proved, performed its job very well.

Yet, when muskets and bullets came along, they took the time-honored principles of armed combat and rendered them immediately null and void. With little pieces of metal propelled at high velocity by gun powder, armor was no longer a major obstacle to overcome. Presumably, now any unskilled foot soldier could stop a heavily armored knight in his tracks. Furthermore, armor created slow moving targets, just what the musketeer liked to see.

At first, even heavier armor was produced to counter this new method of destruction. But the damage could not be repaired. Sturdier protective gear merely caused those who wore it to abandon it all the more quickly. Lugging bulky mounds of metal plates around was both hot and exhausting, tiring a soldier even before he reached the battlefield. In actual fighting, it also retarded new scientific warfare tactics, based on mobility and troop organization, that were then being espoused by the military leaders of Europe. There was no doubt — the self-preservation methods of old had to go.

By the end of the 1500s, the wearing of armor for personal defense had been virtually abandoned. At this point, the man of the sword was abruptly thrown out into the cold,

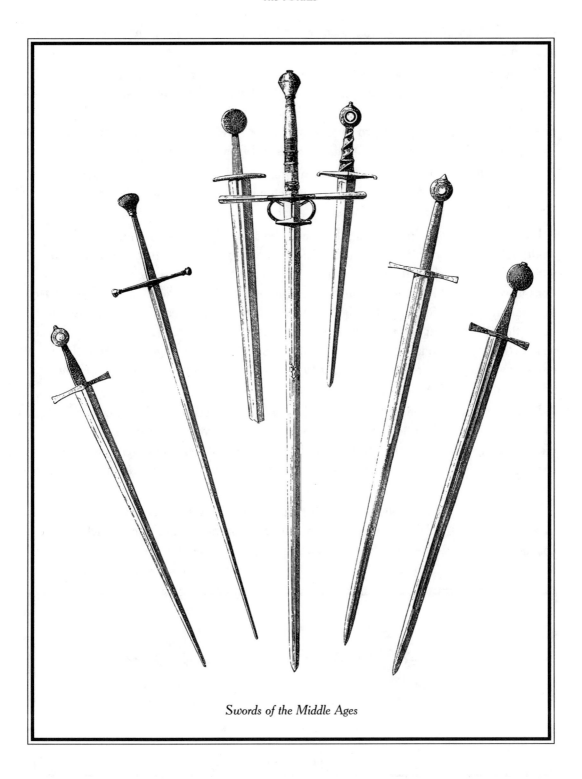

Swords of the Middle Ages

so to speak. Defensively-speaking, once armor had been abandoned, there was now a great void.

Knights and nobles turned for assistance to those whose fighting experience had depended little on armor, the common soldier. Lacking funds to purchase expensive helmets, breastplates and so on, these individuals more often than not depended on personal ingenuity with the sword for survival. Defensive sword skills were ardently sought after. The term "fencing," in fact, is derived from the word "defense."

Many of the skills that were taught during this period employed liberal amounts of kicking, tripping, tumbling, wrestling and punching, but at least it was a starting point for the development of a system for sword combat.

Unofficial "schools" for teaching the use of the sword had been around since the Middle Ages. These early congregating spots for swordsman, however, had little to do with academics. In fact, they were usually little better than robbers' dens. Such operations were outlawed in England during the 13th and 14th centuries because they tended to attract the worst elements of society. Fencing masters, moreover, were considered no better than thieves, vagabonds and actors. An edict enacted in London, England, in the year 1286 stated emphatically, "Whereas it is customary for profligates to learn the art of fencing, who are thereby emboldened to commit the most unheard of villainies, no school shall be kept in the city for the future."

Historian Arthur Wise noted in his book, *The Art and History of Personal Combat* (1971), that the reputation of fencing schools "did not encourage lively, analytical and discriminating minds into the profession." For centuries, at best, they were places where even the most innocent practice session could lead to bruises, eye loss, broken bones and even death.

The first attempt to establish a single, organized approach to fencing was generated in Germany during the 14th century, with the founding of the Fraternity of St. Mark, commonly known as the Marxbruder. With their headquarters located in Frankfurt, they set up a university where aspiring swordsmen in the country could come to earn their

Early Swordsmen

A 16th century fencing school

degrees in arms. Before long, no one could teach in German territory without their approval. The Marxbruder effectively enforced their rules with their swords for nearly 100 years. Eventually, though, other fencing groups, representing differing schools of thought, were formed and, by shear weight of numbers, remained in operation.

As time went on, all across Europe, with dueling increasingly coloring the fabric of everyday life, men of the sword, influenced by the scholarly bent of the Renaissance, began studying and analyzing swordplay with hopes of finding and isolating scientific principles based on human responses that could be counted on to work time and again.

In 1536, Italian fencing master Achille Marozzo, considered the greatest teacher of his time, wrote the first book to approach sword fighting with anything that could be vaguely linked to art or science. Known in his later years as the "Master general of the art of fencing," Marozzo thought that there was nothing more noble in life than the study of sword combat. His teachings, primitive by today's standards, depended heavily on violence and inspiration as their underlying strength. Nevertheless, they were far advanced beyond any other fighting systems of the period.

In light of Marozzo's fantastic success, new fencing styles developed quickly. Camillo Agrippa simplified fencing technique, emphasizing logic rather than romantic fancy. Salvator Fabris brought together the best ideas of numerous fencing masters to create one well-defined style. Ridolfo Capo Ferro established the lunge as the primary method

*A fencing master from the
16th century*

of delivering an attack. Now, with every reliable idea that was advanced, two old bits of useless nonsense fell by the wayside.

Perhaps the greatest transformation in fencing technique came with the development of the rapier in the 16th century. A long-bladed sword designed exclusively for thrusting, the rapier set the fencing world on its ear. For centuries, swords had been envisioned as edged weapons, designed for cutting important parts off of one's opponent. Suddenly, men were poking neat, lethal holes in one another. This newfangled approach, it should be noted, did not sit well with the entrenched fencing establishment. Controversy raged for years over which method of combat — the cut or the thrust — was the superior one. So heated was the disagreement among the two schools of combat that proponents of both systems often fell to dueling whenever they encountered each other on the street.

Masters of the old school, men who carried the sword and buckler (the buckler being a small, round shield worn on the free arm), looked on rapier play with contempt. The English, the last holdouts of the cutting sword in Europe, were particularly brusque in their appraisal of what they perceived as a foreign invasion to their way of life. Their attitude was best summed up in the writings of fencing master George Silver. His *Paradoxes of Defense* (1599) heaped much derision on the rapier and its practitioners. He fiercely dismissed rapier play as "Schoole-tricks and jugling gambalds." He then went on to say, "To seek a true defence in an untrue weapon (the rapier) is to angle on the earth for fish, and to hunt in the sea for hares .... And if we will have true defence we must seeke it where it is, in short swords, ... or such like weapons of perfect length, not in long swords, long rapiers, nor frog pricking poniards."

Despite the staunch opposition, even hatred, directed toward the rapier, it eventually won the day over its competition. By the end of the first quarter of the 17th century, the point weapon was supreme. And the reason was simple: guided by an economy of movement, and possessing a needle sharp point likely to be devastating when it hit home, the rapier proved to be the most efficient tool for dispatching one's enemies. To give an example: in France, between the years 1600 and 1780, 40,000 noblemen were killed in sword fights, mainly due to the death-dealing potential of the point weapon. There's no arguing with success.

Along the way, two distinct approaches to fencing became dominant in the European community, the French school and the Italian school. The French method was one of academic deliberation that depended heavily on strategy. The Italian style favored a strong physical game. As time went on, the two developed a rivalry that continues to this very day.

By the 18th century, in an effort to make swords even more versatile, the rapier was pared down and streamlined into the small sword, which came to be looked upon as the epitome of killing implements. With its shorter, slimmer, lighter blade, and small, unobtrusive hand guard, the smaller sword brought further unique alterations to fencing.

Weighty rapiers had generated slow movement. Reaching out too far to hit an opponent, or trying any action that was too elaborate, meant putting one's self in a position that could not be easily defended and, therefore, wide open to counterattacks. Rapiermen, like the swordsmen who came before them, usually fought in a circular fashion, something like modern boxers, which allowed them to keep themselves protected — even while on the offensive. The small sword freed up the sword fight in ways earlier fencing masters could only dream about. First, it increased the speed and intricacy of weapon maneuvering. Second, it increased a fencer's mobility. And, third, because of the weapon's lightness, opponents found that the only way to get up enough forward momentum to produce effective hits was to approach one another in a straight line (linear fencing), which is a hallmark of modern fencing technique.

Something else took place in the fencing world during the 1700s: fencing gained respectability. With the invention and adoption of the fencing foil — a blunt tipped,

Swordplay in the 17th century

Fencing in the 18th century

flexible version of the small sword designed specifically for training purposes — the mechanics of swordplay could be explored and practiced to a much greater degree. The fencing master became a learned man of breeding, a combination teacher, historian, artist, scientist and philosopher, and the fencing school became a place where noble families sent their sons to gain refinement. (It is from this period that many of today's negative misconceptions regarding fencing spring: that you have to be rich to fence; that fencing is snooty; that fencing is some kind of arty, esoteric game that has no place in our modern world.)

The leader of the movement, who elevated fencing from its bloodthirsty, roughhouse origins as a brutal killing art, was a London-based Italian fencing master named Domenico Angelo. In his book, *The School of Fencing*, published in 1763, he insisted, for the first time in any writings dealing with the use of the sword, that fencing could be practiced merely as a game of skill, a game that, if diligently pursued, would positively effect one's health, poise and grace.

The more academic fencing became, the more its emphasis shifted to its aesthetic elements. This, coupled with the increased reliability of guns for personal combat, brought an end to the carrying of swords. By the latter part of the 18th century, the sword was no longer part of a man's everyday dress. The epoch of the sword as the queen of weapons was over.

The 19th century further solidified the sword as a tool of sport. Great fencing masters defined and redefined fencing technique. These included Henry Angelo, Baptiste Bertrand, A.J. Corbesier, Emile Gouspy, Joseph Keresztessy, Louis Lafaugere, Beppe Nadi, Eugenio Pini, Pierre and Camille Prevost, Louis Rondelle and Louis Senac.

During this period, the sabre and the épée were introduced to fencing, expanding the game dramatically. The épée, the dueling sword of fencing, initially reflected a need for a weapon that taught practical fighting technique for the private affairs of honor that still took place. The sabre, of cavalry origins, encompassed a distinctly military bent in its employment.

Also, the fencing mask was adopted for regular use. Around in one form or another since the mid-18th century, it was perceived for decades as an object of scorn among skillful fencers who thought it the refuge of cowards and poor swordsman. Finally, however, the desire to free the game up from the somewhat rigid and stylized form it had fallen into — and thereby allow for more a natural, quicker style of play — led to a reevaluation and abandonment of the old prejudices.

During the late 1800s, Italo Santelli, Luigi Barbassetti and Laszlo Borsody developed new sabre techniques in Hungary that revolutionized the use of that weapon. In England, Alfred Hutton did much to breathe new life and interest into fencing on a popular level. In 1891, the United States founded its own official fencing organization, the Amateur Fencers League of America, to develop and guide its fencing efforts.

The 20th century might truly be called the Age of Competition with regard to fencing. In 1913, the Federation Internationale d'Escrime (F.I.E.) was founded by France, Italy, England, Germany, Holland, Bohemia, Hungary, Belgium and Norway to oversee fencing worldwide; and from this congress came the standardizing of rules that make international tournaments possible. In 1896, when the modern Olympic Games began, they became the key outlet for the greatest fencing talents from all over the globe. World Championships were eventually set up to further expand the sport's scope. Other major fencing events soon followed.

Great modern fencing personalities include Nedo and Aldo Nadi, Lucien Gaudin, Edourado Mangiarotti, Roger Ducret, Christian d'Oriola, Giorgio Santelli, Jean-Claude Magnan, Helene Mayer, Joseph Levis, Aladar Gervich, Ellen Preis, George Calnan, Phillipe Riboud, Adrianus de Jong,

Turn-of-the-century British fencing master Alfred Hutton

*Modern sport fencing at the
1992 Olympics*
(USFA/Photo credit: Roger Mar)

Pal Kovacs, Julius Palffy-Alpar, Ettore Spezza, Ralph Faulkner, Peter Westbrook and Ilona Schacherer-Elek, to name only a few.

Perhaps the most notable innovation in fencing in this century has been the development of electrically-oriented sport weapons. These register their own touches automatically with the aid of a special scoring machine that is connected to a fencer's foil, épée, or sabre via cords and cables. In effect, the fallibility of the eye in detecting touches, a sticking point throughout fencing's long history, is no longer a problem. The épée was the first weapon to go this route in the 1930s. The foil came next in the 1950s. The sabre was last, finally giving in to technology in the 1980s.

Today, fencing is as dynamic an activity as it was in centuries past. Moreover, it is no longer confined to Western nations. It is a sport of worldwide influence, with participants in the millions. Countries such as China, Japan and Korea now engage in top flight international competitions. The United States Fencing Association (formerly the Amateur Fencers League of America), estimates that there are roughly 150,000 to 200,000 fencers in this nation. Fencing schools, once hated and outlawed, are now found virtually anywhere.

The lure of the sword, constantly reinforced by our literature, movies and television, continues to be powerful. Even time cannot dim its appeal. Apparently, we cannot escape the sword, in any of its many guises — as a killing weapon, an artistic implement, an exercise tool, a piece of sporting equipment or a symbol of bravery, war and courage. Truly, the history of the sword, as was so aptly observed by 19th century writer and fencer Sir Richard F. Burton, is the history of mankind.

RALPH FAULKNER: THE OLD MAN AND THE SWORD

I include, here, a brief outline of my own fencing master's life. When one drinks from a well, one should consider its source. And since I will be offering my knowledge of fencing, it should be noted by whom my foundations were laid and constructed. To Ralph Faulkner I owe a debt for instilling in me an old-world respect and love of fencing, and an abiding sense that fencing is an art as well as a sport.

Ralph Faulkner never set out to be a fencer, a fencing champion or a fencing master. Born in the dusty cattle town of Abilene, Kansas, in 1891, his everyday existence was far, far from the civilized combat of the fencing strip. But, always the athlete from very early on, he began fashioning and sharpening the physical and mental attributes that would eventually lead him into that world.

Faulkner's early adult life was rather eclectic. Fresh out of college, he became a forest ranger, spending most time in the wilderness of Washington state. Then came a successful theatrical career in New York, where he established himself as both a stage performer and silent film actor.

Still, no fencing.

But quite suddenly, things changed. "Fencing came to me out of the blue, one of those quirks of fate," Faulkner often said. "But it must have been a pretty strong quirk. I came to the sport not so much by choice as by pure necessity.

"I had a bad accident in 1922, during the filming of a movie called *The Man From Glengarry*. It was an outdoor, adventure yarn. I played a Canadian lumberjack. I was running over a pile of wet, slippery logs during a river action sequence when I fell and broke my left knee.

"I had an operation, major surgery, but it didn't improve my condition. If anything, it got worse. I was faced with being an invalid on crutches for the rest of my life. In fact, my doctors gave up on me. At this point, I realized I had a choice. I could fall apart, or I could do something for myself.

"First, I moved to Los Angeles, where I thought the warm climate would aid in my recovery. Then, I joined the Los Angeles Athletic Club and began experimenting with various exercises that might help heal my leg. And, after a while, I came up with two that were especially beneficial. One was rowing a gymnasium shell. The other was fencing. I tried rowing, but frankly, it was one of the most boring things I'd ever done.

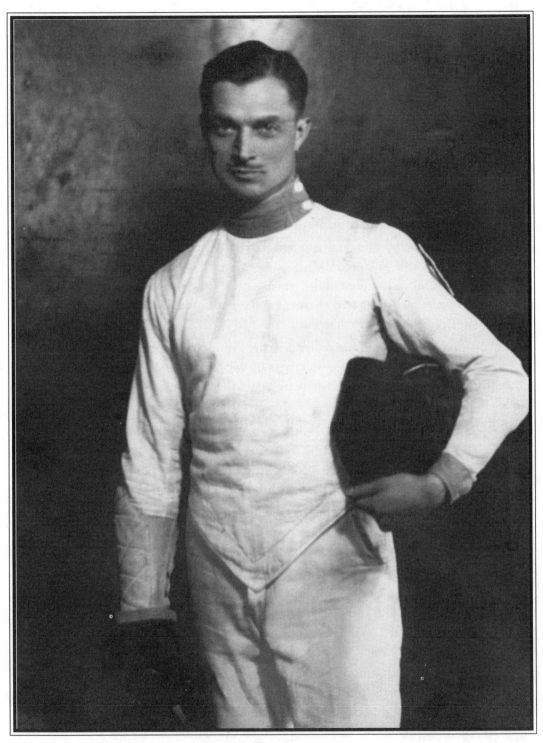

Ralph Faulkner at the 1928 Olympics (Photo from the collection of Ralph Faulkner)

You just sat there; it was all so mechanical. Fencing, on the other hand, gave me the precise therapy I needed and was fascinating besides. Fencing passes the highest intellectual test of any sport known. More than anything else, it was a game of physical chess.

Faulkner fenced for 50 hours a week for months, selling real estate on the side to keep himself going. After about a year, his knee was completely healed. He later admitted, "It's a strange thing to say, but I think it's actually stronger today than my undamaged right knee."

By this time, Faulkner was hooked on fencing. He enjoyed the competitive aspect, the physical workout, the mental stimulation — everything the sport offered. Then, when he felt ready, he plunged into the world of organized amateur fencing.

"At first, I fenced only in Southern California," Faulkner said. "In time, though, I worked with most of the great fencers in the world. Lucien Gaudin, Cornick, Glichai, Ducret, Puliti, Cattiau. Gaudin was probably the greatest fencer who ever lived. I kept my eyes open and learned all that I could. I spent a long time analyzing what was going on and was criticized by some in this country for thinking too much. But that was my approach to fencing.

"There are four basic factors, questions, you should always be asking yourself on the fencing strip. The first is, what is your opponent doing? The second, how does he accomplish what he is doing. The third, what can you do against it? And, last but not least, can you accomplish what you've decided to do? Working with this viewpoint in mind paid off for me."

Faulkner won numerous titles and honors over the years. In 1928, in France, he captured a major sabre championship. He also participated in two Olympics, the 1928 Amsterdam games and the 1932 Los Angeles games. In the latter, his sabre team took fourth place, the highest a U.S. sabre team had placed in an Olympic competition up to that time.

"I didn't train in any special way for the big events," Faulkner stated. "I fenced the same way for everything. And I simply entered everything in sight. I fenced and fenced and fenced. That's how you get to be good.

"Fencing on the international level, of course, meant infinite training. But there was one preparation to competition some fencers adhered to that I never could accept. They would sit and contemplate by themselves and curse the people they were going to fence against. They'd become savage, hating them. This was supposed to help them reach their fencing peak. I never found this necessary. I always approached my opponents calmly, trying to zero in on their particular characteristics, strong and weak, to beat them."

The Faulkner School of Fencing in the 1940s (Photo courtesy of Polly Craus August)

As a fencer, Faulkner traveled all over pre-World War II Europe looking for fencing experience. Old-world concepts were still prevalent, especially among men who called themselves swordsmen.

"I nearly had to fight a duel once," Faulkner recounted. "It was in Dieppe, France, in 1928. I was fencing in an épée contest. The épée is the dueling sword of fencing and its use reflects what would happen in a real fight. The entire body is the target; and, in those days, you fenced one touch — just like it would be with live weapons. It was a climax, a showdown. Today, you fence for five touches. You can make mistakes. It's just a game now.

"Anyway, there was this Frenchman in the tournament; Leon DeLauoye was his name. He was very provincial and old-world, and like many Frenchmen, emotionally volatile. He was also the editor of a magazine called *The Fencer and the Shooter*, a somewhat martial periodical. Basically, the man was in, what you might say, a dueling syndrome. And I had a fencing bout with him.

"One of my favorite spots to hit my opponent was on the knee, and this chap's knee was quite prominent. So I immediately whacked him a good shot there and beat him.

Unfortunately, he took my win rather personally. His attitude was that if any stumbling American, who, as far as he was concerned, couldn't know anything about fencing, beat a classical French fencer like himself, I must have somehow cheated; and this was the greatest of insults to him. So, he sent a challenge to me, through the Oxford fencing team, to fight a duel stripped to the waist.

"The Oxford boys, however, decided to handle the matter diplomatically. They refused the challenge as it stood, because they knew I hadn't broken any code. They convinced DeLauoye to change his challenge to a meeting with fencing masks and jackets on, and sport weapons rather than the épée de combat.

"We finally had our bout, a 10 touch barrage, and I beat him again. After that, he got over his hurt feelings. I'd proved myself to him, you see. He even sent me an autographed photo of himself praising me as a fencer."

Eventually, Faulkner left amateur fencing competition and found he really enjoyed teaching. "I opened a theatrical/fencing school — Falcon Studios — with my wife, Edith Jane. She was the dance teacher, and I handled the athletic and business end of it. We were successful from the very start. Over the years, we have provided training to many successful stars. Alexis Smith, Nanette Fabrey, Anita Louise, John Barrymore,

Faulkner works with one of his young students, Bernie Meislahn (Photo courtesy of Polly Craus August)

Jr., Sheri North, Ken Berry, Richard Thomas, Robert Hays and Bo Derek have passed through our doors."

The theatrical school soon led Faulkner back to film work. Now, instead of just acting, he was a professional swordsman, who both performed in fencing scenes and trained actors in the art of stage swordplay. Over the years, he worked on such films as *The Three Musketeers* (1935), *Captain Blood* (1935), *Anthony Adverse* (1936), *The Prisoner of Zenda* (1937), *Zorro's Fighting Legion* (1939), *The Sea Hawk* (1940), *The Thief of Baghdad* (1940), *The Fighting Guardsman* (1944), *The Bandit of Sherwood Forest* (1950), *The Purple Mask* (1955), *Jason and the Argonauts* (1963), *The King's Pirate* (1967) and *The Clash of the Titans* (1981). The stars he trained included the likes of Errol Flynn, Louis Hayward, Douglas Fairbanks, Jr., Tony Curtis, Ronald Colman, Danny Kaye, Basil Rathbone, John Derek, Anthony Quinn and Cornel Wilde.

"Film work always kept me on my toes," the fencing master said. "In a way, it was every bit as challenging as getting out there on the fencing strip. I must say, I brought my own strong ideas into what I was doing. I gave my actors a solid foundation in fencing basics before we ever worked on routines. That way, they understood what they were doing, and why they were doing it. And, because they understood what was going on they could put more intent into what they were attempting in front of the camera and still retain safety. It wasn't just two people clanging swords together. I did my best to display a knowledge of swordplay in the movie duels I was involved with."

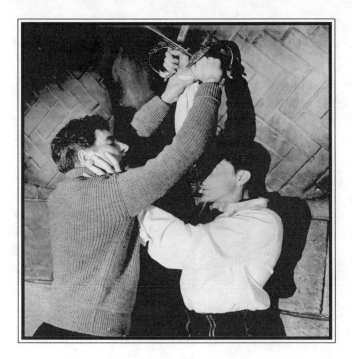

Faulkner opposes Ronald Colman in The Prisoner of Zenda *(1937).*
(From the collection of Ralph Faulkner)

Ralph Faulkner training one of his many champions, Polly Craus (Photo courtesy of Polly Craus August)

Faulkner also made a name for himself coaching fencers for competition. Teaching a classic style of fencing based on the French school, he instilled in his students, young and old, a sense of pride and confidence. He demanded that no matter the outcome of any fencing encounter, his fencers always give their best effort; and this, he invariably, received. His champions included National fencing champions and Olympic competitors Polly Craus, Sewell Shurtz and Janice-Lee York. He also had numerous teams that competed successfully at the highest levels in U.S. fencing.

In his later years, Maestro Faulkner's involvement in film work slowed down, but his school still kept him busy. He took pride in the fact that after 50 years at Falcon Studios,

Faulkner School of Fencing, 1975 (Photo by Anita Evengelista)

he was still teaching. Everyone received a private contact lesson from him — whether he had five students in an evening or 30. He explained, "I don't believe it is possible to really learn what fencing is about unless you learn it in contact with someone who knows fencing intimately and gives you the precise responses of a fencer." He was certain that was what made his school so successful.

Ralph Faulkner lived to the ripe old age of 95½, and like many of the great masters of fencing before him, continued to teach the art and sport he loved right up to the end of his life. Suffering a stroke immediately following a Saturday fencing class, he died quietly two weeks later, on January 27, 1987.

Ralph Faulkner in his 90s (From the collection of Ralph Faulkner)

MY LIFE IN FENCING

I wasn't born to fencing the same way the great swordsmen Henry Angelo, Nedo and Aldo Nadi, Giorgio Santelli, Leon Bertrand and Edouardo Mangiarotti were born to the game by having famous fencing master fathers. Yet, somehow, I was inexorably led to the sword. A metaphysically-oriented person would call it fate. A religious person might term it a calling. A psychoanalyst might talk about compulsive behavior. Whatever the case, I can think of nothing else I might have done with my life that could have given me more satisfaction or a sense of accomplishment.

I began my fencing career in 1969, at the age of 19, when I bought my first fencing equipment at a local sporting goods store. I knew of no fencing schools at the time, but I had to have the equipment. It was like finding buried treasure. Or something magical. It was definitely finding the rest of my life.

I'd always been interested in fencing — from movies, of course — and I knew in my heart that one day I'd learn to fence. For me it was a foregone conclusion. Then, one day, I came across an ad for fencing in the Los Angeles Yellow Pages, and I knew it was time to start.

I began fencing with Ralph Faulkner, "Fencing Master to the Stars," and former Olympian, at the famed Falcon Studios on Hollywood Boulevard. He was 79 years old the day I walked into his school; I was barely 20.

My first lesson was rather traumatic. I found out rather quickly that I was not D'Artagnan, and, most of all, that fencing was not as easy as it looked in the movies. I heard the word "no" at lot.

After my first experience with fencing, I was somewhat shaken, so much so that it took me a full two weeks to build up my nerve to go back again. But I realized that if I didn't go back soon, I never would. So, I took the plunge one more time. I haven't stopped since.

In those days, I fenced three days a week, six hours a day, and at home

Taking a lesson from Ralph Faulkner

Giving a lesson

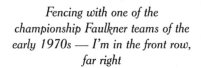

Fencing with one of the championship Faulkner teams of the early 1970s — I'm in the front row, far right

I worked on the things I could practice on my own, footwork, lunging and point control. I also kept notebooks of what I'd learned. I devoured fencing.

It was a great time to be at Faulkner's. It was like a huge family. There'd be 30 or 40 fencers there every evening, and you never had a chance to sit down. It was just fencing, fencing, fencing and more fencing! I fenced against the best fencers in Southern California and, without a doubt, many of the worst. Later, there were competitions. I was lucky enough to fence with some of Faulkner's best teams of the 1970s.

As I went along, my learning process consisted of constantly putting myself into situations that tested my fencing abilities. I wanted to really understand fencing — not just try to "get touches." Sometimes it was ego crushing, because "enlightenment" did not come instantly. I made every mistake a fencer could make and developed most of the bad habits a fencer could develop; but I analyzed everything, picking every move I made apart until I made it right.

Mr. Faulkner, of course, was the cornerstone of Falcon Studios. He made fencing more than just a sport. He taught a respect for fencing that made you take what you were doing seriously. There was tradition. There was art. There was science. It wasn't just a game of getting touches. Fencing meant control. Fencing was special. It had substance. Fencing was alive.

In 1972, I went to Europe on an extended fencing trip. I wanted to find out about the European approaches. I fenced in France, Italy, Germany, Austria and Switzerland — in big schools, little schools, anywhere I could find fencing. It didn't matter.

Fencing in Europe was tough, a real education. Sometimes no one in the school I was visiting spoke English — or cared to. I had to let my weapon talk for me, which was all that was expected on the fencing strip anyway. No one gave me an easy time of it, or a second chance. The history of the sword, with all its bloody glory, was their history. If I wanted to be part of it, I was the one who had to fit in.

In Europe, fencing was a way of life, not just a pastime. When it was time to leave, I took home a new way of thinking, not to mention a scar on my chin from an accident in a hard fought bout in Italy.

Back in the U.S., I returned to Falcon Studios and studied once more with Ralph Faulkner. There was more to learn. Much more.

In time, Mr. Faulkner got a notion to take an assistant. Well into his 80s, he decided he needed someone to lighten his work load, someone whose ability he could trust. One day, he called me into his office. "Do you think you can teach?" he asked me. "Yes," I said without pause; but inside I was thinking, "What am I saying? Can I teach?" I was terrified. It was a big responsibility. Yet, Mr. Faulkner had faith in me, and I guess that was enough to start with. I apprenticed myself to the fencing master.

Up until then I'd never really thought of teaching fencing before, not seriously, anyway. Maybe occasionally in a flight of fantasy I'd picture myself leading a class. I don't think I'd ever have pursued it on my own, though. Teaching was pretty much laid in my lap.

At first, I was little more than an echo of Mr. Faulkner. He once said that I told his

Becoming a teacher

fencing stories better than he did. But, as time went on, working under fire so to speak, I learned to teach, really teach. I taught when I enjoyed it. I taught when I didn't want to teach. I taught when I was ill. I taught in all kinds of weather. It was my responsibility to be there, to make things easier for Mr. Faulkner and to give students their money's worth. I started by being molded by the job; then I began to mold the job.

I developed my own ideas and perspectives. More and more, my understanding of fencing grew. I picked everything I did apart just as I had with my initial education in fencing. It was important for me to know what I was teaching.

At the end of 1980, after spending 10 years with Ralph Faulkner, I decided it was

The Evangelista School of Fencing

time to set out on my own. It was a difficult decision. Falcon Studios was family. Mr. Faulkner was like a grandfather to me. But I was limited in the scope of my teaching out of respect for the Boss. I had to adhere to his line. Mr. Faulkner, realizing it too, gave me his blessing.

I opened my own school. I turned my garage into a fencing studio. I also coached at the Pasadena YMCA. I taught both sport and theatrical fencing. I also acted as a consultant to the film industry. One of the highlights of my theatrical teaching was having four former students in a production of Shakespeare's Richard III at L. A.'s Ahmensen Theatre. I also assisted in the creation of a fencing related episode of Magnum P.I., and I was a guest teacher at the theatrical department at U.C.L.A. In 1984, I also helped put together a theatrical fencing program for the San Diego Opera Company.

On a sporting level, it was gratifying to see students who I'd taken from scratch enter USFA tournaments and win medals. A number of my younger students qualified for the Junior Olympics. This was a highly satisfying time for me.

In 1985, with my school growing, I decided to make a change in my life. For family-related reasons, I set aside my own career aspirations and bought a farm in the Missouri Ozark Mountains. In June of 1985, we moved.

Talk about changes. As much as I'd planned the move, it was a shock to my nervous system. There was no fencing, and, in the beginning, no one was really interested. When I told people what I did for a living, they sort of smiled oddly and nodded with a kind of blank look on their face. When people called on my various ads, they usually wanted to know what kind of fences I taught the building of. They still do.

I had to find contentment by teaching fencing to my children and my wife, reading about fencing, and writing articles about fencing.

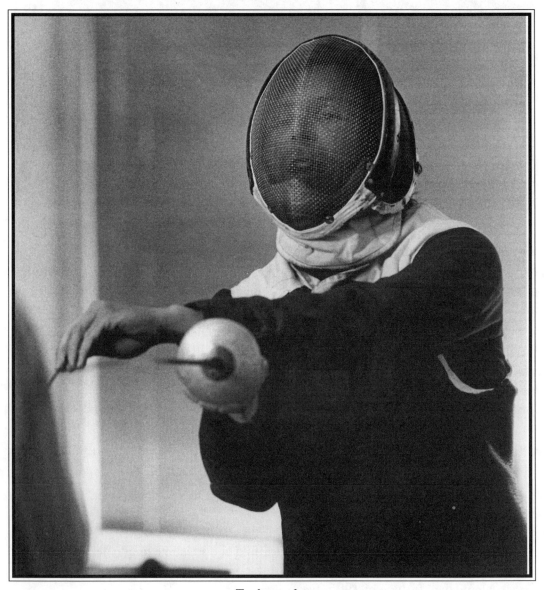

Teaching today

After two years of virtual fencing isolation, though, students started appearing, and I was on my way again. Now, after 11 years in the Ozarks, I have a small but dedicated group of fencers. Strangely, in these 11 years, I believe I've learned more about fencing than I did in all my years in Los Angeles.

My first book, *The Encyclopedia of the Sword*, which came out in 1995, is a compendium of sword knowledge. Five years of work. A volume covering swords, fencing history, modern sport fencing, fencers, and fencing masters, swashbuckler movies, fencing on television and literature of the sword.

As for my approach to fencing, it's pretty simple: Pay attention to the art of fencing (which through form and technique spells personal control), pay attention to the science of fencing (which is strategy and psychology), and the sport of fencing (which is getting five touches before the other guy) will take care of itself. Don't be in a hurry. Don't opt for quick fixes. Devote the time it takes to build a strong foundation and learn the "language" of fencing. And always treat what you do with respect.

My future in fencing? Simply to teach anyone who wants to learn to the best of my ability.

And to keep learning.

PART II
A FENCING
PHILOSOPHY

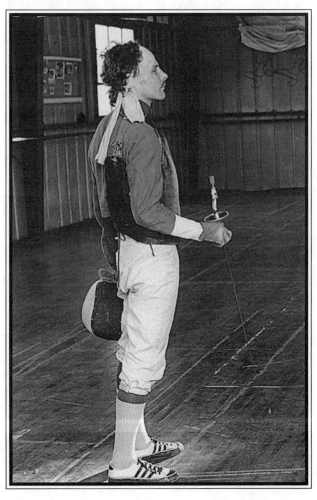

MY FENCING PHILOSOPHY

One of the main themes of my fencing approach is the importance of classical fencing. The classical style, one that seeks to promote personal control, where fencing actions are both economical and effective, has fallen on some pretty hard times lately. Most of the fencing photos published these days in prestigious fencing journals illustrate the basic physical moves ("toe-to-toe," "bowl-'em-over," "hit-or-miss"), exemplifying the modern approach to personal combat. Yet, the classical game — either French or Italian — was, with occasional revisions, good enough for nearly 300 years of constant use. There must have been a pretty good reason for this dogged adherence. I believe it is based on something real — universal principles dealing with the way human beings think and move. By mastering the application of these concepts, through long, hard study and practice, a fencing student is led logically to personal control — first over himself, and then over his opponents. This was once a given among the fencing community and also among the great teachers, the Aldo Nadis, the Giorgio Santellis, the Ralph Faulkners.

So why has classical fencing been virtually abandoned in the latter half of the 20th century? To be honest, its very nature manifests its downfall in our fast lane, fast food world. To follow classical fencing means anything but an instant path to success. It takes time to learn the "language" of fencing, which is an anathema to those in a hurry. Who has time for dedication and patience these days? Yet, when that control does materialize, it is a formidable thing, indeed. Ultimately, in metaphorical terms, it is the difference between the precision laser and the crashing stick of dynamite.

Today, with the way fencing is taught in so many schools, you often never have to get the sword arm straight for an attack; develop point control, distance, timing or sentiment du fer; or employ your free arm in a way that it may actually improve your balance, your lunge, your return to on guard. You just go out there and "fence," man! If you are strong, fast and aggressive, people will probably tell you you're a great fencer.

In this last point rests a certain irony. We judge ability entirely on scores — rather than how the results are achieved. So often the underlying truth of the matter is obscured. What is my actual ability? What is the ability of the opponent I just defeated? Did I really out-fence him, or did he simply make more mistakes than I did? Can I be better than just winning now, this moment? Few fencers ask these questions anymore. You're more likely to hear, "Well, it worked," or "I'll beat him, that's what counts," than anything introspective. A really good fencer can always find ways around any purely physical game. It isn't that difficult; that's what classical training compels one to do.

As a teacher of fencing, I must be true to my origins and stay with classical style — even if it might ruffle a few feathers among coaches who teach "competitive" stuff.

One of the notions that I hope to underscore here, for beginners and advanced fencers, is that true fencing takes place between the brain and the sword hand rather than between the tip of your weapon and an opponent's chest. When Maestro Aldo Nadi made the statement, "There is only one fencing," I have no doubt he was observing that the underlying truths of fencing, truths encountered through connecting your head to your weapon, bridge all schools. It always gives me a funny feeling when I read some piece of fencing literature from 100 or more years ago, and run across a statement right there, in black and white, that I've been laying on my own students, word for word, for years. At the time, I thought I was making an original point based on my own perceptions and experience. If it's not reincarnation, there must be some validity in the old ways.

Fencing is more than just a game, it's a living thing, the sum total of every person, good or bad, who's ever picked up a sword, a rapier or a foil. That life, that energy, is what I really want to convey in this volume, so that the technical points and the abstractions covered will be more than vague, foreign concepts. They will make perfect sense.

We will now discuss the *Language of Fencing*.

PART III
THE BEGINNING
FENCER

THE LANGUAGE OF FENCING

The language of fencing is the interaction between two fencers. It may be simple or complicated. Yet, if you speak the language, you may gain an understanding of what is happening on any fencing strip, whether the play is taking place in London, England; Paris, France; Los Angeles, California; or Tokyo, Japan. The language of fencing, then, is a universal form of communication that transcends national boundaries and cultures.

Evolving relentlessly over the centuries, the language of fencing comes to us after being studied and tested in the blood of our ancestors. It is a language of physical movement and mental responses, overlaid and colored by emotional content.

To speak the language of fencing fluently, to think in it, to express it distinctly and artfully with foil or épée or sabre in hand, makes you not only an athlete of distinction but a citizen of the world and a participant in history.

The Language of Fencing

WHY FENCING?

Nonfencers often ask me, "Why should anyone want to fence? After all, no one fights with swords anymore. What can fencing do for me?"

True, it's probably unlikely that you're ever going to be fighting a duel, flashing blade in hand down at the local park, or go into battle wielding a broadsword. Yet fencing, for all its anachronistic splendor, has much to offer anyone who decides to give it a try.

To begin with, fencing is a superb and unique form of exercise. On a basic level, it gives a good, solid workout that is fairly inexpensive to engage in. You'll build endurance, strength, flexibility and the capacity to relax under fire. Coordination — which includes physical balance, timing, grace and poise — will be improved. Fencing aids both circulation and respiration, adding further physical health benefits. Mentally, it is as stimulating as chess. It enhances observational skills and the ability to think in an abstract manner (important for problem solving). Ultimately, fencing blends both mind and body into an effective whole.

Psychologically, fencing develops self-confidence. Responding with a sense of authority during times of mental and physical stress becomes second nature. Fencing provides an outlet for those who possess a highly competitive nature. It may also be used to channel aggressive impulses that might be otherwise frowned upon by society at large. It also teaches self-control over a person's reactive nature. Fencing, of course, develops patience.

Furthermore, you should remember that any physical workout of a static nature runs the risk of becoming boring to those who partake in it. Fencing may be many things, but it is never that. Every time you pick up a foil, épée or sabre and step onto a fencing strip you are in new, uncharted territory. Is this a new opponent? What challenges will he bring to you? Is he aggressive or passive, fast or slow, tall or short, brutal or light of touch, smart or dumb, knowledgeable or inexperienced, reactive or responsive? Old opponents' abilities change with experience, with age. How will you handle that? Your own abilities change. How do you modify your fencing as you grow older? What attack might you better perfect? What combinations of attacks might you employ? What defensive maneuvering might you work on? With these thoughts in mind, the game of fencing remains ever fresh for the athlete, something you are not likely to give up easily. Exercise ignored does nothing for you. Fencing is difficult to ignore.

The gains you make in fencing, however, don't necessarily end on the fencing strip. I can give a number of examples of how the attributes enhanced by fencing might be employed in other areas of your life. For instance, the problem solving skills I have learned in dealing with fencing opponents have aided me with such diverse activities as car repair, home electrical wiring, appliance maintenance and plumbing, where I had to not only diagnose problems, but fix them. Psychological skills honed through fencing — reading other people and dealing with them effectively — have aided me in personal and public relationships. The self-confidence I've gained as a fencer was of particular use to me both when I sold advertising and collected money as a professional fund-raiser for community groups. I also believe that fencing has helped me with my organizational skills as a writer. And I'm absolutely certain the mental calm I've developed over the years on the fencing strip stood by me well when I helped deliver both my children at home. The physical balance I have established as a fencer was useful to me when I learned to ride horses. It even made playing tennis easier.

Outside my own personal experience, many individuals have given me further evidence of fencing's additional value. Numerous martial artists have come to me over the years to learn fencing to improve their footwork, timing and concentration, stating time and again that it brought them physical challenges their own disciplines did not. (It is a well known fact that famed martial artist Bruce Lee employed numerous fencing principles in his own fighting discipline Jeet Kune Do.) A musician student of mine found that the finger dexterity he gained in manipulating his foil improved his guitar playing. An exercise of some intensity, fencing burns those calories like mad, making it an ideal vehicle for weight loss. My own fencing master, Ralph Faulkner, initially took up fencing as physical therapy for a badly injured knee, a physical condition his own doctors had given up on.

Certainly, fencing's accessibility is an important, even vital, selling point. Schools are everywhere. Equipment can be easily obtained through mail-order purchases. Lessons are affordable. And equipment is relatively inexpensive, especially when compared to other sports. A really good tennis racket can run you as much as an entire fencing outfit. And don't even talk about skiing gear! You can shell out hundreds of bucks with that sport — just for clothes.

Fully suited to women as men, fencing is one of the few truly equal opportunity sports. Even if you find yourself somewhat less incredible in your physical makeup, you can still become a decent fencer. One of the acknowledged all-time greats of fencing, Helene Mayer, was a challenge for every male fencer who ever faced her on the fencing strip.

Fencing is an ideal activity for kids, boys and girls alike, as it develops self-confidence, self-control and self-awareness, three factors necessary for turning children into successful adults.

A sport for both men and women

Being a very social sport, it is something the whole family can enjoy together, improving intra-family relations. (I met my wife at the school where I fenced; the first thing I ever said to her was, "Are you taking a fencing lesson tonight?") I once had a high school student who made fencing her senior class project, earning an A grade for her presentation. More recently, another student was offered a fencing scholarship at a prestigious Midwest university. Of course, fencing is a skill few actors should be without.

Lastly, there is a hidden plus to fencing that is rarely mentioned. Dedicated fencers have a propensity for living a long time. Not only that but they experience lives in which they remain aware and physically active. In other words, fencing keeps you young!

For example, the great 18th century fencing master Domenico Angelo lived to the ripe old age of 86, teaching right up to a few days before his death. Giorgio Santelli, one of the most acclaimed modern fencing masters, was 88 when he died. Never even contemplating retiring from his art, he often commented on how fencing kept him going. Movie fencing master and Olympian Ralph Faulkner was 95 when he died. He, too, taught fencing to the end of his life, often exhibiting more energy and enthusiasm than many of his younger students. Famed Spanish master Julio Castello was 91 when he died. Beppe Nadi, father and teacher of champion fencers Nedo and Aldo Nadi, lived to the age of 84. Coach of countless sabre champions, Csaba Elthes, died recently at the age of 83. Still living fencing master Lajos Csiszar, 91, maintains an active interest in the fencing world. The list goes on and on.

I believe this "fountain of youth" feature of fencing comes from the unique way in which it couples and stimulates mind and body. And it has long been observed that folks who stay interested and involved in life tend to live longer, healthier lives. Fencing great Aldo Nadi, in his classic book *On Fencing* (1943), observed, "In Europe, I have seen men of seventy who could easily defeat young fencers of average strength. This does not happen in any other sport."

I might add in closing, that no other sport contains the romance, the extended history of centuries, the plethora of traditions, and the sense of honor that fencing houses within its confines. Even the beginner can partake in the thrill of the swashbuckler movie and the historical novel.

There is something for almost everyone in fencing.

Getting Started in Fencing

GETTING STARTED

So, you've decided to learn to fence. How do you begin? What do you do? Where do you go? You don't just pick up a stick, and start whacking away at the first person you meet on the street. You go to jail for that.

FINDING A FENCING SCHOOL OR CLUB

A fencing school is the obvious and best place to start your career in fencing. Once upon a time, during fencing's dark and somewhat disreputable origins, fencing schools were dangerous dens, full of the dregs of society, men who learned the use of the sword to prey upon their neighbors. Schools of fence were often outlawed and feared by the common folk. Fencing masters were placed in the same category as common criminals. Hopefully, today, this is not the case in most fencing schools.

If you live in a large urban center, like New York City, Los Angeles or St. Louis, finding a fencing school should be a simple enough task to accomplish. In most large cities, there are usually as many as 10 or 15 schools to choose from. Smaller cities and towns, although it's not always obvious at first glance, often boast at least one school. Fencing schools, for instance, can be found in Colorado Springs, Colorado (pop. 300,000); Belleville, Illinois (41,000); and West Plains, Missouri (pop. 9,000).

Your initial reconnoitering should be done through the obvious route: the *Yellow Pages*. If this yields nothing, your next queries should go to the chamber of commerce, local colleges, YMCAs and athletic clubs.

If all these institutions fail to provide you with any useful information, your final contact should be the United States Fencing Association (see appendix). This internationally recognized organization, which guides amateur fencing in America, has listings for fencing schools and clubs all over the country. If you have a plethora of listings to wade through, they may be able to help with recommendations. If there is no fencing in your immediate area, they will, without doubt, be able to give you the address of the nearest fencing group.

SORTING THE GOOD SCHOOLS FROM THE NOT SO GOOD

It is, of course, difficult for the potential fencer to make judgments regarding the quality of the school or instructor you initially encounter. But there are a few simple general questions you should ask when first entering a new fencing situation. To begin with, although this isn't always a given, what are the teacher's credentials? What is his

Teacher and student

or her background in fencing? Has the instructor been fencing long? Who was their teacher? What was the extent of their training? Competition experience? How formal was their teaching education?

I should mention, however, just to complicate matters, that while vast competitive experience is exceedingly valuable, it doesn't always make a good teacher. I've known champions who couldn't explain in a logical way why or how they performed moves on the fencing strip. Of course, taking lessons from someone who's only been fencing for a year or two probably won't be of much value to you either.

There are a few things you should watch out for when you enter a school for the first time:

First off, how well does the teacher explain what he teaches? Can he give you a beneficial reason for what he is telling you? Some teachers will simply say, "I'm the teacher. You are the student. You will do what I say. Period!" It's always been my contention that if a teacher can't answer any question his student throws at him, he shouldn't be teaching. And I encourage questions.

Another important point, how soon does the instructor allow novices to begin bouting? I've visited schools that allow first time students to "fence" right after their initial lesson. This, I think, is one of the worst beginnings a fencer can have. The student isn't really fencing, anyway, and all sorts of bad habits can become rooted in this early introduction to personal combat. Just because you are paying for the lesson, and want to mix it up on the fencing strip, is no reason to let you go ahead and do it. Ideally, I would say, a student should take lessons for at least six months before they start bouting. A teacher should be looking out for your best interests, not just the short term effect of keeping you happy.

Does the instructor start his students off with the foil, or does he allow them to pick and choose the weapon they will be fencing? The épée is certainly a dramatic weapon, and the sabre is doubtlessly the flashiest; but I've been taught, and I find it to be the case, that the foil is the only weapon for the beginner. I once heard a rather stupid teacher say to a student, "Do you want to fence foil, or do you want to fence with a man's weapon?" and he held up a sabre. This implied, of course, that the foil is somehow a lesser weapon, which is utter nonsense. The foil was created to be the teaching weapon of fencing. By its very nature, by the rules, or conventions, that guide its use, it teaches control that ultimately influence and improve your mastery of the other two weapons. If a teacher doesn't know this, or chooses to ignore it, he is giving his students less than they should be getting.

Another point, if the instructor does begin his new people with the foil, how soon does he allow them to go on to fence épée and sabre? I've seen students who'd only been training for three or four months being allowed to bout with both épée and sabre. Then I watched as their fencing became an uncontrolled jumble of whacking and poking. A firm foundation should always be laid with one weapon before the next is undertaken. It's been my observation that a student should fence foil for at least a year before he picks up an épeé, and at least two years before he picks up a sabre. A teacher who allows a student to rush headlong into fencing all three weapons almost guarantees that that fencer's overall technique will be stunted to some degree. How good might a fencer be if only he approached each weapon in its proper order, and in due time? A fencing student should approach his training with a sense of patience, and if he doesn't have the capacity to do so, the instructor should have the wherewithal to hold him back.

The factor of fencing safety should be vital in choosing a teacher and club. Does the teacher allow his students to work together in any capacity without masks, jackets or gloves? Is brutal, undisciplined fencing or horseplay allowed? Any good instructor will nip such behavior in the bud.

Lastly, how's the fencing etiquette in the school or club you are thinking of joining? Are students versed in the traditional values of fencing? Do they salute before matches. Do they acknowledge touches on the fencing strip? Or do they argue over who touched whom? Do they shake hands after a bout? These practices would be important items to me because they demonstrate the level of respect fencers have for their sport and school, and hence, reflect on the instructor's influence on his pupils.

BUYING FENCING EQUIPMENT

Purchasing the proper, and appropriate, fencing equipment is a must if you are to ever become a serious fencer. Some schools and clubs will provide equipment initially to the new student; but, used by many fencers, it is often well worn and of minimum quality. Weapons

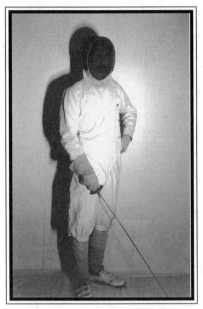

The standard outfit of fencing

may be poorly balanced; jackets stained, baggy and frayed; masks dented and ill-fitting. You should get beyond these self-limiting tools as soon as possible if you are to make any real progress.

The value of equipment that complements your undertakings cannot be minimized. Utility gear — the finely balanced foil, the form-fitting jacket and pants, the pliable glove, the comfortable mask — only enhance the fencing experience. Moreover, I believe that owning your own equipment brings you closer to the game. This ultimately aids in developing the fencer mind-set that turns you into a true fencer and keeps you anchored in the sport, perhaps for a lifetime.

So where, then, do you come by fencing gear? Sporting goods stores, by and large, don't sell it. And this is probably a good thing. To be sold specialized equipment by an uninformed individual can be a horrible experience, if my own experience is any indication of such things.

The sporting goods store in Hollywood was the first place I had ever encountered fencing equipment. There, in a deserted aisle towards the back of the store, were foils, masks, sabres, jackets, gloves, épées, all the wonderful accoutrements of fencing. When I saw it, I just stared. Immediately, a salesperson, a middle-aged gentleman, descended upon me out of nowhere and asked if I needed any help. I said yes, I wanted to buy fencing equipment. He replied that he'd see that I got everything I needed. He then proceeded to sell me a woman's fencing jacket (I should have been suspicious: it kept riding up at the chest), two gloves (one for each hand — did I look particularly ambidextrous?), a child-sized fencing mask (the snug fit would insure that it would never come off accidentally), an Italian foil purported to be French, and a French épée purported to be a sabre. The only thing the fellow got right was the knickers, fencing pants (they fit, and ended up lasting me five or six years). Let the buyer beware, to be sure. The salesman, no matter what he said to the contrary, knew as little as I did about choosing fencing equipment. But I was the one who paid for his ignorance. I learned the hard way.

The best place to purchase fencing equipment is from a fencing equipment supply business. Not every city has one. In fact, most cities don't. That's why they all engage in mail order selling. They are expert. They can answer all your questions about fencing equipment. They'll send you a price catalogue of their wares. And they won't sell you a

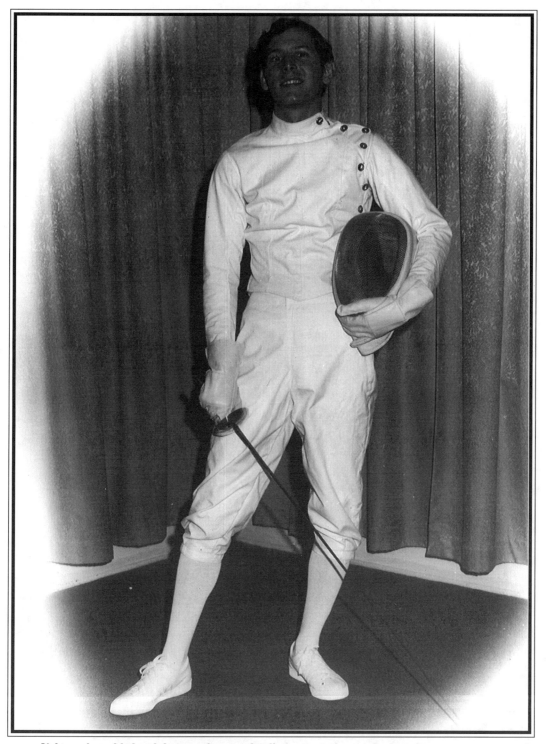

If this awkward kid with his two gloves and girl's fencing jacket can learn to fence, anyone can.

woman's fencing jacket unless you're a woman, or you just happen to want a woman's fencing jacket. (A listing of fencing supply houses appears in the appendix of this book.)

EQUIPMENT NEEDED

At the very least, a student just starting out in fencing should acquire a weapon and a glove. Owning your own weapon accustoms you to its weight and balance, and hence, makes using it a simpler proposition. The weapon, as I've said, should be the foil — not an épée, not a sabre — because it is the teaching weapon of fencing. You will learn more about fencing if you start with the foil. A leather fencing glove, either for the right or left hand, follows, because it makes holding your weapon easier, and, obviously, it protects the sword hand. These items will see you through your first lessons.

Of course, the ultimate object of fencing lessons is to guide the student into bouting. If this is your goal, then your next acquisition will be a fencing jacket and a fencing mask. Jackets come in traditional (white) cotton duck and stretch knit. Which is better? Cotton duck is canvas, and it is highly durable. Stretch knit is cooler than duck and is a bit more form-fitting. In the end, it becomes a matter of taste. Too, jackets are cut specifically for either the right-handed or left-handed fencer (this will determine which side of the chest the jacket opens on, and which arm gets more padding). Furthermore, jackets may be fastened with buttons, zippers or velcro™ (I prefer buttons — more traditional, you know). Lastly, women's jackets have extra padding in the chest area or have pockets in the chest where breast protectors may be inserted (a must for all women fencers).

I should add that there are also fencing jackets known as "half-jackets." These are, as the name implies, half of a jacket (the weapon-holding side, of course). Offering only bottom-line protection, they tend to be used only by beginners during informal practice sessions and may not be worn for official competitions. Their main value is that they are cheaper than full jackets.

As for fencing masks, you will encounter three types: foil masks, sabre masks, and three-weapon masks. Each variety is self-explanatory; its design, as its name implies, being geared toward a specific weapon. A foil mask will probably be the least expensive of the group, but it should never be employed against a sabre or épée: its trim will be chewed up by the sabre's cutting edge, and its mesh may be damaged by the épée's stout blade. A sabre mask is designed with head attacks in mind. Thick leather trim, molded along the top and sides of the mask, cushions against the continual jarring cuts a sabre fencer must endure. On the negative side, this makes it a bit heavier than the other masks. The three-weapon mask is the most versatile mask you might buy. Its design is light and airy if you are fencing foil; it has effective leather trim for sabre; and its mesh is designed to stand up to épée thrusts. It may be the most expensive mask; yet, if you plan to eventually take up all the weapons of fencing, it beats buying three separate masks. (It should be noted that fencing masks come with either snap-in bibs or ones that are sewn in. Sewn-in bibs are required for official USFA-sanctioned competitive fencing.)

For casual bouting in the fencing salle, any loosing-fitting pants will do. However, white fencing pants — knickers — are a must for tournaments. They come in either cotton duck or stretch knit varieties. (Knee-high white socks go along with the knickers.)

Finally, for shoes, you should look for an athletic shoe with good traction. You can buy fairly expensive, or really expensive, fencing shoes, but anything that is comfortable and grips the floor will do.

CHOOSING A WEAPON

It should be understood, at this point, that you should begin your fencing career with a foil. But now comes the tricky part. What style of foil? Essentially, there are three to choose from, each being designated by the type of grip it employs: French, Italian and anatomical. Each has its own particular traits, which, in turn, influences its use. Each embodies a different approach to fencing.

Originally, a foil was any weapon that had been rendered harmless for practice by placing a cover over the dangerous portion, edge or tip, of the blade. This was followed by weapons with already blunted blades, which, however, still pretty much resembled their deadly counterparts. In time, though, specific practice weapons were created to promote the study of fencing. These, with minor changes, are foils as we see them today.

Since I teach the style of fencing known as French, and so only recommend the French foil to my students, I will first speak of it. The French foil, patterned in its appearance

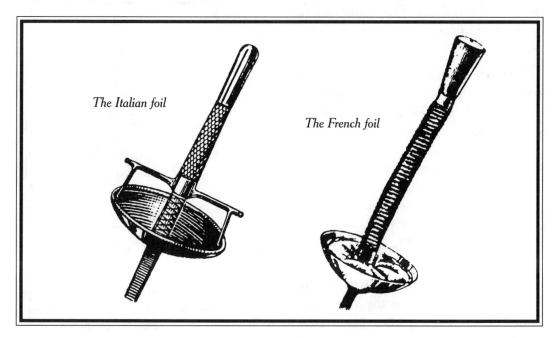

The Italian foil

The French foil

after the small sword of the 18th century, comes, as you might expect by its name, from France. It has a grip, slightly twisted, which fits neatly down middle of a fencer's sword hand. Because of its design, it promotes finger control of the weapon (sentiment du fer), a prerequisite for efficient, economical fencing. It is a weapon that lends itself to pliability and versatility in the multitude of fencing situations you might find yourself. A fencer who is less athletically-inclined than his opponent may, with practice, find the French foil an equalizing factor in the encounter. Admittedly, it takes some time to learn to use it effectively. I would not, however, use anything else.

The Italian foil, as Italian in its inception as the French foil is French, was modeled after the rapier, the dueling sword of the 17th century. It possesses a straight grip, most often strapped to the wrist by a leather thong (martingale), and short crossbars (gavigliano) set just beneath the hand guard, around which the fencer wraps one or two fingers. The design of the Italian foil, plus the way it is fastened to the fencer's personage, encourages a rather physical style of fencing that often brings the sword arm into active play. Nevertheless, it allows for much precision. Famed fencing champion and master Aldo Nadi observed, "In my opinion the Italian weapon is by far the better from all points of view. Its outstanding advantage lies in its superior power. The handle is bound to the wrist by a leather strap about one-inch wide which insures a strength and firmness of grip that simply cannot exist in the French foil. More important, it lightens the burden of the fingers, thus permitting most of their effort to be employed in directing the point (offense). Furthermore, the strap in-creases effectively the power of the parry (de-fense)." This opinion of superiority would, of course, be disputed by proponents of the French school.

The anatomical grip foil is the most recent arrival on the fencing scene, a creation of the 20th century. Its design, which employs ridges and short, finger-supporting prongs, has basically been molded to the structure of the sword hand. Some-times called a pistol grip (its shape resembles a pistol) or an orthopedic grip (it was originally introduced to benefit fencers whose sword hands were either deformed or damaged), this weapon creates a muscular approach to fencing that, if left unchecked by one's opponent, can, in fact, be quite overpowering on the fencing strip. On the other hand, it engenders neither the dexterous finger-control of the French foil nor the directed strength

An anatomical grip

of the Italian blade. It is simply a tool of power for the sake of power. Period. Frowned upon by more classically trained fencers, it is by far the most popular type of foil among fencers today. Its proponents are those who have found the French technique too difficult to master and the Italian, with its wrist strap, too confining or bothersome, and who mistakenly believe that strength is the most important key to successful fencing. Sadly, the anatomical grip often produces a style of fencing that is, because of the grip's design, self-limiting. Tending to facilitate a hand hold that runs the risk of becoming a veritable death grip, the anatomical foil may produce a fencer who rarely develops a style of play that grows beyond its heavy, forceful nature. Certainly, there are more fencing injuries being inflicted these days with anatomical weapons than in previous years when the French and Italian foils held sway. Simply put: there is no give when they make contact with an opponent's body; and this can be a problem when blades snap and become jaggedly sharp.

There are a number of incarnations of the anatomical grip. These include: Belgian (standard/modern/large), Visconti (traditional small/medium/ long) German, American (standard/large), Gardere, Spanish (modern/offset), Rambeau, Cetrulo and Russian. British fencer and writer E.D. Morton, in his book, *Martini A-Z of Fencing* (1992), called this group of foils "this monstrous brood." Personally, having tried anatomical grips, I would never use one on a regular basis.

Are you still undecided as to which type of weapon to purchase? Maybe fencers you know have told you how great the anatomical grip is. Here's an analogy. You have two types of screw drivers, the flat head and the Philips. Each one fits a specific, unique purpose, just like the French and Italian foil. Then, someone comes along and designs a new screw driver that looks and feels somewhat like a hammer, and instead of twisting a screw into a piece of wood, like the other two tools, this one beats the screw in. Like the other two screw drivers, it achieves the goal of driving the screw into the wood, but in the process, it bends the screw and bashes the heck out of the wood. That's the anatomical grip. Understand?

Whichever foil design you decide on using, there are some incidentals you should be aware of when purchasing a weapon. The first has to do with blade length. Length in blades is designated by the numbers 0, 1, 2, 3, 4 and 5 — 5 being the longest (35 inches from tip to hilt); 0 being the shortest (30 inches from tip to hilt). The shortest blades are for small children; the longest, for adults.

Blades most often come from France or Italy. These have the best reputation. You might also encounter foil blades of lesser quality from Poland, Russia and China. The latter may be cheaper, but blades that break are of little value to you. My advice is to spent the bucks and get a blade that has decent temper and will last awhile.

Another point: Do you want a standard blade? One with a dummy electric tip? Or one that is set for electrical use. A standard blade is simply a basic unadulterated foil blade. A dummy electric blade is one that has been fixed with an electric tip to simulate an electric fencing foil. An electric blade is one that has been electrically wired for use with a scoring machine (we will speak of electrical fencing equipment in more detail). The electric blade is basically for the competitive fencer. The dummy blade is for the fencer who wishes to familiarize and accustom himself with a weapon resembling an electrical weapon in weight and balance without actually having to use the more expensive blade. Neither are necessary to the student just starting out in fencing. A standard blade is what you want.

Blades come in light, medium and heavy weights. A light or medium blade will probably do for a first weapon.

Grips come either right-handed and left-handed. When ordering by mail, you should always specify RH or LH.

Finally, if you decide to go with a French foil, the French grip (poigneé) may be covered with leather, twine or plastic, or be made of metal. Leather endures and is easy to grasp. Twine grips are cheap, but they fray easily with much use. Plastic is easy to hold onto, but not very traditional. The metal ones last forever, but they're cold. All work to one degree or another, so it becomes a matter of preference, what you happen to be looking for. (I've found that going with the twine covered grip, which is the cheapest version you can get, and wrapping it with baseball bat tape, gives the best gripping surface of any covering available; and you can re-wrap it any time the tape starts to wear out.)

Italian and anatomical grips are made of either metal or plastic, or combinations thereof.

ELECTRICAL FENCING EQUIPMENT

Once upon a time all fencing was accomplished with standard weapons, and touches were either spotted by a director or left up to the honesty of each fencer. However, the 20th century has caught up to even an ancient activity like fencing. Weapons, with blades electrically wired to sense touches, have been devised to take all the guesswork out of who has hit whom on the fencing strip. All three weapons of fencing — foil, épée, and sabre — have their own electrical relative.

An electric fencing vest (lame), worn over your fencing jacket when fencing with the electrical foil and sabre, is must for tournaments. Yet, it is nothing a beginning fencer need worry about.

A body cord, an electrical cord that connects your weapon to the scoring apparatus, is another requirement for the "electrical" fencer.

Furthermore, for electrical sabre fencing, a special fencing mask and glove are necessary.

Of course, none of these items are essential for the new student of fencing. I merely mention them here for informational purposes, to let the beginner know they exist.

ADDITIONAL SUPPLIES

Cotton or nylon underarm protectors, worn under the fencing jacket, should be considered when you begin bouting. Extra protection isn't a bad idea, and these are required for organized competition.

A martingale (a leather or cloth strap) is often worn by the fencer using an Italian foil or épée to fasten his weapon to his wrist. It has long been considered an integral part of Italian fencing technique and so should not be overlooked.

Lastly, an equipment bag, in which to stow all your newly-acquired fencing equipment, will be an intelligent and useful purchase. It will make transporting gear much easier (no poking people with foil blades on the bus); and you won't tend to forget something integral to fencing at home, like your mask or jacket, if you find yourself in a hurry. (Be prepared, however, for the inevitable question you will undoubtedly encounter about which musical instrument you play by carrying such a bag around town.)

Now that you have your equipment, or at least have access to it, it's time to move on to that first fencing lesson.

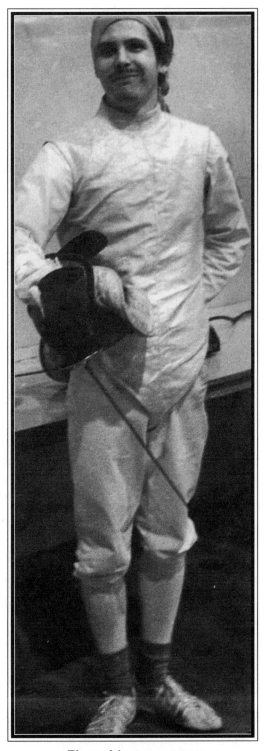

Electrical fencing equipment

THE FIRST FENCING LESSON

It's important to remember that every fencer who has ever lived, great ones included, has had his first day, when he knew nothing at all about the game of fencing. When you go to lesson numero uno and watch those experienced fencers on the floor engaged in lightning fast exchanges — lunging, parrying, riposting — they may seem as if they're in world apart from you and that what they're doing is probably unattainable. But remember, no one has ever emerged full-blown into the fencing world, knowing all there is to know, and fencing like Robin Hood, Zorro and D'Artganan all rolled into one.

Fencing above all takes work. It is a martial art, and hence, a discipline. Patience and practice. It has been said that the mastery of anything is simply repetition; and that, ultimately, is true (although it should be noted, you'd better be repeating what you're doing correctly, or you'll just end up with one heck of a reinforced bad habit).

If you go into fencing thinking you will or must be really good in a few weeks or months, you will be disappointed. You may be a decent fencer in a year or two, but, to be honest, fencing is an ongoing, lifelong process, and you will still be learning after you've been fencing for 50 years.

Again, be patient! And relax. I often tell my beginning students, "Don't be in a hurry. It took 500 years to develop this sport. You're not going to absorb it all in a single lesson." You'd be surprised how many novices get discouraged when they they're still not "expert" after six months of practice. Your goal should be merely to learn to fence. You will have ups and downs, and there will be times when you think you'll never get any better. Just take a deep breath and go on. You only fail when you quit.

My own first lesson is a case in point. After 25 years, I can still recall it as though it was yesterday. (It was that traumatic for me!)

Having seen that venerable classic swashbuckler film, *The Prisoner of Zenda*, perhaps one too many times, I entered my first fencing lesson with the thought that fencing would be easy for me, that I would shine above all others, that I would, in fact, be wonderful. Needless to say, I was not. I believe I was one of the worst first lessons I've ever witnessed. I made every mistake that could be made, my arms and legs deciding on their very own that they had no relationship to my brain (and vice versa). Worst still, my teacher, Ralph Faulkner, who was in his late-70s at the time, yelled a lot. Every time I

About the first fencing lesson

failed to follow one of his commands, he would grab the tip of my foil blade with his free hand. "No, no, no!" he would shout, banging his own blade forcefully against mine. People stared. A few, I noticed, were giggling. Worse still, all the terms sounded like Chinese to me. Nothing made any sense. Talk about sobering experiences.

I felt crushed. And certainly disillusioned, as anyone would have, starting with illusions of grandeur I'd had in my head. After my lesson, I slunk from the fencing school, thoroughly depressed, and I went home.

I was faced with some hard truths. I was not a born swashbuckler. And fencing was something that was not simple to learn. It would, in fact, take a lot of work to master.

Two weeks later, I still hadn't returned to the fencing school for another lesson. I spent a lot of time staring dejectedly at my fencing equipment. Then, one day, I said to myself, "If you don't go back for another fencing lesson now, you're never going to go back." That realization scared me. I wanted to be a fencer! So, I gritted my teeth, and, on the very next scheduled fencing day, I was there, nervous and subdued, but ready to learn.

Remember, most people only think about learning to fence. I've met hundreds of them over the years. "I always wanted to learn to fence," they invariably say, shaking their head, "but I just never got around to it."

So, as with everything important, that first step must be taken. You have to make that decision and follow through with it. That's maybe the hardest thing you'll have to do with regard to fencing. That first lesson. It means separating yourself from your comfortable, ordinary, predictable, everyday, unchallenged life and putting yourself and your ego on the line. It means taking a stand, and sticking to it. It will be well worth it, though. If you take, or have taken, that first step, you can be proud of yourself. You are part of a singular and honored minority, with a tradition and history that stretch back hundreds of years.

FENCING THOUGHT

Fencing thought is an exercise in abstraction. You must put together diverse, unrelated elements to create a cohesive and logical whole, a whole that will serve you in an efficient, effective manner. This means blending your assorted abilities with your opponent's varied responses. It's a puzzle waiting to be solved.

You might say developing the fencing thought process is like learning a foreign language. I've heard it said that to really speak a foreign language well you must be able to think in that language. And this is so true with regard to fencing. You must learn to think fencing to do fencing. Approaching fencing with regular, everyday thoughts is the equivalent of learning a language phonetically. You make the sounds, but you have no idea of the true meaning of what you're saying. In the case of fencing, the latter promotes a game that is no more than a shadow of what it might be.

At the start of your fencing training, there are a number of obstacles to overcome. Some of them are built into the training process, some are self-generated. Of the two, the second variety is the most formidable. It has been said that the greatest opponent a fencer will ever encounter is himself; and truly, to overcome our own mentally-imposed roadblocks becomes one of our greatest challenges. (This is not particular only to fencing, of course.)

Ideally, in fencing, you must be able to direct the physical actions that guide your offensive and defensive movements and think strategically at the same time. If this ability is not nurtured, the fencer will never be more than a machine on the fencing strip. The more athletic the individual, the more he will be able to overpower his opponents; but this will only last as long as his opponents remain weaker than him. The physically less capable fencer will merely trundle along, never fully achieving much success on the fencing strip. The mind must be there, or else!

Many people, both men and women, come to fencing with the societally-conditioned feeling that it is wrong to attack or strike another person. Hopefully, those students suffering from this concept get over it. I tell all my younger students that the fencing school is the kind of school where it's okay to hit the teacher and one another. To step onto the fencing strip without the full intent to succeed in every action will only lead to failure.

In the beginning, to be attacked by someone else is also a great shock to the nervous system. We may tell ourselves intellectually that we're not actually going to be hurt or killed by that masked form coming at us aggressively and that the blunted foil, sabre or épée they're pointing in our direction is harmless; but we react by seizing up emotionally. Eventually, if approached properly, confidence grows, and this perceived violence simply translates into nothing more than movement to be dealt with. Period.

Like most martial arts, fencing promotes a calm, knowing control over your behavior, a feeling of grace under fire. Anger and brutality have no place in the fencing thought process. Neither do fear and panic. All negative mental states cut you off from unruffled deliberation and lead to overreaction.

So, how do you get in touch with the mind-set of the fencer? It's not easy. If it was, there wouldn't be much need for fencing teachers. Everyone could just go out after a couple of introductory lessons and fence away like Zorro.

The road to fencing thought is two-fold. First, exercise patience. Basically, take your time. Frustration and haste will get you nowhere. Second, practice. Learn the mechanics of fencing. Learn the mental steps it takes to connect yourself to your opponent. Develop the foundation actions of fencing: the on guard position, the lunge, the recovery, the ability to advance and retreat. Needless to say, everything should be accomplished with balance. Next, perfect your offensive and defensive maneuvers in the lesson. Hold off bouting until you've gained a sense of what you're doing. That is when you don't have to think about getting your sword arm straight before you lunge, or when you don't forget to riposte after a parry, or when you don't have to recall the difference between a coulé and a doublé. Then, when you finally get around to bouting, fence as much as possible. Fence and fence and fence and fence. But, when you do, pay more attention to how you get your touches rather than just getting them. A touch should merely be an indication that you are on the right track. Relax, experiment, make mistakes, test yourself, and develop a sizable, effective repertoire. Keep the brain active. Absorb everything that happens on the fencing strip like a sponge. This approach will always keep you moving in the proper direction.

Finally, with all of this in mind, only time and experience will give you a fencer's mind. No amount of talking or intellectualizing will do it. You simply realize the process is there to be developed; and, through deeds, you accomplish that task.

If there is a secret to achieving fencing thought, this is it.

LEARNING THE WEAPONS OF FENCING — PROGRESSIVELY

The foil, épée and sabre each represent a unique approach to the art of sword fighting. Each has its own particular origins and character that reflect the way it is employed. Each demands a different set of skills be acquired. Yet, surprisingly, there is common ground for all three.

If a student of fencing wishes to truly learn the art of fencing, he should, in time, master each weapon; but the order in which they are tackled is of great importance. Although it is acknowledged that the foil was designed to be the teaching weapon of fencing, the weapon a student should begin his learning process with, it is a fact that many fencers begin their careers with the épée or sabre. These individuals would argue that such a move didn't harm them in the slightest. I believe, though, it ends up being a big mistake.

A fencing student should always start with the foil, first, and foremost, because its usage best develops abilities necessary to overall fencing mastery. It was, after all, designed for that reason. Within its structured play, the foil educates the fencer in all the elements of swordplay so important to personal control on the fencing strip: timing, distance, balance, point control, strategy, a sense of offense and defense, weapon handling and conventions. It's all there, and more. A fencer may acquire these skills outside foil fencing; but perhaps, never to the fullest extent that he might with the foil. The foil is the fine-tuning tool you need to crystallize your fencing talent.

The next weapon a fencer should move on to is the épée, the dueling sword of fencing. While fencing épée is basically a game without overriding rules to govern the way in which it may be used, it is, like the foil, a point weapon. Therefore, the point control you have already developed with the foil will be of major benefit to your épeé fencing. There are differences in foil and épée fencing, to be sure, but these are minor when compared to the importance of point control. The épée may strike anywhere on an opponent's body; yet, when you are attempting a touch on the wrist of a sword arm, on a knee, or on a foot, precise placement of the blade point is paramount in the equation. Here, too, the point control you continue to hone in the épée bout will further enhance your foil performance. Of course, the foil, unlike the épée, is a conventional weapon, with very specific rules of conduct; but I think it is easier to develop a sense for conventions, and then set them aside for épée than it is to start fencing without them in épée, and have to suddenly acquire them for foil. I've known fencers who started with the épée, and more than a few of them had the hardest time adapting to the rules foil imposed on them. Some never could get the hang it, giving up the latter in frustration.

The last weapon to be approached should always be the sabre, as it is the most divergent of the three weapons. While the point is used to some extent, the sabre is basically a cutting weapon; hence, the arm guides its manipulation, something you should avoid like the plague with the foil and épée. Yet, if the fencer has put sufficient time into learning the two point weapons, encountering this new style of play will not dramatically alter his control. Go to sabre first, however, and all the arm action needed to make cuts and parries with the sabre will definitely cause problems when it comes time to establish command over a weapon point. I can assure you that being "cut" violently with a foil or épée blade across the chest, arm or leg by an entrenched sabre person is no fun. Apologies don't help either. It still hurts like heck!

Another reason to put off studying the sabre until after the foil: the sabre is a conventional weapon, like the foil, so mastering foil conventions first will make picking up sabre conventions all the easier. Also, being a sometime point weapon, the sabre will be greatly enhanced by the study of the foil and épée. It's a sad fact that many modern sabre fencers do little or nothing with the point within the confines of their game. Think how much more effective your sabre work would be with a maneuver almost no one else employed!

Finally, we are left with this realization, that while the épée and sabre are indeed dynamic and exciting weapons to fence with, neither fully promotes basic fencing skills the way the foil does. They can, in fact, if made your initial weapon, set up habits that detract from further growth as a fencer rather than aid it.

If approached in a thoughtful, step-by-step manner, each weapon ends up complementing and improving the others. The like elements enhance one another, while the dissimilar ones, hopefully, remain isolated, and have no adverse effect.

Many, I know, will see this approach as radical or unrealistic. To me, it just seems logical.

APPROACHING YOUR FIRST BOUT

Everyone who comes to fencing wants to start bouting as soon as possible. That's only natural. To fence is the point of taking fencing lessons. You want to bout!

Yet, there is a danger of jumping into bouting and mixing it up with other fencers too soon, before you are ready for it. Some will say this is nonsense, that you really only learn to fence by bouting. It's true that the bout is the proving ground of the lesson; but, ultimately, you must ask yourself what you are accomplishing out on the fencing strip. Are you engaged in a one-on-one, intimate relationship with your opponent, studying him, probing for weakness, planning strategies, molding and manipulating his responses, undercutting his strengths? Or are you fencing without regard to his actions, reacting blindly, approaching him in exactly the same manner you cross blades with every other fencer you meet? Simply put, is your bout a conversation or is it a boring monologue? If it's the latter, no matter what anyone tells you, you're not truly fencing. If there is no thought, there is no control; and if there is no control, your entire fencing experience becomes a game of chance. In the 17th century, the fencer who approached bouting without thought or ability was called an "ignorant." In the 18th century, he was a "poker." In the 19th century, a "stabber." Today, he's just a plain old bad fencer.

It has been my experience that bouting too early in your fencing career tends to stunt a beginning fencer's overall development. A student, therefore, should come to his lessons with a sense of patience. Bouting should be set somewhere down the line for a time when he has been prepared for it as much as possible. Not only does this allow for the building of a strong foundation in your technical and mental approach to the game, but it also sets fencing up as something special, something to be taken seriously, to be respected, not just some frivolous poking with a foil to fill in a couple hours.

I know what I'm talking about. I began bouting before I was ready for it, and my early technique suffered badly for my mistake. On class days, my fencing master had many students to be concerned with, sometimes as many as 40. It was difficult for him to keep tabs on everyone all the time. Some students, like me, fell between the cracks. No one told me I would be doing anything wrong by fencing before I was prepared for it; so, one afternoon, maybe two weeks into my training, when someone asked me if I wanted to bout, I said sure! I couldn't wait to get started. And why not? First, by being asked to fence, I was being accepted by my peers into the group, and second, I was, I thought, finally achieving my dream. I was fencing, right? I poked away wildly without any concern for my opponent's defensive moves. I parried attacks with pile driver force. I never riposted once that I can recall. I was one big, unthinking reaction waiting to happen. And no wonder. I didn't know anything. I managed to instill quite a few bad habits firmly in my blossoming fencing technique that day.

It took me a full year of fencing to get myself in check, to turn myself back, to slow down, to basically start learning to fence all over again. This turnaround was inspired by a deep-seated dissatisfaction with my fencing. I felt like I was missing something important. And I was.

Eventually, through much labor on my part, I was able to reprogram my fencing by picking it apart, by finding out how it ticked. But many students, thrown into the ring too soon, never get this opportunity. Either it never occurs to them that there might be something more to fencing, or worse, they think they're pretty darned good when they really aren't.

I've been to schools where new students were allowed to bout right after their first lesson. When this happens, as far as I'm concerned, the instructor is stealing the student's money. Even if the student wants to bout, he hasn't the wherewithal to make the correct decision about what he should be doing. It may seem like fun at the moment, but the damage it creates is in some cases irrevocable. I've taken on students who had, like myself, been allowed to fence well before they were ready. Without exception, they were purely physical fencers with bad habits in almost every gesture they made, bad habits that were almost impossible to eliminate. They, of course, had no idea they were doing anything wrong.

I never let my students bout before they have gone through a progression of learning that includes a thorough blend of both physical and mental approaches to fencing. This enables the student to fully understand his relationship to his opponent on the fencing strip. This is followed by a period of engaging in conventional exercises (discussed in detail later in this book), which has often been described as the half way point between the lesson and the bout. Only after this is a student allowed to bout. This initiation period regularly lasts up to a year. As for competition, I would never allow a student to enter a tournament until he had bouted for at least a year. This may seem excessive, and perhaps a bit daunting if you are contemplating taking up fencing. But consider, if you are really serious about learning to fence properly, how much more you will get out of fencing if you begin by building a solid foundation for yourself. If you plan to fence for years, what's a few extra months preparation? When you do engage in that first bout, it will be like launching a well-built ship on the sea. You'll float and continue to float. You'll travel forward with confidence. You won't sink the first time a big wave slams into you.

Approach fencing as a fencer. When you are fencing, really fencing, you are in touch with something that stretches back hundreds of years to those early pioneers of the sword who took their weapons in hand and created a science out of whole cloth by observing the way men moved and thought in armed combat situations, art and science combined into an effective whole. That isn't something to be treated lightly.

Be ready for that first bout.

Practice.

Learn.

Earn it!

CONVENTIONS: BEHAVIOR ON THE FENCING STRIP

The fencer's behavior on the fencing strip is guided by conventions, or rules. Some of the rules cover sportsmanship; some of the rules cover the administration of the fencing bout; some of the rules cover the way a fencer should, and must, approach the fencing process.

Once upon a time, men fought with sharp swords, and the object was to kill your adversary. There were no rules. Anything it took to achieve your goal in the duel was accepted as part of the game. This was a recognized part of existence.

When fencing first became a non-lethal activity, an activity to promote personal growth, it still retained much of the "anything goes" quality of earlier times. Before specific rules were established, when fencers wished to debate certain points of fencing theory, or test their skill, they would sometimes fence with practice weapons called sharps. These sharp-tipped foils were rendered "harmless" by being fitted with a small metal cap called a gafflet. The blade tip was slipped through a hole in the cap until perhaps a quarter of an inch of point was exposed. The blade was now able to wound but not kill. The fencing that was done with these weapons was decisive play, because an outcome that featured pointed blades was beyond doubt. It was recommended by some fencing masters of the period that poor fencers be "enlightened" to their deficiencies with these weapons.

At this time, though, fencers as a rule prided themselves on their personal control and gentlemanly conduct on the fencing strip. Brutality, lack of weapon control, and poor etiquette were despised, and those who engaged in such behavior were shunned. Written rules were almost unnecessary, as true swordsmen followed a personal code of honor as strong as any edict.

Nevertheless, as fencing grew in popularity, entrenching itself as a competitive sport, it became necessary to adopt specific formulas for the sake of uniformity and clarity of purpose on the fencing strip.

In the latter part of the 19th century, famed French fencing master Camille Prevost first set down the precepts that would become the basis for international fencing conventions. However, they were not accepted at once, and certainly not universally. As might be expected, this rejection of standardization led to a certain amount of ill will when fencers from rival nations met in fencing contests.

In 1914 the rules of foil fencing were set down in an official code by two highly respected men of the sword, Marquis de Chasseloup-Laubat and Paul Anspach. This was done at the behest of the Federation Internationale d'Escrime, the organization founded in 1913 to govern worldwide fencing. Épée and sabre rules were adopted at the same time. The countries initially adhering to these rules included France, Italy, Great Britain, Germany, Holland, Bohemia, Hungary, Belgium and Norway. Later, the United States, under the guise of the Amateur Fencers League of America, would place itself under the auspices of the F.I.E..

At last, fencing had a standardized set of conventions. Nevertheless, their implementation still faced one major obstacle. Their introduction to organized fencing was interrupted by World War I, a fairly imposing barrier. It was not until 1919, when peace was restored to Europe, that Chasseloup-Laubat and Anspach's rules were put into play; and, without a doubt, fencing benefited greatly from their presence.

It should be noted that, while the general structure of fencing's conventions remains basically intact to this day, specific points have occasionally been altered and/or amended over the years to reflect modern needs.

Yet, what exactly do these conventions regulate? What do they accomplish? In part, they influence proper manners on the fencing strip. But, more specifically, they promote proper technique by guiding the way in which each weapon of fencing may be employed. The foil, the épée and the sabre each have their own set of rules.

The cultivation of proper fencing responses is essential to fencing in general. But it is especially vital in the implementation of the foil, which, as the teaching tool of fencing, establishes your foundational abilities and attitudes, which ultimately influence the learning of the épée and sabre. Furthermore, it is important to understand that foil rules were not created arbitrarily. It's not like Monopoly®, where someone sat down and made up a game plan out of thin air. The majority of rules reflect a logical process of

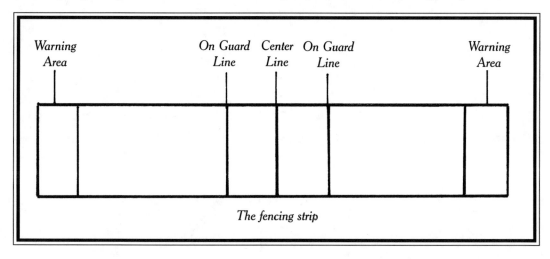

The fencing strip

thought and action, a built-in common sense, based on the practical application of the sword stemming from a time when blades had sharp points on them. There are things you should do with a weapon and things you shouldn't do. The rules, then, mold behavior by limiting it to correct actions. This is accomplished by rewarding beneficial responses and discouraging dangerous ones. Learning to stick to these rules promotes self-control. It's like being able to hit the bull's-eye on a target over and over with a bow and arrow. For the fencer, rules are the bull's-eye. They give you something to aim for.

The sabre, like the foil, is a conventional weapon, with a firm set of guiding principles. In this way, it is much like the foil, although the specific techniques of sabre usage differ, by and large, from that of the foil.

The épée, a weapon that most reflects behavior in a real sword fight, has the fewest rules governing its use. However, it still has regulations regarding sportsmanship and brutality on the fencing strip.

In closing our initial discussion of conventions, it should be noted that without them, most modern fencing would closely resemble swordplay as it existed in the 16th century. Watch a game of ice hockey on television sometime, and you'll understand what I mean.

SOME PARTICULARS OF SPORT FENCING

Besides being an art and a science, fencing is also a sport. Here, then, are a few bits of general information regarding this side, the competitive side, of our discipline. Knowing them will help you better understand how the game is played.

THE FENCING AREA

Fencing takes place on the fencing strip, or piste. The area is described as a rectangle, 46 feet long and 6 feet, 7 inches wide. The fencer must stay within its bounds while fencing. If he steps off the strip, an immediate halt is called in the action.

THE OBJECT OF THE GAME

While the underlying object of fencing is obviously to hit and not be hit, when engaged in a bout — which is the sport aspect of fencing — the goal is to hit your opponent five times before he hits you five times.

Not long ago, when a fencer was hit, a point was marked against him. Now, when that same touch occurs, the point is awarded to the successful attacker.

Either way, of course, the winner still wins and the loser still loses.

MANNERS

Good manners should be a given on the fencing strip. The first show of respect for the game, and those who engage in it, is to salute your opponent. If there is someone directing the bout for you, that person should also be saluted. Long ago, a number of elaborate salutes were employed in fencing. Today, for the most part, the salute is performed by simply inclining your blade slightly toward the person to be honored.

Another point of fencing manners is to avoid arguing over touches. Not only does this promote bad feelings, but it subverts the point of the game, slows the action to a standstill, and ultimately ruins your own concentration.

TOUCHES

In friendly bouting, a fencer should always be willing to acknowledge every touch received. On target and off. There is a truth expressed on the fencing strip that exists whether a fencer admits to

The salute

it or not. When you're hit, you're hit. Period! To avoid the issue by denying a touch —
for instance, by saying that a touch was off-target when it was really valid; or that your
opponent's touch was flat when he actually hit with the point — only ends up diminish-
ing the fencer who does it. This is so, even if you manage to fool your opponent. The
reality of an error in behavior or a lack of skill still exists; and you can't trick those things
into disappearing. Only with an honest appraisal of your own merits can you improve.
Moreover, there's no shame in being hit by a splendid attack. It happens to the best of
fencers. Besides, what's a touch, anyway? As long as you're not using sharp pointed
weapons, not much. Just a moment in time. Learn from it.

In the official fencing bout, scored on an electrical scoring machine, you need not
acknowledge touches. The box, via bright, blinking lights and loud buzzers, will do that
for you.

SAFETY

Even in the most casual of fencing settings, a fencer should always wear the proper
equipment for safety purposes. A fencing jacket, a mask and a glove are the bare minimum. A pair of athletic shoes with decent traction will keep you from slipping around,
and perhaps, twisting an ankle or pulling a muscle.

WOMEN FENCERS

For many years, women were only allowed to compete with the foil in official fencing
situations. This may seem somewhat odd, but it had to do with tradition and mistaken
notions about the physical capabilities of women. Today, women fence all three weapons.

As it should be.

Women fencers in the 19th century

THE FREE ARM AND HAND

During the days of dueling, your free arm and hand — the arm and hand without the weapon — might have been usefully employed by wielding a dagger, a cloak, a lantern or even another sword; or they might also, on their own, been used to block or grab an opponent's blade. Today, a fencer may not use his free arm or hand to block or parry his opponent's attack.

The free arm is used specifically for balance.

THE DIRECTOR

In free bouting, or loose play, fencers usually keep track of their own touches. When the fencers get a bit more serious, they may ask a third party to guide the action and keep score. This person is called the director, the president or the referee. All play on the fencing strip of official tournaments is guided by such a functionary.

The director places the opposing fencers in his charge on guard, gives them permission to fence, decides on the sequence of fencing actions, figures out who has the right to hit whom at any given time, observes and announces on and off target touches, and calls a halt to the action. He may also place penalties on a fencer for poor behavior on the fencing strip.

At one time, when bouting was judged by eye alone, the director was aided by four judges. Today, with the electric scoring machine registering touches, these assistants have been rendered obsolete.

TIME LIMITS IN THE BOUT

Fencing casually with an opponent can last as long as the fencers involved wish it to. In tournament play, a five touch bout must be completed within six minutes. Most bouts fenced do not last that long.

THE WEAPONS OF COMPETITION

Today, without exception, all fencing in organized competition is done with electrical weapons. The electrical épée was the first to be introduced to tournament play in the 1930s. The electrical foil followed in the 1950s. The sabre, the final weapon to be enveloped by technology, was brought into the electric fold in the mid-1980s.

SOME TABOOS WITH REGARD TO THE FENCING TOURNAMENT

Body contact on the fencing strip is penalized. As is deliberate brutality. Swearing and threats are no-nos. Moreover, a fencer may not leave the strip he is fencing on without permission. Nor may he employ weapons that have not been checked and approved by the tournament officials. And it goes without saying — but I will, anyway — that drugs and alcohol do not mix with fencing in any form, at any time.

YOUR FIRST TOURNAMENT

Everybody I knew at my fencing school told me I was going to win my first tournament. I thought so, too. Then, on the night before the contest, I said to myself, "Gee, what if I don't win?" That was my downfall.

I went into that tournament with thoughts of doom and impending disgrace. To say I was nervous would be an understatement. I crashed. I was too cautious, too tense and too mentally numb. I was overwhelmed by it all. I lost my first four bouts. I only started to fence by my last encounter in the preliminaries. I beat my opponent 5 to 0. Unfortunately, I was done fencing for the evening after that.

A first tournament can be very traumatic. But it doesn't have to be. And it shouldn't be. If you treat it like everything else in fencing — a learning experience — it needn't be anything more than a test of what you've learned thus far in your fencing lessons. If you approach your first tournament with the thought that no one ever remembers who came in second, consider this fact: no one really recalls who came in first either. In the end, for all the posturing and shouting, a victory is just a statistic on a book page. So what goes on out there on the fencing strip had better mean something more to you than a series of wins and loses. It had better be a real experience, full of feeling and honest self appraisal. And don't forget to have a good time.

If you do win, that's fine. But, if you don't, you've still gained valuable experience. That means you've grown as a fencer, and your chances for doing better in the future have increased.

After my disastrous first contest, I said to myself, "From now on, I'm not going to try to prove anything. I'm just going to fence like I know how to, and enjoy myself. I like fencing too much to mess it up by giving myself an aneurysm!"

And I meant it.

In my second tournament, which happened to be a highly ranked event, I took sixth place in a field of 45.

I never again worried about how I'd do in competition, and strangely enough, winning became part of my game.

I became a fencer.

Don't be in a hurry to become a champion.

Become a fencer first.

PART IV
THE FOIL

The target area of foil fencing

THE FOIL

We start our fencing training with the foil because it was designed with this purpose in mind. Its rules, the guiding force of the game, compel us to act in a particular, beneficial manner on the fencing strip. And, by continually following the rules, called conventions, we gain control over ourselves and then, hopefully, over our opponents. This control over behavior and movement is the art of fencing.

ORIGINS

This art, however, was not always the polished activity it is today. In its earliest form, even in practice, it was a rough, violent activity, and there were no special weapons with which to train. When a man wished to hone his fencing skills, he would simply place a covering over the dangerous portions of his blade, so that it could be employed for practice purposes. A sword blade with a cutting edge might be slipped into a sheath of leather; a sword's point might have a piece of wood stuck firmly onto it. This technique was called "foiling" your sword. The dictionary defines the word foil as "to prevent from being successful," and certainly by rendering a sword harmless, defeating its initial purpose — to destroy — that's just what was done. In fact, to begin with, any weapon that was treated thus was called a foil.

In time, practice swords, called "rebated" swords (rebated meaning, "to turn back," in essence, "to foil") were created especially for teaching purposes. In most respects, they were copies of the actual swords they represented, except their edges were dull, or their tips were fitted with large metal balls. Otherwise, they were just as heavy and rigid as the originals, and could still do much damage if they connected with sufficient force.

Eventually, a special weapon was designed with both practice and safety in mind. It was lighter than a real sword and more flexible. This was the foil proper. Here, the verb "to foil" became the noun "foil."

The first foils were fairly stout implements, when compared to their modern counterparts (their blades might be as much as four feet in length, with tips the size of golf balls), but they were nevertheless a big improvement over foiled or rebated swords. With them, a fencer stood a good chance of getting out of a "friendly" bout with bones, flesh, eyes and teeth pretty much intact.

The 18th century brought a more refined foil form. The blade was shorter and less weighty than that of its predecessor and could be employed quickly and with much precision. The Italians patterned their foil design after the rapier, the dueling sword of the 1600s. It employed a shallow cup guard, a straight handle and crossbars around which the fencer could wrap his fingers for added strength. The French, on the other hand, based their foil on the small sword, the dueling weapon then in use, creating a hilt that was basic in the extreme. The hand guard, now resembling a figure eight in shape, was minimized in size for lightness. The grip, which was for some time straight, finally assumed its distinctive, ingenious design, employing a slight twist and bend that caused it to fit neatly and comfortably into the hand. The crossbar, also retained for a while, was at last eliminated.

Today, besides the French and Italian foils, we also have the anatomical foil. Sometimes called a "pistol" grip foil, or an "orthopedic" grip foil, this type of weapon, of which there are numerous designs, specifically enhances hand strength, and so create a fencing mode that is both as heavy as it is aggressive.

SCHOOLS OF THE FOIL

The Italians and French developed the two dominant schools of foil fencing. The Italian style was a highly physical approach, emphasizing strength and agility. The French technique, best described as "academic," relied chiefly on control of the foil stemming from the fingers, creating a flowing, precise, efficient game, aided by a well-developed sense of strategy. To this day, these distinct attributes continue to be characteristics of the Italian and French schools of foil play.

We will not be discussing the Italian school of fencing in this book — at least not in any detail. It has certainly served those well who have followed it, and do follow it, and I have much respect for the Italian method; but I was brought up in the French school of our art. That is what I have followed for 25 years. That is what I know. And so, that is the approach we will be taking.

CONVENTIONS

But before we get to the specifics of French foil fencing, there are some general details concerning the weapon that are relevant to all foil play.

It is a fact that the conventions of foil fencing have altered from age to age. In their present form, they represent the best of fencing thought as was observed in ancient times. They reflect an ideal of fencing behavior that fencers do their best to maintain. Without these conventions, of course, it would be difficult to either teach or learn the art of foil fencing, because, minus a set of standards, the use of the foil could then be whatever the individual imparting information said it was. Foil fencing would be chaos.

We will talk now of some of those ideas that guide the use of the foil.

To begin with, the foil is a point weapon. That means that it may only touch with its tip. Blade contact made with the edge of the blade does not count.

The foil has a specifically designated target area, which is the trunk of the body. Any valid hit here will score a point. The arms are off target, as are the legs and head. The bib on the fencing mask, although it covers an otherwise on-target spot, is also off-target. The target area, by the way, was limited in this manner to promote point control.

Another important feature of foil fencing is the convention of priority, or "right-of-way." It's the same principle as when two cars arrive at an intersection at the same time. For safety sake, the convention is that the car on the right is given the opportunity to make the first move. In the same way, the foil rules establish safe behavior by delineating attacker and defender status, reflecting the notion of what should be done if the weapons being employed had sharp points.

This idea of priority, and the rules that revolve around it provide foil fencing with its most compelling element: intelligent, controlled action.

We begin with this simple concept, in an exchange between two foil fencers, the fencer who extends his sword arm first, pointing his weapon directly at his opponent's target area, becomes the attacker. The other fencer, being threatened, automatically becomes the defender and must protect himself with his blade by knocking away (parrying) the incoming blade before he may attempt his own offensive action. If he attempts to hit without first defending himself, even if he manages to touch at the same moment as the attacker, his touch is rejected by the rules. He has, in effect, initiated an outcome that would have been disastrous if, again, the blades had sharp points. Ties with sharp points are no good. You kill your adversary, but he most certainly kills you, too.

On the other hand, if the defender does successfully block the offensive maneuver that threatens him, his status immediately changes. He is now, by the rules, the attacker (actually, counterattacker) with the right, finally, to attempt a hit. Consequently, the initial attacker, no longer having priority, must revert to a defensive position.

And this is the way it goes, back and forth, back and forth, between two fencers, each vying to gain priority, until, at last, one of them manages to get one step ahead of the other and gain a touch.

This, to be sure, is a simplified version of a fencing encounter. It is, however, the basic idea underlying foil play. It may not seem "real" to some people; but real, in this case, is not as important as gaining control over your actions. We save "real" for épée fencing.

There are many other conventions that deal with proper foil usage. But we need not go into them all in this book. They may be learned and fully absorbed when you begin lessons.

THE BODY OF THE FRENCH FOIL

Now that we have seen how the foil may be employed, let's take a look at what the foil is. Specifically, the French foil.

Initially, the foil is divided into two basic portions: the blade and the hilt. The blade may be defined as the portion of a sword intended for offensive and defensive purposes. The hilt is everything else.

But now, we will break the weapon up even further.

THE HILT

The hilt is made up of four distinct and separate parts: the pommel, the grip, the petite coussin and the hand guard.

We find the pommel on the very bottom of the foil. The term "pommel" in French means "little apple." Although not so today, once many sword pommels were round, and I suppose, looked to those who employed them, like apples, poetically speaking. The pommel serves two functions. First, being somewhat hefty, it acts as a counter-weight on the weapon, drawing its balance down close to the hand, rather than leaving it

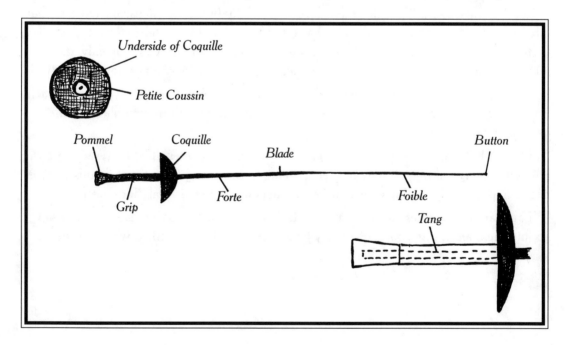

higher on the blade. The latter situation would make the foil top-heavy and unwieldy. And, second, it acts as a nut that, screwing onto the blade, keeps all the foil parts fitted tightly together.

In olden times, however, the pommels had another use. When two combatants came too close together to use their sword blades effectively, one might draw back and strike his adversary sharply with the pommel, which being a rather sturdy piece of metal, would certainly have done some damage. The modern, nonfencing, usage of the word "pommel" (or pummel) meaning "to beat," comes from this violent utilization of that part of the sword.

The next portion of the foil we encounter is the grip, or handle. In French, we call it the poigneé. This term comes from the word "poignant." For instance, a poignant story is a gripping story. A poigneé then is a grip.

The petite coussin, or little cushion, is located on the underside of the hand guard and protects the fingers from assorted sharp jolts.

The final part of the hilt is the aforementioned hand guard, or coquille (meaning "shell"). On dueling swords. the hand guard, in its various forms, was there specifically to protect the sword hand from cuts and thrusts. On the foil, it provides a general kind of protection, since the hand is not part of the foil's target area.

THE BLADE

The foil blade, which is rectangular in shape, is made up of five separate parts: the tang, the shoulder, the forte, the foible and the button.

The tang is the portion of the blade that fits snugly through the grip. It is also the blade part onto which the pommel is fitted.

The shoulder of the blade is located where the blade proper attaches to the tang. It is a narrow rim of metal that fits up against the hand guard.

The forte is the widest and sturdiest blade section. It is the lower part of the blade, nearest the hilt. Forte means "strong."

The foible is the narrowest, most flexible blade section. It is the higher part of the blade, nearest the point. Foible means "weak."

The button is the blunted tip of the foil blade.

THE SET OF THE BLADE

At the exact spot where the tang becomes the blade, a slight angle, or bend, is placed in the metal. For a right-handed foil, the bend inclines to the left. On a left-handed foil, it is to the right. This bend, called the "set," is what endows the foil with its proper balance. With a poor set, or no set, the foil will always feel clumsy in the hand. With an expert set, the foil fairly becomes part of the fencer's hand.

What is a correct set for a blade? What is too much or too little set? This is a difficult question to answer. Each blade you encounter, no matter how similar to other blades, has its own distinct personality. And the set necessary for this blade may differ slightly from what is required to produce decent balance for that blade. Each blade, then, must be taken on with that in mind.

So, how do you establish a set? The way I do it is to place the tang portion of the blade in a vice, and then give the blade a light tug so that a bend is created right where the blade and tang join. Now, assemble the foil. See how it feels in your hand when you make a circular blade movement. If the motion feels smooth and comfortable, you've got it. If, on the other hand, it feels somehow awkward, increase or decrease the set and test it again. The action should flow. Repeat the process until the weapon feels as though it is merely an extension of your fingers.

That's the way I learned to set a foil blade. Trial and error. The first time I tried it myself, it took me two solid hours of experimentation before I had what I was looking for. Now, it takes me close to twenty seconds — if I'm being extra careful.

All this may seem a bit esoteric to start with, but once you get a feel for it, you'll never have to depend on anyone else ever again for how your foils feel in your hand.

That's a good thing for any fencer.

HOLDING THE FRENCH FOIL

The great 19th century French fencer Louis Justin Lafaugere gave us one of our first enduring observations concerning the grasping of the foil: "Hold it as though it were a small bird, not so tightly as to crush it, but sufficiently firmly to prevent its escape."

How you end up holding the French foil will determine how effectively you will be able to manipulate the weapon, both offensively and defensively. Grip it properly, and it will become a deft extension of your hand. As time goes by, it may even seem to bond with your fingers. When this occurs, a perceptible sense of touch will be infused into your blade to such a degree that the weapon fairly becomes part of your nervous system. We call this development "sentiment du fer," or "the feeling of the blade." Grip the French foil awkwardly, however, and it will be never be anything more than an unwieldy club in your hand.

As a point of reference, the French grip (poigneé) has a bend in it that curves downward and to the right on a right-handed foil (to the left and downward on a left-handed foil). These characteristics, when lined up accurately in the sword hand, guarantee that the grip is being held correctly.

Another indicator for establishing accurate finger placement on the poigneé is that you'll always be holding it with your thumb and index finger (manipulators) on its two widest sides, which, it should be observed, correspond to the two widest sides of the foil blade. This should be accomplished at the spot where the grip attaches to the hand guard. Finally, to complete the process, the handle should be cradled steadily between the tip of the thumb and first two joints of the index finger. This, however, should be done without squeezing. Mindless finger pressure should be avoided at all costs. Rather than being jammed vigorously into the

Holding the french foil (Photo by Anita Evangelista)

palm of the hand for support, the poigneé should be set in place with a firmness tempered by relaxation. It then fits neatly down the center of the hand, with the last three fingers (aids) merely folded lightly over the grip to hold it in place.

Achieve anything less than this, and you're probably not holding the foil correctly. At the very least, you'll set up a paralyzing death grip that'll make you feel as though your sword hand is ready to fall off. At worst, you'll never master point control, one of the great essentials of foil fencing.

This, of course, sounds pretty awful. "Why would anyone want to use a French foil?" you might ask. "It sounds like some kind of a medieval torture device!" Don't be put off by the pitfalls I've mentioned. They exist, yet they are not insurmountable. The French grip is a natural one and may, therefore, be brought under control with perseverance.

We will approach this problem honestly. In the beginning, be prepared for your French foil to feel foreign, even clumsy, in your hand. It may slip around. You might even drop it from time to time. These setbacks happen to all beginning fencers who employ the French foil (it happened to me, too); so, as a matter of course, it is best to check its placement in your hand periodically. Then, check it again, recheck it, and recheck it once more after that. Your own awareness, and constant tinkering with the grip, will be your greatest assets in making the French foil your ally.

Regrettably, a great percentage of novices, when they encounter such momentary difficulties, immediately drop the French foil for the presumed security of the anatomical grip. Yet, don't be fooled by the lure of this grip. For all its instant "ease" of handling, it ultimately destroys any hope for sentiment du fer by producing a hand hold that is both vice-like and numbing.

Stick with the French foil, and, in time, your hand will gain an effortless strength that will fix the grip where it belongs. Then, the advantages of fencing with a French foil will become readily apparent.

ON GUARD

The first point of actual fencing we'll be discussing is the On Guard ("en garde"). It is the position from which all fencers work, so the stance you establish should be both comfortable and efficient. It is the physical foundation upon which we will build our entire approach to fencing.

It is important to remember that being "on guard" refers not only to a defensive attitude, but also an offensive one. It is, in effect, a position of readiness. The guard adopted then should allow for an effective, flowing transition from one mode of operation to the other. To be bunched into a contorted, unbalanced posture dooms a fencer to failure on the fencing strip.

Of course, for almost every beginning fencer, the on guard position will feel somewhat odd. It is obviously not a position we use in everyday life (although ballet dancers might find it somewhat familiar). It is, however, the posture best suited to fencing.

Once upon a time, historically speaking, the on guard position was whatever a given fencing master said it was. The stances adopted were based not so much on truly effective fencing but on the fencing master's own personal fancies. This, as one might expect, did not lead to many universal concepts with regard to fencing technique. It kept things fairly fragmented.

Only with the utilization of widespread standards did fencing thought solidify into a real science. It also became easier to teach and learn.

The French were pretty much the first to insist upon a common on guard position. The on guard position that the French created, and kept refining into the 18th century, is, in most respects, the same on guard position we employ today. It is one of form and balance, a perfect vehicle for promoting grace of movement and decisive play.

THE FEET

We begin with the feet, for that is where we rest our body weight, our physical balance. A fencer with poor feet placement will possess a top-heavy, uneven fencing style.

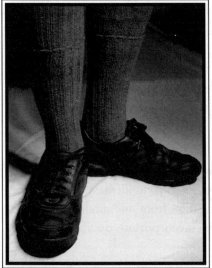

The intial placement for determining foot placement

To place the feet properly, we start by bringing the heels together so that they form a right angle. The right foot (and now we will be speaking primarily in the text of right-handed fencers) we will call the front foot; the left foot becomes the back foot. This setup forms the relationship between your feet that must be maintained. Whenever the feet fall out of alignment, the balance will go.

To help you visualize the foot setup, think of this: there is an invisible line that runs forward from the back heel upon which the front foot rests. By maintaining this image, you will be able to keep the feet proper aligned.

The right foot is, in effect, pointing in the direction of your opponent. The left foot points directly to the left. Now, with your front foot, step forward 12 to 15 inches. The exact measure will be determined by your height. Placing the feet too close together will make it easy to lose your balance; too far apart, and you will establish an overextended on guard in which it is difficult to relax.

Once you have established a comfortable and effective distance between your feet, work hard to maintain it. It is a detail that, once fixed and constant, will aid you greatly in maintaining control.

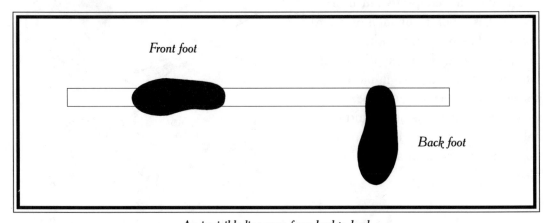

Front foot

Back foot

An invisible line runs from heel to heel

THE LEGS

The weight of the body should be placed equally on both legs. Too much weight shifted to either leg will unbalance a fencer and/or slow him down.

THE KNEES

Bend both knees equally. This will aid in distributing body weight effectively. The bend should not be so great that it causes undue strain. It will also effectively lower your center of gravity. Straight legs, on the other hand, promote loss of balance by shifting your center of gravity to your head. Find a middle ground.

THE TORSO

The torso should be erect. No leaning allowed. Coupled with properly bent knees, you will feel the balance of your body dwelling somewhere around your belly (this is a good place to keep it, too) and equally between both feet.

The torso should also be angled at about 45 degrees to your opponent. Too little angle will present too much of your target area for easy touching. Too much of an angle, although exposing very little target area, will promote a stiff, tense on guard that will quickly tire the fencer out. A correctly angled torso will be both defensible and relaxed.

THE SWORD ARM

In other ages, the sword arm was held nearly straight. This was done to keep the point continually placed in a fairly offensive manner. In the modern French style of foil fencing, the sword arm is bent. The bend should not be constricted, that is, a bend that brings the elbow in close to the body; nor should it resemble that old-time straightness. It should be a comfortable bend that places the elbow approximately over the bent front knee.

THE SWORD HAND

The sword hand should be held at chest level. The thumb of the hand should be stationed at one o'clock, a position of partial supination (palm up). We use very little pronation (palm down) in the French style of foil fencing. We will underscore it when we do.

To clarify matters, a sword hand is said to be supinated when the thumb is placed anywhere from a one o'clock position (partial supination) to a three o'clock position (complete supination). The sword hand is said to be pronated when the thumb is placed anywhere from eleven o'clock (partial pronation) to nine o'clock (complete pronation). The thumb stationed at 12 o'clock is said to be a neutral hand position.

The sword hand should also correspond with a line that runs up and down the center of the torso, dividing the body in half. This spot, when combined with the chest level position of the hand, establishes what is called the "axis" point. It is where the "high" and "low" and "inside" and "outside" portions of the body (lines) come together. I follow the concept that this should be a position of balance, each section being no more opened or closed than any other. This allows for equal attention to be paid to the entire target area.

There is another school of fencing thought, however, that suggests that the sword hand should be held in a placement that noticeably closes off one portion of the body or another. That section of the target area is then, according to this technique, impervious to attack. This is called "closing off the line." It is a standard practice in foil fencing today; yet, I see it as setting up an unbalanced response, one that leads easily to wide, exaggerated, sweeping blade movement, and general overreaction.

Better a fencer should learn economy of movement with his foil. And this is achieved only when a well-defined, balanced axis point with the sword hand has been established. In the end, it enhances your ability to maintain fencing responses that will always have an underlying sense of control.

THE FOIL

Proper foil tip level should be another constant for you. It sets up a given from which effective blade movement can be maintained.

The tip of the foil should be held at your eye level. Not at the eye level of your opponent. Not at your opponent's throat. Not, for the most part, at any other odd, undisclosed level. Your eye level is where it should be. Why?

When the point of the foil is too high, the weapon is naturally drawn back, which allows your opponents to get in too close before they might be stopped. When the point is too low, it creates a defensive response whereby the foible (weak part) of your weapon is coming up against the forte (strong part) of your opponent's weapon. Weak against strong? Not a good way to oppose your adversary.

THE HEAD

The head should be erect. Never tuck in the chin; this is constrictive. Nor should the head be leaned forward. This tends to throw your balance off.

THE FREE ARM

The free arm is one of the most important, and, from what I can see, most neglected, tools in modern fencing technique. Probably because most fencers see it as extraneous to what they are trying to produce: a touch. After all, it holds no weapon. How important can it be, right? To most fencers, it's just there, a piece of nonfencing meat. So, it just flops or hangs without purpose; and consequently, the fencer deprives himself of a vital asset of control.

To begin positioning the free arm properly, the elbow should be raised until the part of the arm extending immediately from the shoulder is parallel to the ground. The arm is now bent at the elbow, so that, with the forearm pointing straight up, a right angle is formed.

Here, the free arm is extended from the body at a 45 degree angle. This arrangement helps to support the 45 degree angle necessary for torso placement and, thereby, improves your overall form.

THE FREE HAND

Lastly, the free hand hangs freely, almost limply, at the wrist. The palm and fingers should be facing forward and downward.

A FINAL NOTE

This, then, is the on guard position. Practice it. Feel comfortable with it. Use it well. It's going to be there for the rest of your fencing career. Once you master it, once it becomes a position as familiar and comfortable to you as, say, sitting down in a chair, you are on your way to becoming a fencer.

THE LINES OF THE BODY

We're going to digress for a moment from the development of foil technique to expand on a concept vital to the basic understanding of the art of fencing.

The lines of the body.

What are those?

In fencing, for the sake of clarity of understanding and purpose, the body is divided into four equal quarters or sections — called "lines" — which give us a definite sense of location and direction concerning any attack or defensive move being made. When we speak of specific lines, then, we create an immediate, universal image that cannot be misunderstood. This is as important for teaching purposes as it is for learning.

In other fencing epochs, these divisions of the body were either simplified to just a few, or multiplied into complicated combinations, depending on the fencing master who was expounding on the subject. Often, they had little to do with actual fencing realities and more with a desire to create something original and unique.

Today, we employ a straightforward set of lines that flow from one to another with a sense of natural progression and purpose.

As we have already noted, the body is separated into four equal quarters. This division gives us a total of eight distinct positions. This is because we have four in supinated hand positions and four in pronated hand positions. Four and four equals eight, the last time I looked.

Now, in foil fencing, depending on which line you are attacking or defending with your blade, and whether the sword hand is held in supination or pronation, that quarter is given a specific name (which is a number expressed in Old French or Latin).

Before we explain these terms in detail, however, we will look at some general line designations as they relate to fencing. The two quarters above the sword hand are labeled the "high" line; the two quarters below the sword hand are the "low" line. The two quarters facing the palm side of the sword hand are called the "inside" line; the two quarters facing the back of the sword hand are the "outside" line. That gives us a "high-inside" line and a "high-outside" line, a "low-inside" line and a "low-outside" line.

Now, back to the specifics — the eight lines of foil fencing. They are prime, seconde, tierce, quarte, quinte, sixte, septime and octave. Huh? In English, it's one, two, three,

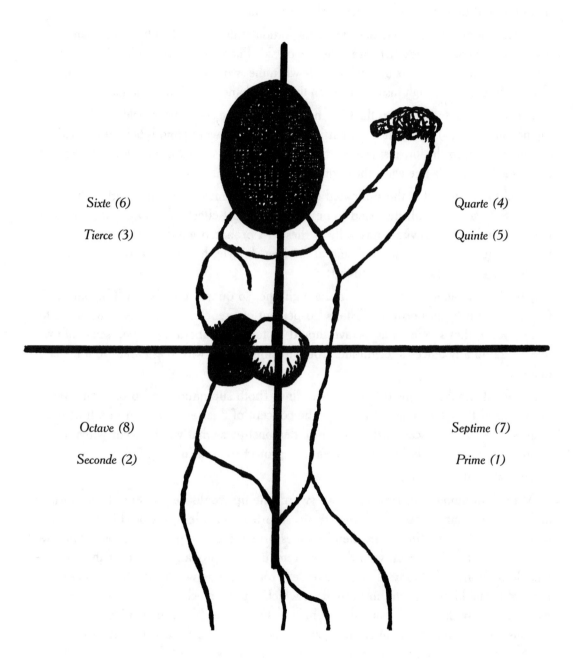

Sixte (6)

Tierce (3)

Quarte (4)

Quinte (5)

Octave (8)

Seconde (2)

Septime (7)

Prime (1)

four, five, six, seven and eight. We use the old terms because they are part of our fencing tradition, and they keep us in touch with our heritage.

The line of prime (1) covers the low-inside portion of the body when the sword hand is held in pronation. Seconde (2) covers the low-outside line when the sword hand is held in pronation. Tierce (3) covers the high-outside when the sword hand is held in pronation. Quinte (5) covers the high-inside line when the sword hand is held in pronation.

The line of quarte (4) covers the high-inside line with the sword hand held is held in supination. Sixte (6) covers the high-outside line when the sword hand is held in supination. Septime (7) covers the low-inside line when the sword hand is held in supination. Octave (8) covers the low outside line when the sword hand in held in supination.

Of all these lines, it is the supinated ones we will be most concerned with. The French foil was, after all, designed to be employed most effectively in a supinated hand position, and so we gravitate naturally to these. A pronated hand tends to promote heavy actions, which are an anathema to the French style; hence, we avoid them to a greater degree (although not entirely).

Most fencing action takes place in the high line, so quarte and sixte will be our main focus. These two lines govern perhaps 90 percent of French foil fencing. This is not to say, however, that septime and octave should be forgotten about. A strong sense of low-line is vital to any fencer's technique. You will simply deal with these areas to a lesser degree.

Finally, it should be noted that all these lines (both supination and pronation) were not assigned their locations arbitrarily. The concept of this setup, rooted in a time when swords were worn in scabbards at the hip, demonstrates what would occur when a swordsman drew his blade from its sheath to protect himself in a fight.

Let's start at the beginning:

At the first moment of exposing your sword, the tip would be pointing downward, and the sword hand would be automatically in pronation. Here, it would be easiest to cover your low-inside line. This then becomes prime, the first position. From prime, we simply move the blade over, with the hand remaining in pronation, to cover the low-outside portion of the body. This is seconde. From seconde we flip the blade point upward to the high line, still in pronation, which, by the mechanics of the movement, naturally covers the high-outside line. This gives us tierce. Now, to avoid a heavy response in the high-inside line, our next destination, we turn the sword hand into supination. This becomes our fourth line, quarte. It is expedient, here, to stay in the same quarter, a popular spot in foil fencing, but with the sword hand turned back to pronation for a bit of strength. This is quinte. From quinte, we shift our blade directly back to the high-outside line, at the same instant turning the sword hand back into supination. Sixte is established. After this, with the sword hand continuing in a supination position, we drop the foil point back into the low line, covering the low-inside portion of the body, septime. At last, with the sword hand still in supination, the foil is moved back to encounter the low-outside line one last time. Octave, the end of the trail. It is all quite natural and scientific.

That's the way I learned it.

Anyway, when I speak of moving from one line to another, these are the divisions I am speaking of.

INITIAL FOOTWORK: ADVANCING AND RETREATING

To be able to travel along the fencing strip with measured smoothness is vital to successful bouting. Losing your balance in the heat of an exchange, or continually fencing toe-to-toe with an opponent in a cramped, jabbing jumble is certainly counter-productive to the goals of our art.

Mobility is obviously accomplished through the application of footwork. Establishing and maintaining proper foot placement during forward or backward locomotion gives us stability. It is especially important for developing balance and distance. Carrying this idea even further, footwork and blade work are ultimately joined in the evolution of that elusive component of fencing: timing. It is, then, more momentous than you might think by watching it being carried out. If your feet tend to operate independently of your sword hand, the result will be that you're always too close or too far from that person you are attempting to score a touch against. A bad thing.

So, extra care should be exercised right from the start to focus on footwork and to practice it over and over and over again. Luckily, footwork is one of those elements of fencing that can be repeated without a partner, and hence, is accessible on a regular basis to every beginner.

When we fence today, we do so in a straight line. Early swordsmen, however, moved around each other in a circular fashion. This was accomplished by placing one foot in front of the other. Such foot movement was called "passing." Sword fighting footwork, at this point in time, was influenced by two factors: one, that cutting swords were being used; and, two, the weight of said weapons. Sweeping cuts from these bulky swords, which were delivered with the entire arm, were best accomplish in a roundabout style. In the 17th century, when the emphasis of blade work shifted to the sword point, a need to create a forward momentum that would produce deeply penetrating hits gave vent to a linear style of play. In the growth of fencing technique, this was inevitable.

In the French school of fencing the term for advancing is "gagner la mesure," or "to gain distance." Retreating is termed "rompre la mesure," or "to break or lose distance."

To advance, take a step forward with your front foot, as though you were walking. Land on the heel, and place the foot flat. The back foot is then picked up, brought forward, and set down. The advance has been completed.

Retreating is simply a reverse of the advance, the hind foot taking the lead in this instance. It is picked up, and moved backward; and when it is set down, it is set down flat. The front foot then moves with its own rearward step. The heel is set down first, after which the rest of the foot is placed flat. The retreat has been completed.

These actions should always be overlaid with a sense of form guided by the taking of properly defined steps. This, of course, is more likely to occur when your steps flow out of circumstances that promote control. Whenever you take a step on the fencing strip, either forward or backward, that step should always be launched from the on guard position, which means, among other things, the knees should remain bent. The feet should also remain in that right angle alignment we have already discussed.

Moreover, for every step taken, the feet should be the same distance apart after the step as they were before the step. This should be a constant factor. An ever shifting distance between the front foot and back foot will cause all sorts of little glitches to appear in your fencing.

It is very easy in the early stages of fencing training for the feet to take on a life of their own, almost as if you've never used them before. Therefore, I will emphasize here how important it is for the novice fencer to continually check his foot placement after each step completed.

A particular practice sequence of footwork might go thus: advance, advance, retreat, retreat, advance, retreat, advance, advance, advance, retreat, advance, retreat, retreat, retreat. The combinations, though, are limitless.

Take on footwork slowly to start with. Get a feel for it. Learn to move with a graceful flow, rather than with a jerk, a lurch or a bounce. This is how you will be getting around on the fencing strip forever after.

THE ENGAGEMENT

Two foils are said to be "engaged" when they are touching or nearly touching in any line. This is a normal position for blades to be held, because it allows for a well-defined, ordered transition from one line to another. The further you must move your blade in any direction so that it may interact with an opponent's weapon, the more that action runs the risk of becoming overbalanced and, therefore, easily taken advantage of.

Nevertheless, the engagement should be anything but static. Being stuck, statue-like, in one spot is one of the worst things any fencer can do. Your engagement should, in fact, be a continually shifting situation. We call this variable blade movement a "change of engagement." In its simplest form — a single change — your blade is simply moved from one line to the line directly opposite.

Changing an engagement from one high line to another is accomplished by passing your blade point beneath an opponents blade. Changing engagement from one low line to another is accomplished by passing your blade point over the top of an opponent's blade.

Yet, we aren't held to the execution of single changes of engagement. Changes may be employed one at a time or in rapid succession. The "double change," for instance, or the "triple change." The list goes on and on. Which combination is most suitable? Only the moment, and your opponent, will reveal this.

Of course, there are specific reasons for employing the change of engagement. Defensively speaking, to continually change your line of engagement makes it difficult for your opponent to get a fix on your foil, thereby making it more difficult for him to formulate a successful attack against you. On an offensive level, a repeated change of engagement is an ideal mechanism for distraction, keeping your opponent continually "off guard" with his defensive posturing. His attention is settled in one line; suddenly you're somewhere else. He must shift his focus back and forth, back and forth, running the risk of fixing his attention in one position for perhaps a moment too long. If done well, this will produce holes in his defenses that you can slip through. You may also change your line of engagement to produce a sought after attack response from an opponent, basically forcing him to attack into a specific line that you are fully prepared for. This forced response, then, because it is fully anticipated, is more easily worked to your advantage. In this particular situation, we would call the change of engagement an "invitation," an action set up to produce a hoped-for response from your adversary.

Of course, these blade movements should merely be a supplement to your overall fencing strategy. Relying on them too much will limit your focus and hence, weaken your own game if your opponent happens to circumvent your ploy.

ABSENCE OF BLADE

When two blades are out of close proximity to one another, we have a situation referred to as "absence de fer," or the deliberate avoidance of contact with your opponent's blade. While it is employed today as a matter of course, with fencers virtually always in this overdone form of the on guard position, I personally think it should be employed sparingly.

More than anything else, absence de fer should be used as a momentary scheme to confound another fencer. To apply it without discretion produces an unbalanced, muscular situation where your blade movement ends up being both obvious and exaggerated, two things blade movement should never be.

However, used sparingly, it may be employed to great effect. Generally speaking, it might be utilized to confound an opponent, especially a beginning fencer, who is not familiar with its application and is, therefore, unable to respond effectively against it. Defensively, it may be used to avoid an opponent's powerful hand, thereby counteracting physical superiority. Offensively, like the change of engagement, it may be brought into play as an excellent invitation.

Fencing with absence of blade

As popular as this form of on guard position might be in modern fencing — and it is most certainly widespread — I would nevertheless caution any fencer against making it his standard form on guard. In the end, odd posturing is no substitute for a well-developed, efficient fencing technique. The latter may take longer to perfect, but it will always be there for you to draw on. The former will not.

POINT IN LINE

To come on guard with point "in line" means that your sword arm is completely straight and that your foil point is directly menacing an opponent's target area. This is sometimes done to confound another fencer, especially if that fencer has no idea how to deal with it. It may also serve as an invitation.

It is, in point of fact, a very threatening, overtly offensive action that demands attention. Furthermore, it is one that establishes right-of-way for the fencer doing it. By the conventions of foil fencing, then, if you encounter it, you are required to deflect the instigator's point before you may execute your own attack. A fully established right-of-way cannot be argued with. You are never encouraged by the rules of the foil to attack onto an opponent's waiting blade point. Once again, if you were fighting with sharp pointed swords, that would be

Fencing with point in line

dumb beyond words. Even if you managed to hit at the exact same moment as the other guy, the conventions would shoot you down, touchwise. Following a common sense approach to fencing, even promoting ties, is a no-no. In our theoretical world of deadly weapons, hitting your opponent as he hits you is not a very satisfying conclusion to your sword fight. He dies, but you die, too. No, you must protect yourself in everything you do. And that is that.

So, now that we've definitely established that deflecting that old point in line is a must, how do you go about accomplishing it? Well, beats and binds are the two most accepted methods (and we will, to be sure, be discussing these in due course).

In conclusion, fencing with your foil point in line can be a useful strategy. But, like anything else in our art, if it is overused, it becomes a crutch just waiting to be collapsed. Remember, while everything in fencing can certainly be used effectively to your advantage, likewise there is nothing you do that cannot be taken advantage of.

The classical Roman writer Terence said in the early B.C.s, "Moderation in all things." In fencing especially, this is a good idea.

THE LUNGE

The lunge, simply put, is the action we employ to propel an attack forward. The French name for the lunge is "développment."

Swordsmen previous to the 17th century, as has already been noted, fought in a circular fashion, passing their right foot in front of the left, or the left in front of the right, to either attack or retreat. With this style of play there was no need for a lunging action and really no way to incorporate one. But, with the advent of the thrusting rapier in the late 1500s, the nature of fencing changed, with point work becoming all important. When fencing took on a linear approach to accommodate this change, a need to drive the sword point forward with sufficient momentum to disable your adversary permanently became of paramount importance. The lunge was the logical answer to this demand.

Still, it took many years for the lunge to be accepted by the entire fencing community. Old concepts about swordplay, entrenched by centuries of use, often die hard. But, in time, the lunge proved to be such a devastating maneuver, it could hardly be argued that it was without merit. Eventually, it was embraced by fencing masters throughout Europe as if it had always been an action of choice. Our modern lunge has not changed much from its early ancestor.

The lunge as it was envisioned in the 1600s by Italian fencing master Ridolfo Capo Ferro

We will now discuss the lunge, how it is accomplished and why it is accomplished in the manner it is. Conventions, it should be noted, play an important role in what transpires.

THE ON GUARD POSITION

To start with, the lunge is always launched from the "on guard" position. I don't know of any other way to do it effectively. It is unfortunate that many modern fencers, apparently in a hurry to mow down their opponent, try to lunge from all sorts of odd body configurations, but I think these gyrations, even if they manage to produce touches, should be avoided. They are not controlled, and hence, have no universal application. Simply put, you can't count on them to produce a successful result.

THE SWORD ARM

The first thing that happens in the lunge process is that the sword arm should be extended, from the shoulder, completely straight. This is a must and is vital to effective fencing. The great teachers have echoed this for ages in their own instruction. French fencing master Camille Prevost, the father of modern fencing conventions, observed in his *Theorie pratique de l'escrimé* (1886), "... it is essential that the extension of the right arm precedes movement of the body." Maestro Aldo Nadi underscored this in his classic *On Fencing* (1943): "Hand before foot, always."

Why? Well, we begin with this premise, based on fencing conventions: to become the attacker on the fencing strip, you must extend your sword arm before your opponent does. This is the prerequisite that produces "right-of-way" in every attack. When it is accomplished, the other fencer is automatically designated the defender and must deflect the attacker's incoming blade before he can attempt to score a touch himself. Anything less than a straight arm, however, will not truly establish priority.

Yet, why should the sword arm necessarily be straight? Remember, the rules of foil fencing are based on a common sense approach to sword fighting (that is, on what we should do if our weapons had sharp points). They attempt to promote the effect of being able to hit without being hit. This straight arm then must produce some very positive results for it to be an attack requirement.

The extension of the sword arm

Here's what the straight sword arm does for us:

First and foremost, when the sword arm is fully extended, the attacker will have the full potential of his reach when he lunges, which gives him the best opportunity to score a hit. An arm that is less than straight during a lunge will obviously foreshorten that lunge. Also, if your opponent decides to counterattack by straightening his sword arm, and the attacker lunges with a bent arm, the opponent will have the longer reach and hit first.

Moreover, when your sword arm has been straightened, your foil point becomes relatively fixed, which improves your chance of placing a touch where you hope to. This, as we know, is called point control.

Finally, the extended sword arm and blade improve your sense of distance by offering a fixed point of reference from which to effectively gauge your offensive approach.

All of this is common sense, or should be; but there are still those who argue that an "extending" arm, rather than an "extended" arm, is sufficient to the attacking process. However, by working the idea out logically, and applying it to what has already been observed, we immediately come to the conclusion that such an arrangement gives us less than we need to produce a successful lunge.

Don't be confused: straighten the sword arm.

SWORD HAND

As the sword arm is extended fully, the sword hand should be rotated from partial supination (with the thumb at one o'clock) to complete supination (with the thumb at three o'clock). Another "why?" This is easy to answer. The French foil grip was designed to be used most effectively when the hand is in complete supination. The up-

An incorrect bent-arm attack

turned hand, combined with the straight sword arm, forces the manipulation of the foil into the fingers, where such ministrations will be both economical and efficient. The less supination you use, the more the sword arm may creep into your game, which tends to produce wide, heavy actions.

THE FOIL

The foil should be held so that its blade is parallel, from button to hilt, to the ground.

THE BACK LEG

We now shift our attention to the back leg, because this is where the lunge is actually generated. The lunge is not created by the front leg stepping forward, but by a forward push from the rear.

The back leg snaps straight, which forces the entire body forward. The action, when performed properly, creates an accelerating, piston-like effect.

THE BACK FOOT

The back foot should stay completely flat on the ground, planted as though it were nailed to the floor. This foot is, after all, the base point of the lunge. If it remains flat, it is likely the lunge has been performed correctly, and you will achieve effective forward motion.

On the other hand, if the lunging fencer rises up off the heel of the back foot and onto the toe, it is a clear indication that the lunge was achieved by a step of the front foot, rather than a push from the back leg. Such a practice may produce both a retarded lunge and a loss of balance.

Now, if the back foot rolls, even slightly, a lean has been added to the lunge. Leaning, of course, throws your weight forward, disturbing your true center of gravity.

THE FRONT FOOT AND LEG

The front foot is picked up as the back leg straightens. The front leg moves forward at the same time. But the action should not be a step. Rather, the front leg should merely be lifted and then set down. Basically, it's just something to land on. If the front leg incorrectly generates the lunge with a pronounced step, the forward action will decelerate or slow down, the closer the attacker's blade gets to his opponent's target area.

THE FRONT FOOT

The front foot sets down heel first; then, drops flat. It is important here that the foot should still be pointing straight ahead. If it's pointing inward, even slightly, you'll likely lose your balance. An inward angle on the front foot is also an indicator that the lunge has been produced by the front foot stepping rather than by the back leg pushing.

THE FRONT KNEE

The knee of the front leg bends forward as the front foot sets down and continues forward until it is directly over the front ankle. If the knee ends up behind the ankle, an "under-lunge" has been produced. This shortens the length of the lunge. If the knee extends beyond the front angle, an "over-lunge" has been produced. While this type of lunge does produce a slightly longer reach, it also promotes leaning, which shifts the entire weight of your body onto the front leg. This both tires the leg and makes it difficult to recover from the lunge easily.

THE TORSO

The torso is inclined slightly forward. Not so much, though, that you feel the weight of your body thrown onto the front leg.

THE FREE ARM AND HAND

As the back leg straightens, the free arm should be snapped backward until completely straight and dropped until it's on a level not quite parallel to the back leg. Dropping the back arm too much, however, may impede the forward thrust of the lunge.

This crisp, backward snap of the free arm, if performed properly, adds to your forward momentum. It's the principle in physics that for every action produced there is a direct and opposite reaction. Simply put, throw the arm back quickly, shoot forward.

Once extended, the free arm also promotes stability in the lunge by maintaining balance. The free hand, palm turned up fully, plus the straight arm, keeps your rear end tucked in and the back shoulder upright. This prevents the fencer from falling inward.

Finally, to give the free arm its full credit, and to strongly emphasize its interjection into the lunge, you should realize that the arm further aids you in the development of point control. When the arm is thrown back, it acts as a rudder, like on a boat. If it is snapped straight back, the lunge will consequently move forward in a straight line, an ideal situation for placing your foil point on target. If the arm is swung back, and pulled in a constricting fashion behind the fencer, it will cause the body to pivot, sending your point in at an awkward angle. If the arm is thrown up and back in a kind of windmill action, it will produce a lunge that likewise arches forward, instead of one that moves in a straight line.

Of course, if the free arm is not used at all, as in the case some modern fencing techniques, it will not help the fencer at all, and a valuable asset will be lost.

Use the free arm. It will serve you well.

Practice the lunge as much as you can. Like the advance and retreat, it is something you can perfect without another fencer being present. But when you do work on it, never

The modern lunge

Practice, practice, practice...

focus in on a single component of the lunge. To learn the action well, all parts of the body must be working in conjunction with one another. The sword arm, the back leg, the front leg, the back arm, everything! That's the only way to properly instill the lunge into your system.

Work on it. If you never learn to lunge effectively, your attacks will always be less than they can be. If you master the lunge, your attacks will be devastating.

THE RECOVERY

Once you have propelled your attack forward with a fully extended lunge — whether successful or unsuccessful in its intent to deliver a touch — it will become necessary at some point to return to the "on guard" position. This is known as the recovery (or sometimes "retaking the guard"). It may simply be a matter of form, a transition from an offensive posture to one of readiness; or it may be a calculated escape from an adversary's counterattack. Either way, it should be accomplished in an ordered, flowing manner.

To carry out the basic recovery, you should begin by pushing off firmly from the front foot while at the same moment bending the back leg. This will initiate a shift of body weight backward. To enhance the move, the free arm must also be employed in a quick, upward pull. Performing these actions in conjunction will pretty much yank you out of the lunge.

Yet, to be truly useful, the recovery must be more than just a mindless throwing of your weight in a rearward plunge. The action must be molded once more into a well-ordered position of equilibrium.

To complete the recovery properly, the front foot should be planted — heel first, then flat — in its original "on guard" starting point. Also, bend both knees, placing your weight equally on both legs; withdraw the sword arm; and return the sword hand to its balanced axis point. Finally, raise the tip of your foil to eye level. Here, the recovery has been completed.

At times, though, you might decide that gaining ground when recovering, rather than losing it, will prove to be of more value to you. This is accomplished through the forward recovery. It is similar in most respects to a standard recovery except that you draw the back leg up and forward when returning to the "on guard" posture.

Now, you are ready to either launch a new offensive maneuver or formulate a defensive one.

THE FLECHE

Fleche means "arrow."

It is a leaping or jumping attack made by pushing forward from the front foot and launching yourself forcefully into the air. With sword arm outstretched, reaching, straining for a touch, and torso leaning conspicuously in the direction of the attack, the fencer performing the fleche is said to resemble, metaphorically-speaking, an arrow in flight. Hence, the name.

The fleche is used specifically to attack quickly and unexpectedly, from well out of distance. It may also be employed to catch up with a constantly retreating opponent.

Immediately upon becoming airborne the fencer must swing his back foot in front of his lead foot, which both adds momentum to his spring and gives him a well-placed foot to land on. If he does not cross over his feet, he will land on his face. I once saw this take place, performed by a fencer who forever after was known as "the Torpedo."

If done correctly, the fleche will hit before the back foot makes contact with the ground.

Because of the unalterable impetus produced by the fleche, its greatest weakness, there is little, if any, defensive response you can generate if the attack fails (its greatest weakness). So, it should be managed with care. If the move doesn't hit, the fencer should just keep going until he passes by his opponent. This will bring a halt to the action and prevent a counterattack he has no hope of stopping.

But, whether successful or unsuccessful, to complete the fleche, the attacker should immediately veer off to the right, away from his opponent. This will prevent a collision of some magnitude.

I once had the misfortune to launch a fleche at the very same moment my opponent set the exact same attack into motion. We collided in midair like some

The fleche as pictured on a Polish postage stamp from the 1950s

111

great aeronautic disaster, mingling, for a moment, arm over head, knee into stomach, elbow against back, foot under armpit. Then, we collapsed in a tangled Gordian knot of bodies and foils on the floor. It hurt. Luckily, such freak mishaps do not occur very often on the fencing strip. I only mention it now to underscore the need for extreme diligence when accomplishing the fleche.

The fleche may also be used in conjunction with other offensive actions, if the situation warrants it.

The surprise generated by a perfectly executed jumping attack will aid considerably in its successful culmination. So, don't overdo it.

THE RUNNING ATTACK

The running attack is fairly self-explanatory. In carrying out your attack, you run at your opponent rather than lunging. Pretty basic. It is used quite a lot in sabre fencing — where the implementation of foreshortened cuts instead of fully extended thrusts makes it feasible — but should be avoided in foil like the plague.

There isn't much complexity to the running attack. You extend your sword arm and charge forward. This looks a lot like medieval jousting. This, of course, doesn't allow for much strategic input.

But the worst thing about the running attack is the lack of precision it generates for the foil fencer. When running — passing one foot quickly in front of the other — it is almost impossible to judge distance sufficiently well to control the placement of your weapon point.

Moreover, foil fencers who engage constantly in running attacks have a nasty habit of initiating cramped exchanges at close quarters; or, even worse, they engage in bone jarring physical contact (corps-a-corps), one of the worst displays of out-of-control behavior a fencer can perpetrate on the fencing strip.

When you have a foil in your hand, forget about running attacks.

THE SIMPLE ATTACK

There are two types of attacks in fencing: simple and composed. In this chapter, we will be dealing with the former. We start with the simple attack because it is fundamental to fencing technique.

Historically, the simple attack is the oldest form of offensive response. In days of old, swords were heavy and cumbersome. Actions performed with them were naturally broad and slow moving, especially when compared to modern fencing exchanges. Actions of a complex nature could not be feasibly executed with such weapons. Hence, the attacks taught then were fairly straightforward and uncomplicated. Flamboyant maneuvering with your sword was considered by most experienced fencing masters to be too dangerous to even contemplate. Any attack taking more than a few moments to perform left the perpetrator open to potentially devastating counterattacks.

Eventually this situation changed, producing a whole new complicated mode of attacking. But we won't go into that now. The simple attack will give us more than enough to discuss for the time being.

So, let's get specific. What the heck is a simple attack, anyway? Basically, it is an offensive process made up entirely of timing and speed — delivered with a lunge — in which the attacking fencer hits his opponent before the latter can respond defensively.

There are four simple attacks in foil fencing.

THE DIRECT ATTACK

The first simple attack we will look at is the direct, or straight, attack (in French, the "coup droit"). It is performed by extending the sword arm quickly in the line one is on guard in and lunging.

As the sword arm extends, the sword hand should be turned into complete supination. This will steady the blade as it moves toward its target.

The direct attack obviously gets its name from its forthright presentation. Yet, for all its perceived simplicity, it is anything but simple to execute successfully. Since there is little to mask its advent, efficient timing must be employed in setting it up.

THE DÉGAGE

The next simple attack we encounter is the dégage, which is French for "disengage." It is by far the most popular of all the simple attacks. Probably because it seems to be physically the easiest to perform.

The dégage is an attack that passes from one line to the line directly opposite by dropping beneath the blade of your opponent. For instance, you may decide to travel from the line of quarte to that of sixte. Or you might move from sixte to quarte. Only the situation will inform you which is best.

It is important here that the attacker's sword arm be extended as his foil accomplishes its passage. (The key word in this sentence is "as" — not "before," and not "after," — "as.") This insures that the sword arm will be 100 percent extended immediately upon reaching the new line. In this same motion, fully supinate the sword hand. This both stabilizes the action and expedites the line change.

When these requirements have been fulfilled, it is time to lunge.

The term "disengage" is derived from two blades being "engaged;" then, when the attack is made, "disengaged."

THE COULÉ

Then, we have the coulé. Which means "running." It is a simple attack that slides along an adversary's blade. It is accomplished by simultaneously initiating blade contact with an opposing weapon and extending the sword arm straight, and then lunging. The attacking blade thereby glides along this route until it hits.

It is important, however, that your forward thrust be made with a very light touch. Any overt pressure may force your opponent's foil out of line and, because of continued blade contact, your own weapon with it. Placing the sword hand into complete supination as you extend, in this case, will promote the desired result.

THE COUPÉ

The final simple attack is the coupé, or "cut-over." It is a simple attack that passes from one line to another by cutting over the top of an opponent's blade. The sword arm is pulled back slightly, which lifts both sword hand and foil point. This allows the attacking weapon to clear the tip of the other blade, making it a simple matter to then drop into the opposite line.

With the lowering of your blade point, the sword arm should be extended fully. Also, as in previous simple attacks, the sword hand should be turned from a partially supinated position to a completely supinated one. In this instance, supination steadies your blade point as it descends, keeping it from dipping below the level of your sword hand.

After the sword arm has been straightened, lunge.

Because the coupé first requires a bending of the sword arm — which, in effect, gives an opponent the opportunity to claim right-of-way — the pulling back and straightening of the sword arm should be done in a single, fluid motion, allowing for the quick completion of the attack.

Which simple attack is best?

While the disengage may be the most popular, in truth, no one simple attack is any better than another, and, in most cases, they may be used interchangeably. So, why do we have so many simple attacks? Well, each one presents a slightly different timing attached to its execution; and each has a slightly different visual effect. By mixing them up, it becomes more difficult for your opponent to lock onto your timing and stop your attack.

Moreover, by cloaking your simple attacks in energetic footwork and numerous changes of engagement, you may sufficiently distract and confound your opponent to make these simple actions quite difficult to deal with.

The great Spanish fencing master Julio Castello was an enthusiastic proponent of the simple attack, stating, "The straight thrust and the disengage with the foil, and the simple cutting attack with the sabre, if done properly with distance, cannot be parried. The reason is one of simple mathematics. The distance to be traveled by the point or edge of the attacking weapon to the target is a little longer than the line traveled by the parry. But the initiative taken by the attacker is sufficient, in terms of reaction time, to make up for the distance fully."

PREPARATIONS

A preparation may be any action performed in bouting to pave the way for an attack. This may include random blade movement, false attacks, light beats, heavy beats, controlled changes of engagement, footwork and feints of attacks. Such moves, of course, are part of your strategic design and must, by necessity, be cultivated thoroughly.

Feints are especially useful in the preparation of an attack, because they help to create a sense of anticipation, even one of imminent threat, in your opponent's mind.

Sometimes you may want to set up a well prepared attack, one that has been molded with craftsman-like precision. Yet, to engage in this constantly can be a mistake. If your opponent catches on to the timing of your preparation, he may launch his own counterattack and catch you flat-footed. Attacking into an adversary's preparation is a highly useful way of gaining the offensive. Certainly, if a fencer's mind is full of offensive thoughts, there is no way he can at the same moment defend himself. This, then, can be a highly vulnerable time for a fencer. Therefore, you should stagger your arranged attacks with ones that spring from the moment. This approach will make it more difficult for another fencer to get the goods on you.

INVITATIONS

An invitation, in terms of fencing, may be any action used to guide or provoke an opponent into a hoped for response. It's like sending an invitation to someone to get them to come to a party. They are a valuable part of strategy development.

Invitations may be subtle, such as a lean of the body, or as overt as a beat of the blade. They come in many guises. They include: opening a line slightly to guide an opponent's attack into a particular direction; straightening your sword arm to induce a bind that can be evaded; allowing your blade to be beaten heavily so that a nonresisting defensive action might be employed; or dropping your guard simply to draw an attack. Even the act of retreating may be employed as an invitation.

My own personal favorite invitation is the one I use against fencers who have a strong habit of having to make blade contact with your weapon before they begin their attack. I simply hold my blade far out of line, so they really have to travel to reach me. And it's a fact that such fencers invariably go for this ploy. It's like cheese in a mouse trap. They are compelled to gain control over their opponent by touching his foil before they do anything. Sometimes this is a psychological thing, a grab for dominance; sometimes it's a behavior ingrained by poor training. Either way, once you perceive it's there, you can count on it to work for you. When they go for my foil, I just slip beneath their weapon, and counterattack in the low line. They're usually still fishing around as my touch lands.

Invitations are highly useful, especially with predominantly reactive fencers. But don't be too obvious with them. If your opponent sees that he is being set up, he may simply feed you the response you are looking for — his invitation — so that he may sucker you into his own trap. The invitation door swings both ways, you know, so be careful.

THE PARRY

A parry is defined as a movement made with the blade to protect yourself from the attack of an opponent by turning his weapon aside. This means it is purely defensive in nature and never offensive. When a fencer is attacked by his opponent, by the rules of foil fencing, he must make a parry. He must attempt to save himself from being hit.

HISTORY

Early parries were nothing like those we employ today. They blocked incoming attacks, it is true, but they were just as offensive in their nature as they were defensive. More than anything else, they were defensive counterattacks, performed by both blocking an incoming attack and hitting in the same instant. These action were described as "stesso tempo," or single time. For many years, stesso tempo was the accepted method of accomplishing a parry, simply because it lessened opportunities for renewed attacks from your enemy. Moreover, the heavy nature of swords was a great deterrent to the development of any other form of defensive weapon maneuvering.

Actual, individual parries were only performed with auxiliary equipment: a dagger, a cloak, a small shield, another sword, even a gloved hand. Sometimes the attacked fencer would merely try to step out of the way of his opponent's attack.

Parrying with a cloak

119

The distinct parry of the 18th century

When swords were decreased in size, making them more maneuverable than ever before, it became possible to perform a parry/counterattack response in the manner we envision it today, as two distinct and separate actions. This timing division was known as "dui tempi," or double time.

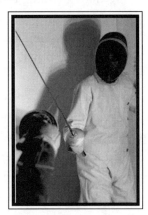

Because of the nature of modern fencing blades, the parry of today possesses none of the jarring, unyielding features of its earlier incarnations. The resilience of our blades, the lively bounce created in a refined metal tempering process, produces a lightning fast response that is often too quick for the unpracticed eye to follow.

A modern parry

PARRIES IN GENERAL TERMS

Here, we move on to the parries themselves. There are two distinct types in fencing: lateral parries and counterparries. Simply put, the former move back and forth in a straight line; the latter go around in a circle.

We will now discuss the specifics of each defensive action in detail.

THE LATERAL PARRY

We begin our discussion of parries properly with the lateral form, because, of the two parry types, this one is basic to the human response pattern. Put a foil in someone's hand who has never fenced before and threaten them with your blade, and they will automatically do something that resembles a lateral parry. For this reason, we call the lateral parry a "reaction" parry. Such linear movement is ingrained in human behavior. It's the odd beginner, indeed, who would perform a counterparry without first being instructed to do so. It is the job of the fencing teacher, though, to turn the fencer's parry of reflex into an parry of control.

In French fencing terms, the lateral parry should always be performed with the sword hand in partial supination (thumb at one o'clock). A pronated hand position will almost always generate a movement that is heavy in the extreme. Using a completely supinated sword hand when making a lateral parry constricts all movement, which causes fatigue and retards the counterattacking process.

The lateral parry then moves in a straight line towards the attacking blade. In terms of outcome, this means that the lateral parry stops an attack in the line into which that attack has been made.

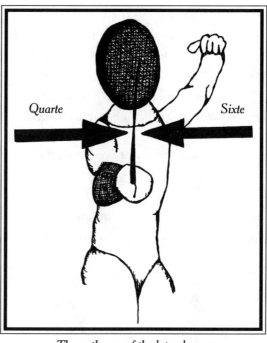

The pathway of the lateral parry

Because we have divided the body into four quarters, we end up with eight lateral parries — four in supination and four in pronation. But, as has already been noted, we have little to do with anything pronated.

The supinated lateral parries of the high-inside line, quarte (4); and the high-outside line, sixte (6), are our two most useful lateral parries, because most of what goes on in foil fencing takes place in the lines they protect.

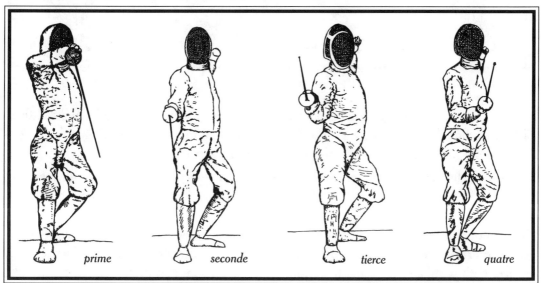

prime   *seconde*   *tierce*   *quatre*

In the beginning, quarte will be the most comfortable of the two to perform. Muscles flow easily toward the inside line. Sixte will be less easy to perform initially because the arm muscles tighten slightly when moving toward the outside line. Practice sixte until you learn to relax with it; then it will be no more difficult to carry out than quarte.

The supinated lateral parries of the low-inside line, septime (7); and the low-outside line, octave (8), will come in handy, but to a lesser degree than those of the high line. They should be practiced thoroughly, though, until their execution becomes a natural response, since their absence leaves half your target area fully exposed to attack.

The pronated lateral low-inside line parry, prime (1); low-outside line, seconde (2); high-outside line, tierce (3); and high-inside line, quinte (5), may be employed occasionally when an extra bit of force might be needed to deal with an overly aggressive opponent; but this should be an extremely calculated move, so that it will not be overdone.

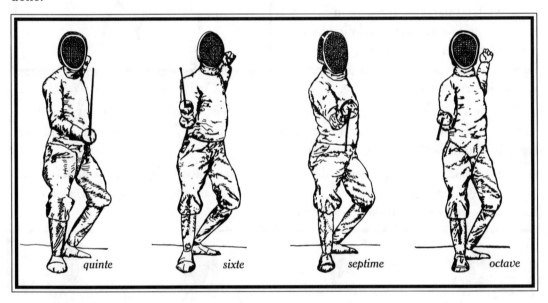

quinte   *sixte*   *septime*   *octave*

THE COUNTERPARRY

As its name implies, the counterparry, or contre, goes around in a circle. We call this action a "thought" parry, because it takes actual mental input to generate it. It is, therefore, a more advanced defensive move than the lateral parry.

As with the lateral parry, the counterparry should always be performed with the sword hand in partial supination. A pronated hand position, when executing counterparries will always create parries far too heavy, parries that, if they miss contact with an opponent's blade, will sometimes sweep clear to the floor. On the other hand, counterparries made with the sword hand in complete supination will be restrictive, and, hence, both weak and unsuited to continued defensive maneuvering.

The counterparry moves in a circular motion, either clockwise or counterclockwise. In terms of outcome, it moves around an attacking blade, forcing it back into the line in which the attack began.

As with the lateral parry of quarte, the counterparry of contre de quarte will be the most comfortable counteraction to perform initially. Contre de sixte, like sixte, almost always feels uncomfortable to the beginner, a condition only practice will relieve.

The circular-oriented defense, like that of the lateral, includes eight parries, four of which will be useful to the French foil fencer. That is the four done in supination.

The supinated counterparries covering the high-inside line, contre de quarte (counterclockwise), and the high-outside line, contre de sixte (clockwise), encompass most of your counterparry work. The counterparries covering the low-inside line, contre de septime (clockwise), and that which protects the low-outside line, contre de octave (counterclockwise), are used less, but should be perfected — just in case.

Unlike pronated lateral parries, pronated counterparries should be avoided at all costs. These include contre de prime (1), contre de seconde (2), contre de tierce (3), and contre de quinte (5). They produce parries that are both unwieldy and awkward, something parries should never be.

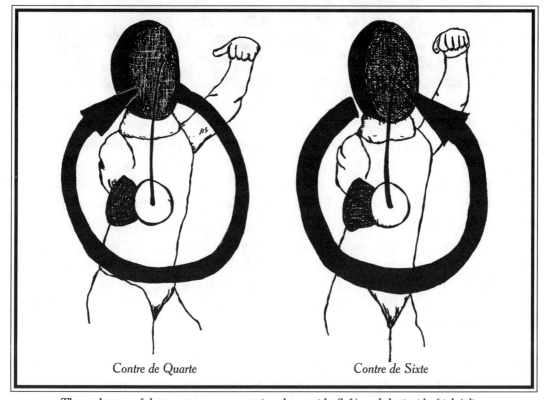

Contre de Quarte   *Contre de Sixte*

The pathways of the counterparry protecting the outside (left) and the inside (right) line.

PARRYING FROM THE HIGH LINE INTO THE LOW LINE

The act of carrying a parry from the high line to the low line is sometimes referred to as a semicircular carry, because the point of your blade, as it drops, moves in a half-circle motion. When the parry is made, whether it covers sixte or octave, the tip of your weapon will always be lower than your sword hand.

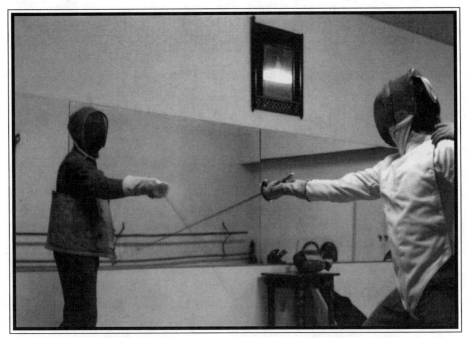

A low line parry

THE THEORY OF PARRYING

When your opponent attacks, you have the option of having one of two things happen. You can defend yourself, or you can be hit. It's your choice. Of course, the former response is the best idea. This may seem obvious. But beginning fencers, operating on a level never very far from reactive, often opt out for being hit by either freezing up or attempting to make a touch when they haven't claimed right-of-way.

When you parry, though, your opponent may evade your blade. In such an instance, you must make another parry. You are required by the rules of foil fencing to continue making parries until you either deflect the incoming blade so that it no longer menaces your target area, or you are hit. If you end up making 500 parries, it is because your opponent has dodged the first 499.

But which parry should you use against an attack? A lateral parry or a counter? In most instances they are interchangeable. For instance, if your opponent attacks into the line of quarte, you may parry quarte or contre de sixte. If he attacks into the line of sixte, you may parry sixte or contre de quarte. In the end, the choice is always up to you. Of course, you should vary your parries often enough to sufficiently confound your opponent. If he cannot discern a pattern in your defensive operation, it will be extremely difficult for him to formulate a strategy to use against you.

There is one case, though, where you would specifically avoid using a counterparry. If an opponent attacked with an excessively wide action that carried his blade noticeably out of line, catching it with a counter might very well pull the point toward you and right into your body, inadvertently causing a touch. But this is an extreme case. I only mention it because, in the realm of possibilities, it can happen.

Once you have made a successful parry, you have claimed right-of-way away from the attacker. Now, you are the counterattacker and may attempt to make a touch. To do this properly, though, your follow-through should be instantaneous. To hesitate may mean losing right-of-way back to your opponent.

This immediate counterattack after the parry, by the way, is called a "riposte."

THE MECHANICS OF PARRYING

There are two specific schools of thought regarding the mechanics of parrying. One group favors the opposition parry, which employs continued force to turn aside an attacking blade. As its name implies, there is a certain muscular application to this defensive move. Produced by the arm, it tends to overpower and, by its very nature, generates considerable blade movement. The other group favors the detached parry, which employs the spring inherent in your blade to deflect incoming attacks. This parry is generated from a snapping motion in the fingers and wrist, which produces a parry that is firm without being overbearing. Because of this, it immediately breaks contact with the blade it has intersected with, which allows the motion created to flow immediately into a controlled counterattack.

The detached parry has as a companion defensive move, the nonresisting parry, which gives way to the force of vigorous opposing blade contact, rather than fighting against it. Channeling the energy it has encountered into a flowing circular motion, the nonresisting parry basically turns all aggressiveness back against its originator. The stronger the blow, the quicker the parry. If done properly, absolutely no detrimental force — force that would otherwise surely slow anyone down — gets trapped in your blade.

It should be noted that the detached parry and non-resisting parry techniques are very much creatures of the French school and, hence, will be the focus of our training. The use of opposition parries is not out of the question; however, we simply relegate them to occasional use.

THE PARRY OF OPPOSITION

When do we use the parry of opposition? After employing a non-resisting parry or two, just when your opponent is expecting another one, throw in an opposition parry to confound him. When he is counting on you to give way to his force in a circular sweep of your blade, come back at him with a firm lateral parry. This will stop him dead in his tracks.

THE CROISÉ

Meaning "to cross," the croisé is a defensive response that is an exception to everything we've been discussing thus far. Basically, it is a parry and a counterattack in a single, flowing action. In a way, it is a parry of opposition, because it certainly does oppose; yet it does not make use of any muscle or force in its execution. The strength of the croisé comes from one distinct ingredient: leverage.

The ancient Greek mathematician Archimedes said, "Give me a lever and I will move the world." With a lever, any object can be impelled out of its present position. And this is just what happens when we apply a croisé against our attacking opponent's weapon.

To set a croisé into motion, catch an incoming foil's foible near the middle of your own. Angling your blade across the attacker's, you have created a lever, which will move the offending point immediately out of line.

Here, your opponent's blade has been overpowered — you have parried successfully — and, even if you did nothing else, it would be impossible for him to force his way back in to make a touch. But, the objective of the croisé is not to simply block, but also to hit. So, at the moment your foil intersects with your opponent's, you must drop your point in an half-circle motion that both serves to maintain firm contact and guide your own blade back into line. This move entails turning the sword hand into complete supination and extending the sword arm simultaneously.

For the right-handed fencer, the croisés in the high-outside line of sixte and low-outside line of octave are the two most feasible actions, because they guide the attacking blade away from your body. This also goes for croisés flowing out of contre de sixte and contre de octave actions. The croisé in quarte may occasionally be brought into play; but it must always be accomplished with a sword arm that has been angled inward in an extreme fashion, this to keep the attacking blade far removed from your target area.

On the other side of the coin, a left-handed fencer, working against a right-hander, has more of an option in placing his croisés. Because of a beneficial body placement, caused by the southpaw's "turned around" stance, he may croisé comfortably to either side of his opponent's blade without distorting the position of his sword arm.

If the croisé is done with proper form, and without hesitation, your opponent will pretty much end up running onto your blade. The entire action, by the way, should be accomplished with the lightest of touches. It is the mechanics of the croisé that makes it work; adding muscle to the equation just overbalances the whole thing and destroys your ability to effectively place your point where it should be going.

The Croisé

The croisé works especially well against highly aggressive fencers, because it negates their energy, turning both their brawn and their belligerence back against them. One or two successful croisés will often give a headstrong fencer reason for pause, slowing down his desire to attack you considerably.

But, like so many of the tactics we've already gone over in this book, use the croisé sparingly.

THE RIPOSTE

We have already noted that the parry is always followed by a counterattack — the riposte. I mention it again here because I wish to underscore the relationship between the two actions. Though distinct in their mechanics and purposes, they should always be thought of as inseparable. In truth, the first is not complete without the latter. And the second one is not possible without the former. That is the truth of the matter. And so these actions should be linked in your mind for all time.

In the next chapter, we will be discussing the makeup of riposte.

THE RIPOSTE

The riposte is sometimes called "the echo of the parry" because, like an echo to an actual sound, the two are linked so finely they cannot be separated. Too, like an echo, the riposte springs instantly from its source.

The riposte is a counterattack launched after a successful parry has been made. It is, in fact, the most common form of counterattack. But it is a counterattack that forbids, generally speaking, the use of the lunge. This is due to the fact that your opponent has already attacked, has lunged himself and is close enough to be hit without generating another such move.

According to the conventions of the foil, once a defending fencer has performed a parry that has deflected an attacker's blade away from his valid target area, he is granted the right-of-way that the attacker initially possessed. He may then consequently attempt his own offensive, or more precisely, counteroffensive action — the riposte.

But, as has already been mentioned, the riposte, to be legitimate, must be delivered immediately after the parry, without hesitation. Any pause may end up nullifying your priority in the exchange taking place.

TYPES OF RIPOSTES

The direct, or straight, riposte is the one most often carried out on the fencing strip. It is made in the same line in which the parry was accomplished.

The parry

The Riposte

We also have simple indirect ripostes that carry the riposte into the line immediately opposite the one in which the parry was executed. This includes, for instance, the riposte by dégage (passing beneath an opponent's blade), and the riposte by coupé (passing over the top of an opponent's blade). Or you might concoct more complex forms of riposting — sometimes called "composed" ripostes — by joining together diverse offensive moves, such as a riposte by disengage-coupé. The manner in which a riposte may be fashioned is only limited by the defensive responses you meet on the fencing strip.

A riposte directed into another line is done essentially for one reason: to evade a parry being made by your opponent. Often the parries preceding an indirect riposte are of an extremely heavy nature and so dictate that an evading maneuver be put into play. Indirect ripostes may avoid either lateral or counterparries.

THE MECHANICS OF THE RIPOSTE

Whether coming on the heels of a lateral parry or a counterparry, the riposte of the French school is always performed in the same manner.

As we've already observed, when you make contact with an incoming blade, your sword hand should be in partial supination. Here, the two blades connecting produce an immediate repelling bounce called the "recoil." To control this recoil, which would otherwise send your foil careening away helplessly, you must immediately rotate your sword hand crisply from partial supination to complete supination (thumb at three o'clock). This turn of the hand not only keeps your blade point in line, but automatically drops it down for an immediate counterattack.

Because the parry we employ separates from the blade it has stopped, we call the type of riposte that follows it a "detached" riposte.

Once the point of your weapon has been properly placed, the sword arm may be advanced with the riposte. But this thrust should only progress as far as you need to go to produce a touch. One time, you might need a full extension; another time, only a hint of one.

The rules of foil play do not require a totally straight arm when riposting, since this would be an impossible mandate to fulfill in every instance on the fencing strip. This is because the defender is working in a distance — sometimes called the "maneuvering distance" — that has been forced upon him by his attacking opponent. It would be an unfair rule, indeed, and an arbitrary one, that demanded something of us that was, at times, impossible to produce. Our conventions, which are always based on common sense, recognize the variability imposed on the riposte; and, hence, leave the sword arm alone, focusing instead on those matters that plainly affect priority.

THE COUNTERRIPOSTE

This is a riposte that follows the parry of a riposte.

RIPOSTING FROM A PARRY OF OPPOSITION

A parry of opposition, because of its forceful nature, may produce an unwanted hesitation between the parry and riposte. Its saving grace is that, in the hands of an expert fencer, it can be an overpowering action, which leaves its victim unable to take advantage of the pause it has generated.

THE SUCCESS OF THE RIPOSTE

Producing a riposte that you can count on may take some time. As long as a fencer remains reactive in his fencing, his ability to counterattack effectively will be, at best, sporadic. It may help, though, to understand why the riposte works, so that these principles may be invoked when practicing the action.

There are basically three reasons for a riposte's success. First, your parry has shaken your adversary's sword hand and, hence, has physically thrown off his timing. Second, if done properly, a riposte can be executed more quickly than a recovery to a guard position. And third, the riposte occurs at a time when your opponent is disconcerted because his attack has been checked, catching him, therefore, in a psychologically weak moment.

In closing, I was once given a sound directive on the art of successful riposting by my fencing master Ralph Faulkner. After you've made a parry, if you're not sure what to do next, go ahead and hit your opponent, and then ask questions afterwards.

COMPOSED ATTACKS

Of the two types of attacks — simple and composed — the composed is both the more advanced and complex of the two. Because the composed, composite or compound attack deals with principles of a slightly abstract nature, few beginners have adequate knowledge to understand the way in which it works. The composed attack is, therefore, an attack of the more experienced fencer.

So, what is this composed attack anyway?

The definition of a composed attack is any attack made up of a feint of an attack followed by the deception of a parry.

In elementary terms: you scare your opponent with a good, sound bluff, into protecting himself; and then you dodge his blade. This effectively creates a hole in his defenses, which makes it easier to hit him.

Now, let's get a bit more specific.

THE FEINT

The feint is an implied threat. My teacher used to say, "The F-E-I-N-T is supposed to make your opponent F-A-I-N-T." But this action is only made for effect, to menace, to induce your opponent into making a parry. No lunge is attached to it. If you lunge, it's not a feint; it's a real attack!

There is a feeling of becoming a magician when executing a feint. In a way, it must be as distracting as a slight-of-hand trick. As with any magician who misdirects his audience with the broad gestures of one hand while he pulls a rabbit out of his hat with the other, the fencer producing a feint must rivet his opponent's attention with his feint, so that the latter, like the magician's audience, will not see what is coming next.

There must be a pressing sense of intent, of resolve, present in the feint. Except for the absent lunge, it should appear exactly like an attack in progress. If it looks like what it really is — a fake — it will not invoke a parry. Why should an opponent who feels no threat defend himself? The answer is, no reason. And if he doesn't parry, your composed attack will be stopped in its tracks.

To begin with, it is a difficult thing for a fencer to generate an aura of intent when it is not, in fact, really there. It is certainly not created by simply extending a sword arm, or pointing your foil at your opponent. It must be infused with subtilties of body language — firmness of movement; tensing muscles; knees taking on a more pronounced bend, as if ready to push forward in a lunge; an ever so slight forward inclination of the body; a focused attention that burns through your opponent. Of course, the aforementioned prerequisite of any true attack — having your point in line and a straight sword arm — must also be present. Add all these diverse ingredients together, and you just may have a successful feint. And how will you know if you do? Simple: your opponent will make a parry.

Moreover, the mechanics of any attack can be designated as a feint. You can, for example, make a feint of a straight hit, a feint of dégage, a feint of coupé, or a feint of coulé. And these can be combined into still more intricate forms. You are confronted by all sorts of interesting possibilities. Still, in modern foil fencing, it is the fundamental feint of dégage that finds the greatest amount of expression.

THE PARRY

In response to your menacing feint, your opponent says, "He's attacking me. I'd better parry." He will then either set a a lateral parry or a counterparry into motion. Which one will it be? Constantly watching his responses on the fencing strip — more specifically , how he reacts under pressure, will give you a good idea of his parrying proclivities.

THE DECEPTION

The deception (in French, "tromper"), remember, is an evasion of an opponent's parry or parries. It should always be a tight, concise action, originating in the fingers, rather than a broad, swooping one from the arm. Split-second timing is the key to masterful deceptions. Performing large, roundabout maneuverings with your blade merely slows the process and invites failure.

ATTACKS

We have two base composed attacks in foil fencing: the one-two and the doublé. Each, we will find, fulfills one specific purpose in bouting.

THE ONE-TWO

The one-two (in French, "une-deux") is made up of a single feint of dégage, followed by a deception of one lateral parry. To institute the one-two, begin by launching the aforementioned dégage feint. It must be a dégage, or the attack will not be a one-two. It may move from quarte to sixte, or from sixte to quarte.

Too, the swordhand should be in complete supination. This will facilitate making the upcoming deception.

When the lateral parry is launched against you, evade it by dropping your foil tip beneath its sideways flow. Once you've cleared your opponent's weapon, raise your blade again to its former position. This entire action is accomplished by tracing a small "u" with your point. You will now find yourself back in the line in which you started your one-two.

Now, lunge.

Contrary to the manner in which it is often accomplished today, the one-two should not be waved from side to side, as if you were simply making two dégages. The one-two is, in fact, sometimes referred to, incorrectly, as a double disengage, but the feint and deception are two distinct actions and should be always be thought of and treated as such to preserve their integrity.

THE DOUBLÉ

The doublé is made up of a single feint of dégage and a deception of one counterparry. This latter detail is its divergence from the one-two: the type of parry it eludes.

The doublé's feint of dégage is performed in the identical manner as that of the one-two (which includes the fully supinated sword hand). But in encountering the circular motion of the counterparry, the mechanics of the doublé's deception alters.

As the counterparry swings around the feint in an attempt to pick it up, the doublé's evasive track flows suddenly forward, in the shape of a small "o." The deception, made from the fingers, ends up traveling in the same direction as the parry. This causes it to stay ahead of the counter, basically outrunning it.

A doublé projected into the line of quarte will evade a contre de sixte parry. One made into the line of sixte will evade a contre de quarte parry.

Instead of reversing its flow — as is the case with the one-two and ending up in the line in which it began, the doublé finishes its spherical course in the line which the feint was made.

Once the parry has been deceived, of course, lunge.

WHICH ATTACK? ONE-TWO? DOUBLÉ?

I must reiterate that the composed attack you end up doing will be determined entirely by the parry you encounter, either through your opponent's choice or his reaction. You do not set up a doublé, then, to make your opponent do a counterparry. You do a doublé because your opponent has performed a counterparry. You do not institute a one-two to make your opponent do a lateral parry. You carry out a one-two because your opponent has done a lateral parry.

Keep this relationship in mind at all times. It will prevent you from acting independently of your opponent on the fencing strip, which is one of the worst traps a fencer can fall into.

However, because much of modern foil fencing is carried out on a reflexive, rather than thoughtful, level, you will, over the length of your fencing career, probably encounter more lateral parries than counterparries. This means you will have fewer chances to do doublés than one-twos. Whenever you come up against this disparity, forget about the doublé — even if it's your best attack. There is no way for you to get an opponent to make a counterparry if he is unable or unwilling to make one.

That is reality.

COMPOSED COMBINATIONS

You are not limited merely to the one-two and doublé when performing composed attacks. Simple attacks can be combined into composed actions, too, such as the dégage-coupé, the coulé-dégage, the double-coupé, the coupé-dégage, and the coulé-coupé. Moreover, the two basic composed attacks can be spliced together to increase your repetoire, creating the one-two-doublé and the doublé-one-two. Further still, simple movements can be combined with composed ones to create even more complex actions: the dégage-doublé, the one-two-coupé, the doublé-coupé-one-two, and the coulé-one-two-doublé dégage-coupé.

The doublé de doublé is a composed attack made up of two doublés, each one going in opposite directions. The one-two-three is a feint of dégage followed by the deception of two lateral parries. The triple is a feint of dégage followed by the deception of two counterparries.

The combinations of composed attacks at your disposal are endless and are only limited by the responses you encounter on the fencing strip.

FEINTS

Besides being an integral component of the composed attack, the feint has a few other useful functions. It may be used in the preparation of an attack, focusing an opponent's attention in a particular line, so that you might go unmolested in another direction. Or, if delivered with sufficient vigor, it may effectively break another fencer's concentration.

It may also serve as a method of finding out how another fencer will react when pushed to his psychological limits. Here, the feint becomes a question: "What are you going to do, buddy?" Your opponent will then answer. If he makes a parry, he will either say, "I like doing lateral parries all the time," or "if you attack me in that line, I'm going to do a counterparry." If he does nothing, he might be saying, "You didn't scare me with that feint. I saw it coming a mile away." By watching carefully how your opponent responds to your "questions," you can, with certainty, set up strategies with which you can manipulate him on the fencing strip — before you ever have to commit yourself to the uncertainties of an actual attack.

The feint, then, is highly serviceable beyond the borders of its initial use.

THE COUNTERATTACK

The counterattack is the embodiment of the old saying, "The best defense is a strong offense."

A counterattack ("contre-attaque") is any attack launched specifically against an opponent's offensive action. The riposte — a counterattack performed after a successful parry — is the most common form of this response. But there are also counterattacks which are totally unrelated to parrying.

THE STOP THRUST

Also known as the "coup d'arrêt," the stop thrust is a counterattack performed — with or without a lunge — on the initial advance of the opponent, whether that advance is followed by an attack or not.

Performed with a fully extended sword arm, the stop thrust is ideally launched against a fencer who insists on attacking, or moving forward forcefully, with a bent arm.

To be considered a valid procedure (one that commands right-of-way in the exchange taking place), according to the conventions of foil fencing, the stop thrust must hit noticeably before the offensive action it opposes. It is, therefore, considered inadvisable to carry out a stop thrust against a properly framed attack.

Learning the stop thrust

THE TIME THRUST

This counterattack (in French, "coup de temps") — best delivered with a lunge — is performed against a composed attack while that attack is unfolding, so that, timing-wise, the counterattacker's move gains a measurable advantage over that attack. (This superiority is measured in "fencing time": the time required to perform one simple fencing action.)

The passata sotto, a counterattack that drops beneath an incoming blade, is one of the more spectacular forms of the time thrust.

Like the stop thrust, the time thrust must hit well before the initial attack it is countering.

The passata sotto

TENSION

Sometimes called an "attack by interception."

"Tension" is defined as performing a counterattack with a fully extended sword arm, so that your blade both blocks an incoming attack and hits in the same instant.

In the viewpoint of the French, it is advisable to carry out tension only in the line of sixte. The Italians, however, perform it in the line of quarte, calling it "inquartata," but add a sideways twist of the body to insure avoiding the diverted blade.

To be an acceptable action, tension must block the incoming attack totally. That is, the incoming attack must not, in any manner, touch the counterattacking fencer.

COUP DOUBLÉ

A counterattack initiating a double touch ("coup double") — hitting at the exact same moment as your opponent — is considered an invalid action.

CONTINUED ATTACKS

A continued attack is any attack resumed after an initial failure to make a touch. In some instances, such an action is very much encouraged by the rules; in others, however, it is heartily condemned.

We will now discuss the reasons for and against continued attacks, of which, by the way, there are four.

THE REPRISED ATTACK

The first continued attack on our list is the reprised attack ("reprise d'attaque"). It is set into motion against an opponent who has avoided being touched during your initial attack by simply retreating out of distance.

The reprised attack is carried out by recovering forward and immediately lunging again. Because the defending fencer has not executed a parry of any sort, this maneuver is always valid.

THE REMISE

The remise is a continuation of an attack set into motion after that attack has been parried. It is executed in the same line in which your blade has been stopped. It should only be brought into play, however, if the defending fencer hesitates before riposting.

You would make the remise the continued attack of choice because, as the defender neglects to riposte, he also opens up the line in which he made his parry.

The remise issues forth from the initial lunge, without pulling your sword arm back.

If the defending fencer does riposte immediately after his parry, his riposte will always take precedence over the remise.

THE REDOUBLEMENT

The redoublement, like the remise, is a continuation of an attack after a parry has been made and should only be instituted if the parrying fencer doesn't riposte. However, unlike the remise, it is directed into the line opposite the parry.

This continued attack is used because the defending fencer, instead of opening his protected line, closes it off with a brutal, smashing parry, which makes it impossible to continue in that direction.

The redoublement further resembles the remise in that it springs from your initial attack and is managed without retracting your sword arm. Also, it is not good against an immediate riposte.

THE CONTRE-TEMPS

The contre-temps is a continued attack launched against a time thrust ("coup de temps"). It is most often performed by first engaging the counterattacker's extended blade in some controlling maneuver.

THE SECONDARY INTENT ATTACK

The secondary intent attack is a unique and interesting process in fencing, for in it you hold the key to shattering a defense that might otherwise seem impenetrable. In shifting your emphasis away from the usual focal point of an initial offensive action — scoring a touch at the end of that action — you set into motion principles that allow you to get the jump, timing-wise, on a difficult opponent, and hence, create an opportunity to successfully hit.

The goal behind the secondary intent attack is to make a touch, not with your opening response, or primary attack, but with a subsequent offensive action that has been planned out in advance. This latter response, which holds your true intent to hit, then is the real attack.

First, let's talk about the makeup of the secondary intent attack. Then we can go on to its varied applications.

INTRODUCTION

The secondary intent attack is made up of three distinct parts: the false attack, the parry, and the counterriposte. Each element, of course, plays an equally important role in the success of the attack, so fudging on any one of them can ruin the entire setup.

THE FALSE ATTACK

The false attack ("fausse-attaque") is the opening ploy of the secondary intent action. As its name implies, it is a fake construction.

The false attack is any simple or composed attack — from a dégage to a doublé — delivered not to hit, but to draw a parry. While in essence a kind of feint, it always incorporates a lunge. But, where a standard feint is made to attract a parry that can be evaded, the false attack is delivered only to be blocked (so that you might instead deal with the riposte that follows the parry).

TECHNIQUE

The false attack should always be forcefully delivered. Without a strong feeling of purpose behind it, it will not elicit the committed parry/riposte you are looking for. This can be a problem, since you must, in reality, hold yourself back from making a touch. The false attack should, therefore, be presented crisply, cleanly and with focus to over-come its actual nature.

By holding back you might include a slightly — very slightly — shorter lunge, with your torso lacking any forward inclination whatsoever. Never present your false attack with a bent arm or deliver it with a weak forward step.

More than anything else, however, this "holding back" in the false attack is a mental state. For it is this intellectual input — the calm knowledge that you are going to be parried for sure because you want it that way — that generates the inner space you need to proceed effectively with the attack.

But remember, as with any fake action, if the false attack looks like what it really is, it will fail. It must look like what it isn't. If your opponent says, "Ho-hum, here comes another bogus attack," he will not parry, and the remainder of your action is doomed.

THE OPPONENT'S PARRY/RIPOSTE

If the false attack is believable, and your opponent is operating with sound fencing principles under his belt, he will make a parry and follow it immediately with a riposte.

Of course, he doesn't know you have extended plans regarding this exchange; and this is your advantage. Knowing what is to take place, you can bump up the timing of the phrase a beat or two, which will, hopefully, overwhelm any counterresponses he carries out.

THE ATTACKER'S PARRY/COUNTERRIPOSTE

When your opponent ripostes, you must make an instantaneous parry while still in the lunge and launch your own counterriposte. By and large, the type of parry you employ should be previously decided upon.

Because of your foreknowledge of what is transpiring, you should be able to launch your secondary action with an overwhelming rapidity. Of course, both your parry and riposte must be performed with as much adherence to proper form as when they are set into motion from the upright on guard position.

WHEN AND WHEN NOT TO INSTITUTE THE SECONDARY INTENT ATTACK

As with all things in fencing, the secondary intent attack has a set of circumstances in which it might be brought into play. You should not think of indiscriminately employing the secondary intent attack. You must first fully recognize the capabilities of your opponent. To not have a well-developed idea of his behavior when launching a secondary intent action is to fence blindly.

Moreover, you should never use these actions if they are unnecessary. If you can hit your opponent easily with a dégage, a secondary intent attack is pointless and may even work against you if your opponent is powerless to feed you the reactions you need to complete your attack.

THE FAILED INITIAL ATTACK

The secondary intent may be directed against an opponent with an extremely strong parry/riposte response. For example, you execute a dégage as your initial attack, hoping to hit, but your opponent parries your blade and counterattacks, touching you soundly before you can get back on guard.

On all primary attacks, there is a time when you are especially vulnerable. Specifically, it is the exact moment when you are parried, where your thoughts must shift from offense to defense. The longer it takes to make the switch, the more likely it is you will fall victim to the riposte. If your opponent is especially skilled, with a brisk detached parry and a lightning riposte, this becomes even more of a problem.

Eventually, you adapt to one degree or another, learning to flow from offense to defense with hardly a second thought. The recovery is finally there for you but even this improvement isn't always enough to win the day against a splendid counterattack. So, what do you do when you need to push the issue, to wring the last bit of possibility out of your exchange?

The answer is the secondary intent.

When you know for certain that your initial attack is going to be stopped, you can frame your own defense and counterriposte in such a way that it puts more weight into the final response. This just may give you the advantage you're looking for — even if your opponent is a bit more experienced than you.

THE STALEMATE

In instances where two opposing fencers are of equal ability, the secondary intent is often the action called on to upset the balance of power. This is especially true among fencers of high attainment.

THE PARRY PROBLEM

It is the business of every defending fencer to vary his parry combinations as much as possible, so that his attacking opponent cannot foresee what is happening. Let's say, then, your opponent is doing just that. His defense is holding you to a handful of simple attacks, which effectively cuts your offensive responses down to the bare minimum. Your opponent has a big advantage over you.

So, you break out the secondary intent. You feed him a false attack, let him parry in any manner he wishes and just deal with his riposte.

In the end, this is easier than trying to figure out any complicated defensive game. Moreover, it greatly enlarges your attack possibilities.

EXAMPLES

One of the most basic secondary intent attacks is the beat/straight hit (false attack), parry quarte, riposte straight (secondary intent). Another would be the dégage (false attack), parry quarte, riposte straight (secondary intent).

A bit more complicated action might be framed as a coupé (false attack), parry contre de quarte, riposte by dégage (secondary intent). Or doublé (false attack), parry sixte with a croisé(secondary intent).

BEYOND SECONDARY INTENT

It should be noted that in the realm of extended attacks, you are not limited to actions of secondary intent. If you find that you need to further increase your advantage over your opponent, you can employ a third intent attack or a fourth. They are, of course, carried out in the same manner as the secondary variety. Your intention to hit is merely placed further down the line.

Needless to say, it is best to keep all extended intent actions as simple as possible. Because they are based on the anticipation of certain behavior patterns, the more complications you interject into the by-play, the more likely it is that unforeseen variables will throw themselves in the way.

ATTACKS ON THE BLADE

Attacks on the blade are employed essentially to open up one line or another. They may be employed to simply push away an opponent's weapon, or they may be used to force him into parrying.

Attacks on the blade come in three forms:

THE BEAT

The beat ("battement") — knocking an opponent's blade away on offense — is one of fencing's oldest moves. In an atmosphere where being able to overwhelm an adversary's sword was a desirable thing, the beat was an ideal action to perform. Its simplicity made it easy to execute, and its effect — keeping an adversary from counterattacking — was immediately apparent. It also had the added feature of being able to disarm your opponent.

The beat is still one of fencing's most valuable tools. When applied with varying degrees of force, it may be used to produce a number of advantageous outcomes.

When executing a beat, it should be performed with a rapid, crisp, snapping motion from the fingers and wrist. As little arm as possible should be incorporated into the action (the more obvious the beat is, the easier it will be for your opponent to avoid it).

The heavy beat will smack an opposing blade out of line. Few actions in fencing are more overpowering than this. A beat of a slightly less forceful nature may also be used to coax a parry out of an opponent, a parry that may then be evaded. The result, of course, is to open up the line opposite to the beat, making it a more convenient spot to attack. The overtly threatening personality of the beat is ideal for pushing the most unresponsive of fencers into action.

Finally, very light beats, done in quick succession, will both irritate and distract — a fine strategy for keeping an adversary off guard.

PRESSION

Pression is the lightest of pressures placed on an opponent's blade. Its strength is its subtlety. Employing it, you may control your opponent's blade, push it away just enough, before he ever realizes he has been taken advantage of.

FROISSEMENT

A froissement is as forceful as the pression is delicate. As your weapon glides forward along an opponent's blade, a prolonged, violent pressure is simultaneously interjected into the action. It is both overpowering and threatening, so that it may be used in either a direct assault or an attempt to elicit a parry.

TAKING THE BLADE

Taking the blade, or "prise de fer," is the procedure of encountering, forcing aside, and controlling an opponent's blade as a prelude to attacking. It is executed with the "forte" of your blade on the "foible" of an adversary's weapon and, normally speaking, with an extended sword arm.

The success of any prise de fer action is determined by two things: first, how much resistance you encounter from your opponent; and second, how quickly and smoothly you are able to institute an attack following the taking of the blade.

There are three forms of prise de fer:

OPPOSITION

Opposition is a firm and continuous pushing of an opposing blade before you attack. It may be done simply to overpower; or, it may be used as a threatening movement to draw another fencer into making a parry that can be evaded.

THE BIND

The bind — "liement"— is an offensive action that takes hold of an opponent's blade and guides its point from the high line to the low line (liement in octave), or from the low line to the high line (liement in sixte). It employs leverage in the same fashion as the croisé, except in this case, the bind is presented with a lunge.

(It should be understood here, that the bind can only be accomplished against an opposing blade that has been fully extended. It cannot, then, be used against a weapon held in the on guard position.)

To bind in the line of sixte: With a bent sword arm, firmly engage your opponent's extended weapon with your own blade in sixte. Immediately, flip your blade tip outward and downward along his blade, describing a half-circle motion (clockwise) as you extend your arm from the shoulder and turn your sword hand into complete supination. Your blade will glide forward, displacing the opposing foil's point. (Here, your opponent's blade will be situated beneath yours, so do not overly raise your sword hand; you will break blade contact if you do.) When your sword arm is completely straight, and your point is in line with your opponent's target area, lunge.

To bind in the line of octave: With a bent sword arm, firmly engage your opponent's extended weapon with your own blade in quarte. Immediately, flip your blade tip inward and downward into the low line of octave, describing a half-circle motion (counterclockwise) as you extend your arm from the shoulder and turn your sword hand into complete supination. As with the bind in sixte, your blade will glide forward, displacing the opposing foil's point. (Here, your opponent's blade will be resting on top of yours, so do not lower your sword hand; you will break blade contact if you do.) When your sowrd arm is completely straight and your point is in line with your opponent's target area, lunge.

To add variety to the bind, the liement in sixte may be preceded by a quick change of engagement from quarte. Because of the circular motion generated by this line reversal, the bind fairly flows out of the change. This produces extremely firm blade contact.

The bind, it should be noted, may only be employed against a fully extended sword arm. A bent sword arm presents an inadequate blade angle for the bind to grab on to.

As a strategy, the bind may be used to simply overpower an opponent, or it may be availed upon to remove a blade point your opponent is deliberately holding in line.

Conversely, if you become a victim of this overpowering maneuver, you should never resist it. That will only insure its success. The best avenue of escape, by far, is a nonresisting parry, which should proceed as follows:

First, drop your foil tip slightly, which both weakens the hold of the bind and causes its trajectory to begin angling away from your body. Then, roll your blade across the top of your opponent's weapon, bestowing a circular flow to the motion of both foils. Finally, as this maneuver flips you into the opposite line, move your sword hand inward slightly to complete the transference and raise your point up to eye level. Suddenly, you are no longer where your adversary placed you. Needless to say, this will be a great surprise to him. Now, riposte.

If you see the bind coming, you can slide lightly off of it (derobement) or evade it entirely (deception).

THE ENVELOPPEMENT

In principle, the enveloppement is much the same as the liement; it merely carries its control a bit further. The enveloppement, rather than carrying an opponent's weapon into another line, returns the captured blade to the line where it was found.

This full circle action completely ties up an opponent's blade, making it impossible for him to respond to your ensuing attack.

MOVING IN THE LOW LINE

Being able to travel with facility into the low line is a highly useful, but much neglected skill, among the vast majority of modern fencers. For these individuals, the low line simply doesn't exist. When they do manage to direct their weapon tips downward, it is most often an accidental happening, a maneuver steeped in poor control.

This, of course, refers to defensive as well as offensive low line techniques. As if it weren't bad enough to severely restrict your access to spots you might assail by neglecting the low line, this fatal flaw also translates into leaving half of your target area totally unprotected. What good is it having strong high line parries if attacking fencers need only slip beneath them to produce a touch?

To incorporate the low line into your game is vital to efficient, effective fencing. High line to low line. Low line to high line. With them connected by ordered thoughts and systematic methodology, we keep our game balanced.

The following are concepts which need to be addressed if you are to gain even the slightest control over the low line.

LOW LINE ATTACKS

The French school suggests that the low line be attacked only occasionally to keep your descending invasion from becoming obvious and stale; but this principle is ultimately influenced by how skillfully your opponent responds to deviations from the high line. The less ability you encounter, the more often you may feasibly visit the low line.

The low line most often approached should be the low-outside quarter. This tactic places the attacking blade beneath your opponent's sword arm — one of the most difficult spots to defend.

The attack into the low-outside line, by the way, is one of the few instances in French foil fencing where the foil is actually manipulated in a pronated hand position. The main objective of this is to make blade point positioning an easier task. But the procedure of getting the sword hand into pronation from supination is not without its catches. The hand isn't just turned over like a flapjack. If you're not careful, the whole process can hit the skids, guiding your point away from your target as though it were being yanked by a powerful magnet.

A number of things must take place simultaneously to produce a well-framed attack in the low-outside line. The extended sword arm is a requirement, of course, as it overlays all attacks. But, as we've already said, we also need to pronate the sword hand and vacate the high line. These objectives are accomplished in the same instant by quickly rotating the sword hand — from its chest level position — outward and downward (with the sword hand thumb moving from one o'clock to nine o'clock) in a tight, clockwise, half-circle motion to about waist level. Such a gesture not only effectively places your blade in the low line, it also aims and steadies your point.

Here, it should be underscored that your foil point must be higher than your sword hand. By maintaining this attitude, you produce a necessary upward angled trajectory for the low line attack, allowing you to come up smoothly under an opponent's sword arm without accidentally making contact with the arm.

Because the sword hand is in pronation, your blade will bend to the outside, rather than the inside when it hits. More than anything else, this aids with balance in the lunge.

When attacking into the low-inside line, the sword hand should be left in supination. However, the blade tip must still be tilted upward.

But, just in case your opponent does have serviceable parries of septime and octave, never try to reach the low line before you have, by some means, focused his attention in the high line. This may be done with a feint of dégage, a series of changes or a beat.

An attack into the low outside line

You may further confound him by presenting your blade into the low line as a feint, and then deceive his ensuing downward parry by returning your attack's final movement to the high line.

LOW LINE PARRIES

In the French school, the low line parries most employed are septime and octave. For these, the sword hand is in supination, and the blade point is angled downward.

These parries, it should be noted, drop into the low line with a half-circle movement. Septime (covering the low-inside line) swings downward with the blade tip in a clockwise fashion. Octave (covering the low-outside line) swings downward with the blade tip in a counterclockwise fashion.

Like in the high line, the parries employed most often will be those of a detached nature. However, octave may, from time to time, be covered with a croisé, which will expedite point placement when this line is especially obstructed by a drooping sword arm.

Today, covering the low line with the parry of prime has become a popular addition to foil technique. Primarily a sabre parry, such an inclusion to your foil repertoire would have once been considered unwise. First, because of the awkward position it places your blade in, it makes it a difficult parry to riposte off of; second, because as a parry adapted mainly to the broad sabre offense, it is fairly easy to deceive with a foil point; and third, because once it has been deceived, another parry is almost impossible to carry out.

But, because prime incorporates a bit of dash and flash suggesting to many young fencers that the downward/upward sweep of its passage creates a kind of all-encompassing, universal parry. A parry that, with a bold across your target area, will stop almost any attack — has been welcomed by the impressionable. Just the same, it is my belief that any fencer possessing solid timing, a believable feint, and a decent coupé can evade this "invincible" parry as though it doesn't exist.

THE LOW LINE COUNTERATTACK

While it is not by any means a creature of the French school of foil fencing, I am somewhat partial to the liement in seconde against an attacking blade. But be cautioned; it must be performed with extreme care. A very strong counteraction, it becomes easily overbalanced. So, calculate the pressure you'll need to produce it. It is strong enough to disarm an opponent.

Engaging an attacking foil in the line of quarte, you immediately roll your sword hand over into pronation and drop your blade tip into seconde. At the same time, angle your sword arm outward and your weapon inward, producing a kind of sideways "v" effect.

If you've managed the bind correctly, your opponent's blade will have been brushed aside like a twig. All you need do now is push your point home.

FOIL TACTICS

Tactics, in fencing, is the utilization of the various ways in which you may attack or defend yourself. Everything you do, of course, is based on the behavior of that opponent in front of you on the fencing strip.

OFFENSE

Only a well-planned attack strategy will succeed. If approached properly, it will not only effectively poke holes in your opponent's defensive preparations, it can negate any offensive plans he harbors as well, rendering him both helpless and ineffectual.

The attacks you make, by and large, should be as simple as possible, for in simplicity there is predictability. Only evoke more complex actions as the need arises. To arrive at a more in-volved attack, build on what you already know about your opponent. Never start with an action based simply on what you'd like to do. Dazzling another fencer with your footwork, so to speak, is not what fencing is about. What if he is totally incapable of responding to your attack of coulé-dégage-doublé-coupé-one-two-three-coupé-dégage-doublé de doublé? How nice to be able to do that against someone. But really, can you realistically count on any fencer feeding you the defensive actions you need to produce such a roundabout attack? The answer is no.

There is a logical growth process to the framing of your attacks. It's like building a pyramid. No one begins a pyramid at the top — the stones will fall on you. You start at the bottom, laying a broad foundation and head up from there. Fencing isn't any different. Start out with a simple dégage. If you're stopped by a counterparry, go to a doublé. After that, if your opponent adds a lateral parry to his counter, do a doublé-dégage. And so on down the line. That guy in front of you on the fencing strip will always inform you of what you should be doing against him.

Never attack with a bent arm. You will shorten the reach of your lunge. Never lean when you lunge. You will lose your balance. And never hold back when you attack, expecting to fail. You will fail.

Don't waste your energy with useless bouncing around on the fencing strip. A fencer's motion should be directed either forward or backward; up and down movement will have no effect on your ability to hit your opponent. It will only serve to hinder your use of timing and tire you out without producing any positive result. Direct your movement to a purpose; that is, know why you are doing what you are doing. A fencer who needs only five attempts to produce five touches has a distinct advantage over a fencer who needs fifty attempts to produce five touches.

Work your opponent. Threaten him, confuse him, misdirect him, block him. Do not let him dictate what is to happen in your encounter. If he uses strength, give way to it. If he is hesitant, push him. If he is tall, and tries to uses his height to his advantage, press in close to him. If he is fast, use your timing to negate his speed. If he is aggressive, employ actions that will tie up his blade, turning his drive back against him.

FORM

Maintain form in everything you do on the fencing strip. The on guard, the lunge, the parry, the riposte, the recovery. No action you do is isolated from the rest of your game. A car engine will run when its out of tune, but it won't run well. The same goes for you. Constantly examine your form. Polish it. That's your tune-up.

Remember, when you perform actions that are inefficient and ineffective, things that work markedly to your disadvantage, you have two people working against you on the fencing strip: your opponent — and you!

REPERTOIRE

It is also important to build an extensive repertoire of actions you can execute with skill. Never fashion a game that relies solely on one or two moves that are merely familiar or comfortable for you to execute. If something you do comes too easy to you, avoid it. Substitute another action, until you can pick and choose your responses at will. The fewer actions you have at your disposal, the easier it will be for your opponent to beat you.

DEFENSE

Defensively, don't be passive. Your opponent will take advantage of you.

Don't use your feet to excess to escape attacks. Your blade is your best protection. Stand your ground. Learn to parry with precision and consideration, even if it means being hit for a while as you perfect your responses.

Mix your parries up. Don't set up patterns that can be used against you. If you use a lateral parry twice to cover your quarte line, next time slip in a counter. If you usually employ a non-resisting parry against a beat, occasionally toss in a parry that opposes to throw a monkey wrench into your opponent's expectations.

MASTERY

Finally, we can sum up a successful approach to fencing in three words: knowledge, will and action. Leave out even one of these components and your play will be diminished. The mind must be there. Emotional content must be there. The ability to perform must be there. No fooling around. That's it!

If you embrace these qualities, absorbing them like a sponge, you will continue to grow as a fencer throughout your life, even into old age. If you think you can find a way around them, good luck!

SOME FINAL THOUGHTS ON STRATEGY

FEINTS

My fencing teacher, Ralph Faulkner, used to say that your best feint is to hit the other guy once. This, of course, is a metaphor for putting the fear of God into your adversary. Once you prove conclusively to any opponent that you can hit him, it is a big inducement for him to thereafter direct a parry at anything you throw at him. The easier you can hit him, the more readily he will respond.

The visually and physically overt nature of both the coulé and coupé make these actions excellent feints. Each projects a personality that is psychologically jarring. The coulé employs firm blade contact. The coupé displays a menacing downward slicing action. For an opponent who is slow to respond to your feint of dégage, press him with either of these, and he will more than likely parry.

CONTROLLED RESPONSES

Never direct parries against actions that in no way threaten your target area. If your opponent is moving forward aggressively with his foil point waving high in the air or directed at the floor, you have no business parrying. Besides, what is there to parry, anyway? A blade angled at the ceiling can't hit you. So, don't mess with it. Hold your ground until the blade can actually do some damage; or, better still, counterattack against the invalid attack. Too many fencers today validate nonsense they encounter on the fencing strip by responding to it as though it were something to be taken seriously.

COUPÉ

I've always liked the coupé as a final action on a composed attack. Pulling your foil blade back takes away an opponent's point of orientation — suddenly the weapon he has been focusing on is no longer within his reach — often causing him to overreact with an extremely large parry.

THE LOW LINE ATTACK

When attacking into the low line, there is no better preparation for it than a beat. A quick beat in quarte followed immediately by a dégage into the low-outside line is the ticket to an easy touch.

BEAT/BIND

If your opponent is on guard with his blade in line, and you can't manage to get him out of the way by simply beating him aside — he keeps popping his point back at you quickly with a stubborn insistence — follow the beat with an immediate bind. This will both collar him and carry off his threat to YOU in one fell swoop.

Moreover, if you wish to perform a bind, but your adversary keeps sliding lightly off your blade, toss in a firm beat first to mask what you really want to do.

PARRYING

If at all possible, parry only the final movement of an opponent's attack.

Photo by Anita Evangelista

YOUR BEST EFFORT

When you walk onto the fencing strip, it is important to always fence your best. Coming up against an opponent you consider less than your equal, it is natural to hold back somewhat; but this is an incorrect response. The moment another fencer squares off against you on the fencing strip, they are putting their talents on the line against yours. They are stating their desire to beat you. This is implicit in the fact that they have walked freely onto that fencing strip. So, to fence at any level but your best is a disservice to both of you. Even if that person comes limping onto the fencing strip in a body cast, you fence to beat him.

Nothing should stand in the way of you expressing your talent. That's not to say that you should be overly aggressive or brutal or argumentative. These faux pas have nothing to do with fencing. But, if you can beat them easily, beat them. Beat them with the skill you have developed. Beat them with your timing, your distance, your tactics. That's what it's all about.

Your time on the fencing strip should be a time of truth. And no one should ask anything less of you. No one should expect anything less from you.

ANTICIPATION VERSUS REALITY

Never anticipate the outcome of parries directed at your attack by an opponent. For instance, it may look as though that blade swinging around in a counterparry is going to catch your dégage; but don't stop what you're doing in response to it. Don't flinch, slow down, or pull up short. When you give up, you toss away all chances for success. Maybe the parry will stop your attack; but then again, maybe you will score a touch before it reaches your blade. You won't know until the action runs its course.

Because of the diverse psychological tricks we humans play on ourselves, many times you will have to grit your teeth and force yourself to follow through with that coulé, that riposte, that stop thrust — whatever you're doing. No matter what that little voice in your head whispers to the contrary, do what you have to do, what the rules direct you to do. Remember, your opponent's possible parry doesn't count. Only successfully competed actions have weight on the fencing strip.

Keep reality in front of you at all times.

THINK

Don't stop thinking. Keep a dialogue going on in your head. Observe, question, reflect, acknowledge, answer. If your only concern is to hit, you will never get beyond a simple physical game, a game that is almost over before it starts. Let your consciousness flow easily between your head and your hand. Don't hang it from the tip of your foil blade.

When you plan out an attack, and it doesn't work, rather than push on ahead, trying to make the best of a bad thing, recover, collect yourself, and find out what went wrong with your action. To go on fencing when you've bungled an attack —even if you do manage to salvage a touch — only masks errors that need to be rectified. A touch is transitory. Problems stay with you. Better to slow yourself down, and fix what needs to be fixed.

FENCE, FENCE, FENCE

Finally, keep fencing.

Fence when you're tired, when you're sick, when it's too hot, when it's too cold, when it's raining, when you hate fencing. You'll never develop a sense of what you should be doing if you wait for just the right moment to fence. There is no such thing. A strong strategy comes out of experience. Having done the wrong thing and the right thing, you are in a position to make choices. But without these moments of insight, you will always be left guessing. So do it as much you possibly can.

This may appear obvious, but the more you put into something, the more you'll get out of it. But, then, maybe it isn't obvious. Over the years, I've had students who came to me for a one hour fencing lesson once a week, and wondered why, after five or six months of work, they weren't more advanced.

Let's be realistic. One hour a week of fencing equals four or five hours a month. Push that to one year, and you get 52 hours of fencing for a 52 week period. That's a little more than two days worth of input out of 365 days.

I have no problem with casual fencing lessons. I think anyone who becomes involved in fencing — for whatever reason — is to be commended. But you have to keep your learning process in perspective. The ability to employ tactics with skill and cunning comes from immersing yourself in the process. It's a fact that you'll never learn the ins and outs of fencing by staying home and watching television.

PART V
BEYOND METHOD:
CONCEPTS

CLASSICAL FORM: FENCING'S YARDSTICK

Classical form is what the art of fencing is all about. Its presence in a fencer's technique is evidence of control, of your ability to purposefully guide your outcome on the fencing strip. It is also believed to be an unessential anachronism by many modern fencers.

In its essence, classical fencing form represents order, a fundamental component of control. You do not establish mastery of anything from chaos. Body parts working out of conjunction with one another, working at a less than adequate capacity, or not working at all, do little to set a fencer on the road to dependable skill.

An example:

I had a beginning student recently who was having problems with his basic lunge. He couldn't stop stepping out with his front foot, no matter how many times I reminded him that he should be pushing from his rear leg. The classical approach. This step, by the way, caused him to come up on his back toe like a ballet dancer and lose his balance horribly. Analyzing his lunge, I noticed that the instant before he attempted any attack, while still in the on guard position, every bit of bend went out of his legs — like he was trying to steady himself for his offensive action. This, of course, was his downfall. Since

Classical form in action — Captain John Duff

the forward motion of the lunge is produced by the back leg straightening, the fact that it was already straight made it impossible for him to put it to use. In fact, he pretty much had to step out with the front leg to gain any ground at all. I told him to concentrate on keeping both of his knees bent in the on guard position until he was able to maintain it naturally. "And make sure there's a bend there just as you're ready to lunge," I added. He did, and suddenly he was lunging properly. Surprise! There is nothing in fencing that is not connected to something else.

Mastery — real, certifiable mastery, not just a few overblown victories here and there — must flow from a set point of effective behavior patterns. Classical form, with its demands for balance, grace, efficiency and accuracy, sets up such a rarefied atmosphere. We are given a sound blueprint that has been tested and polished for centuries.

But the establishment of classical form is not an overnight proposition. It takes time, a lot of time, to develop something so important. It is, then, rather unappealing to many modern fencers, especially highly competitive ones, who view traditional style as old-fashioned. Better to get out there on the fencing strip as soon as possible and prop up whatever abilities you already possess.

Yet, logic would suggest that any kind of natural talent, bolstered by a rock hard ability to direct your energies and actions with finesse, would be superior to a mere "fast food" approach to fencing.

Finally, with its ability to soundly anchor us in a process that is both centered and intrinsically correct, form allows every fencer the luxury of being able to occasionally deviate from the norm with absolute control and, thereby, get away with it.

Proper form may no longer be a major concern among today's young fencers, but does that make it any less relevant to the reality of excellent fencing? When I see photos of fencers hunched and bunched on the fencing strip, jabbing, toe-to-toe, with arms angled and foils flailing, I don't think so.

FENCING WITH THE FINGERS

In the French school, learning to manipulate your foil with the fingers is the hallmark of the skilled fencer. Using your fingers effectively negates enlarged arm movements, bringing all blade work down into smart, flowing motions, motions that are highly efficient. The fingers become the needle and thread of your technique, attaching everything together tightly.

We've already talked about the French foil grip, which, of course, was specifically designed to enhance fingerplay. But this fact cannot be overemphasized, since it is the cornerstone of French technique. The gentle twist of the French grip's design inserts it neatly into the sword hand, allowing the fingers to enclose on it without difficulty.

The French weapon is held and guided primarily with the thumb and index finger; and since these do most of the work, they are sometimes called the "manipulators." The last three fingers fold lightly over the grip, basically holding it in place. These are called the "aids."

But how are the fingers actually brought into play? It doesn't simply happen. Two things must first take place: first, the sword arm has to be fully extended; and, second, the sword hand has to be turned from partial supination to complete supination. These movements effectively restrict arm use by constraining certain muscles, forcing all control to be assumed by the fingers.

But avoid gripping the French foil too tightly. Nimbleness, which is essential to successful fingerplay, is killed by squeezing. Excessive pressure will both throw off point control and turn your sword hand into a dead piece of meat. At most, the foil should be held with a firmly directed insistence.

In time, with much practice, your fingers will develop a special affinity for the French grip.

This mingling of weapon and hand is eventually transformed into sentiment du fer — the feeling of the blade — where your foil is no longer a separate object, but an extension of your own nervous system. Suddenly, foil, hand and mind are linked in an intricate alliance, as your blade transmits subtle signals of pressure and movement. This is fencing with the fingers at its best.

TIMING

Timing, it has been said, is everything. Strike when the iron it hot. Time and tide wait for no man. There's no time like the present. And, of course, there's no time to lose.

Timing is the intangible mechanism by which we blend and employ body movement and speed. It is feet and hand interacting in perfect conjunction. It is the soundless music of our energies. It is the beat, the tempo — sometimes smooth, sometimes uneven — by which we execute our thought out strategies on the fencing strip. And it is the single most important component in fencing.

And, like timing in comedy, the timing of fencing cannot be taught, only found through experience.

In the beginning, we have no idea what is going on when we stand there, weapon in hand, in front of an opponent whose only intent is to cause our symbolic downfall. Our moves are hesitant, lacking both purpose and determination. We are slow, our feet are lead. Then, one day, we see the light, but only in retrospect. This is frustrating, to be sure. Finally, movement flows. We are plugged into the process. We mold, we manipulate. Our movement becomes an ebb and flow. One moment we're here in quarte; the

Timing is everything

next moment, we are there in septime. Our foil point floats with calm, but firm, purpose, like the bee hopping from flower to flower in the warm summer sun. We weave through an opponent's defenses as though they didn't exist. We have the power to stop any attack in its tracks.

Suddenly, timing is there!

Where did it come from? And when, exactly, did it arrive? We usually only become aware of timing long after it has ingrained itself in our person.

Practice, I think, makes the journey a quicker one. But each fencer must make the journey alone.

DISTANCE

Distance, in fencing terms, is that collection of feet and inches that separates you from your opponent on the fencing strip. On a more personal level, it is an elusive chasm stretching between your blade and your opponent's target area.

Distance, once called "measure," has always been a chief concern in fencing. Over the centuries, it has been studied and categorized. And, while occasionally cloaked in fanciful theories, it has always retained one firm and true concept: the proper manipulation of distance allows a fencer to be able to hit while not being hit.

Today, we boil distance down to three basic forms: being too close, being too far away, and being in just the right spot. As to be expected, each of these designations has its own distinct qualities. We will now discuss them in detail.

OUT OF DISTANCE

"Out of distance" refers to the situation of being too far away from your opponent to hit him, even when lunging. Most of the time a fencer works in this situation, because, while he may not be able to hit, he most certainly cannot be hit. Being out of distance, then, is highly protective.

Of course, lunging out of distance will get a fencer nowhere. No matter how artfully or energetically he performs an attack, if it falls short of its objective, he has wasted his time. Attacking on the advance — stepping forward before lunging — is the standard method of alleviating this deficiency.

CLOSE DISTANCE

"Close distance" is the situation of being so near an opponent, he may be hit simply by extending your sword arm. No lunge is necessary. In fact, in such cases, lunging is impossible. Many beginners tend to gravitate to close distance, because it seems to them

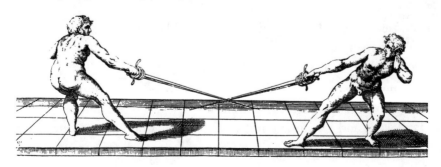

that being right on top of one's opponent will make getting a touch easier. This, of course, is a mistake. In point of fact, if you are close enough to hit your opponent by simply extending your sword arm, he may just as easily hit you.

Moreover, when fencers get too close to one another, exchanges tend to become cramped. There's no way around it. Jabbing and poking, amid twisting and squatting, is the usual outcome of such situations. We legitimize fighting at close quarters by giving it the nice, clean label of "in-fighting;" but, to me, it's just sloppy distance maintenance. Forget the excuses. Some instructors actually encourage their students to engage in it, but how much better it would be for a fencer to develop a balanced approach to distance.

The attacking fencer on the right exhibits a poor sense of distance (photo courtesy of USFA/Roger Mar)

In-fighting may even initiate a corps-a-corps (meaning body-to-body), where actual physical contact is made with your opponent. This action is frowned upon by the conventions of fencing, since it is the ultimate expression of out-of-control fencing.

PROPER DISTANCE

"Proper distance," is that single distance where, by extending your sword arm and lunging, you are able to comfortably hit your opponent. This distance will differ slightly from fencer to fencer.

To keep yourself protected, proper distance should be attained only at the moment you are completely ready to lunge. To stay within its confines too long leaves a fencer open to immediate counterattack.

Distance, it should be noted, is influenced chiefly by how you employ your footwork. To practice footwork constantly, then, is a must. Over and over and over. Forward and backward. Backward and forward. Until your movement becomes second nature.

This is the key to distance.

SPEED

While many fencers believe that speed is the most significant factor in a fencer's makeup, this is not the case. To be sure, speed can be useful, but it is, in fact, subordinate to both timing and distance. Therefore, relying on speed as your primary fencing asset is a major tactical blunder. A fencer who has taken the time to develop both timing and distance can easily take a "fast" fencer apart.

There's nothing wrong with speed, of course. It can be overpowering. But it should be bonded tightly to proper technique. In the beginning, an aspiring fencer should focus on form rather than quickness. To try fencing with the alacrity of D'Artagnan before you are ready for it only confuses matters. When you have a solid grasp of what you are doing, when you can get your blade to go where you want it to go, then, and only then, add speed. Otherwise, you'll end up being one of those hapless fencers who always gets where he's going before he's gotten there. And there are plenty of those, you know.

(Photo by Arnold Jacques)

STRENGTH

Muscular strength has no place in fencing. Endurance, yes, but not strength. A fencer who relies on strength is usually an unbalanced fencer, whose pounding, slashing blade actions often end up bouncing off the floor. He constantly opens up his lines with defensive moves that are all over the fencing strip. He is very reactive. This individual, by the way, is easy to circumvent.

I've fenced against this type of fencer over the years, and they are quite predictable. Sure, if you allow them to push you around, they will certainly beat you up; but we have numerous actions in the French style of fencing that may be used to counteract raw power.

Muscles just get in the way. I can tell you that the most difficult students I've ever taught over the years have been those who were hard-core bodybuilders. With all their ability to lift hundreds of pounds, they could never learn to fence well. They just couldn't relax with the foil in their hand. The tension they used in weight lifting, the tension that created their bulging muscles, always worked against them when they picked up a foil. That weapon, that 16 ounce object, caused their sword hands to shake as though they had some severe nervous disorder. They couldn't loosen up to save their lives. And, finally, they had to stop before their arms fell off.

If you have normal strength, strength to hold yourself upright, and an ability to relax under pressure, you can be a good fencer. You learn to pace yourself, to use your energy wisely.

My teacher, Ralph Faulkner, used to say, "The best exercise for fencing is fencing."

Forget strength.

Timing, distance, dexterity, strategy — these are the things of which fencers are made.

Strength isn't always an asset

BALANCE

Balance is a hoped-for outcome of fencing. When we speak of balance, though, we're not just talking about physical balance, the kind of balance that keeps you from falling on your face. We are also describing the mental sort. Moreover, we constantly strive for a combining of both attributes into a useful, effective whole.

PHYSICAL BALANCE

Physical balance is derived from the proper placement of the feet, a bend of the knees that lowers the body's center of gravity to a position of optimum equilibrium in the general area of the belly.

It is also the skillful and precise application of your weapon against your opponent. This comes from the establishment of a centered placement of your blade and the proper and continued practice of those fencing actions that achieve control. It is in doing only what it takes to carry out any fencing action and no more than that. Your blade movement, both offensive and defensive, will then never be overstated and work against you.

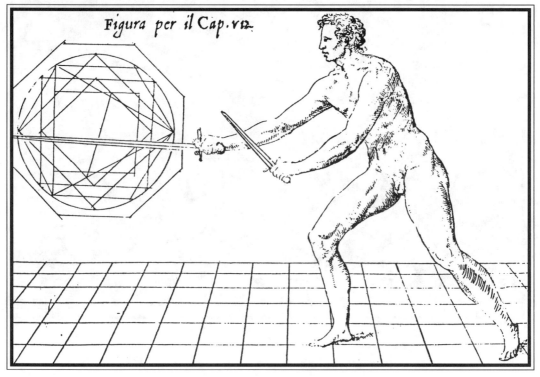

Figura per il Cap. vii.

MENTAL BALANCE

Mental balance comes from a respect for fencing, a stubborn adherence to and thorough understanding of, the precepts of the game. It is a calm, unemotional outlook toward actions taking place on the fencing strip and a self-confidence that is based on experience.

When you can look at that weapon-waving opponent barreling down on you on the fencing strip and see, not a violent attack, but simply movement to be dealt with, then you will have achieved mental balance.

SYNTHESIS

Bringing mind and body together on the fencing strip is the ultimate goal of fencing. (And you though it was getting touches, didn't you?) A blending of thought and action supercedes all true effectiveness on the fencing strip. Touches, therefore, become the expression, the outcome, of superb fencing, not the determing factor of its existence. (Simply put: you are not a good fencer because you get touches; you will get touches because you are a good fencer.)

From this point in time, you will have a centering, an anchor spot, from which to fence. You will be connected to yourself, your opponent and the moment at hand.

This is balance.

HONOR

The last few years have given us public demonstrations of athletic behavior, on and off playing fields, that has been anything but admirable. It was once said that sports built character. Today, we see, as a matter of course, fits of temper, greed, drug abuse, incredibly poor sportsmanship, elitism, laziness, vanity and brutality acted out by sports participants on the diamond, rink and court.

Perhaps, with fencing, we can do better.

TRADITION

Fencing has had its share of unpleasant individuals over the ages, to be sure. I've known some of the modern ones personally. But our art also has a side to its long history that is proud, noble and brave. The honor of fencing has been hard won over the centuries through the sweat and blood of our predecessors. Fencing, then, provides us with a built-in opportunity to express ourselves in ways that show we appreciate our heritage and to rise above the common denominator.

Fencing offers us control.

We can choose our behavior.

RESPECT

We should always respect our teachers and our schools. Here we honor our foundations. On the fencing strip, we must never forget to salute our opponents and shake hands after bouting. In tournament play, we show respect for those who officiate our bouts, for without them, competition would be chaos.

TACTICS

To me, the fencer who physically intimidates his opponent with brutality of blade movement or downright, knock-down fencing, or who attempts to side-track an adversary through obnoxious, argumentative behavior, is an ignorant amateur, a thoroughly bad fencer, showing little regard for his learning or the institution of fencing. Beat your opponent with fencing excellence — with your superior blade movement, timing, distance and strategy.

That is what it is all about.

TRUTH

We acknowledge touches. When we cheat, we cheat not only our opponents but ourselves, because we rob ourselves of the truth of fencing and cease to grow as fencers.

FRATERNITY

We fence against anyone who asks us to a friendly crossing of blades. We can always learn from both good and bad fencers. We admire the expert touch, and look with tolerance on the less than adequate fencer. Everyone starts in the same place, awkward and unknowing. To forget this is to forget we are human.

HONOR

To act in any way but the abovementioned manner would be to denigrate the art of the sword. We maintain a sense of good will, we persevere, we are patient, we always strive to do our best and we take pride in the uniqueness of fencing and in our skills. When we win, we win through fair play or not at all. No matter what anyone else tells you, standards count.

We express our respect constantly for fencing and, therefore, demonstrate through our unflagging loyalty, our own personal honor. Such sentiments are often looked upon with cynicism in today's world. But fencing attempts to ground us in solid reality, not in the trendy behavior of our times. If we allow ourselves to become ugly on the fencing strip, then we lose no matter what the record books say.

PART VI
THE ÉPÉE

THE ÉPÉE

The épée is the dueling sword of fencing. In this single statement we frame the entire character of the weapon. Descended from the rapier — the personal combat sword of the 17th century — the épée in both design and use recalls the days of early morning duels on mist shrouded hillsides and sword-toting musketeers.

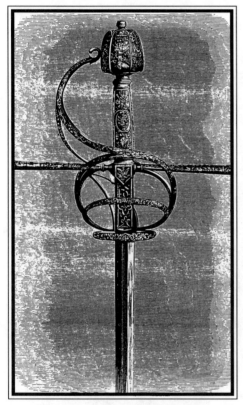

The rapier, the dueling sword of the 17th century

There are general principles of fencing that are the same for both the épée and foil. The épée, then, becomes the natural second weapon in your learning process. Like the foil, the épeé may strike only with its tip. Like the foil, the épée incorporates the exact same body lines. And, like the foil, the épée is guided primarily by a supinated sword hand. Timing, footwork and distance are likewise as important to the épée as they are to the foil. Most of all, the épée demands a healthy control your blade point, which has its origins deeply rooted in the precise maneuverings of foil play.

But, of course, there are some major differences.

The exact application of the épée takes its lead from the circumstances encountered in a real sword fight. Indeed, the épée was devised in the latter part of the 19th century as a method of teaching a fencer these stark principles, something the well-defined conventions of the foil could never do. The foil should not be dismissed as extraneous, however, for it teaches the overall self-control that makes mastering the épée a much easier endeavor. In fact, I believe a fencer who has not studied the foil first will never fully realize his épée and sabre capabilities.

When you have fully absorbed the foil, then, you usually are ready to tackle the épée.

THE NATURE OF ÉPÉE FENCING

The épée is a nonconventional weapon. This means that there are no rules of right-of-way, or any limitations on the target area that might be attacked. The idea is to simply get in and deliver a touch before your opponent does, and that's all.

Generally looked upon as a practical weapon, a very straightforward weapon, the épée, if observed with a keen eye, actually possesses a side that is most esoteric in nature. There are moments when the épée encounter is very much a freewheeling experience, embodying all the spontaneity and energy of a real sword fight. Developed to its fullest possibilities, the épée game offers the opportunity to develop your ability to improvise under pressure, to take advantage of situations that are here one moment and gone the next.

The basis for épée fencing is the duel

It was this somewhat unplanned quality of épée fencing, in fact, that once made it much despised among purists in the fencing world. The épée was called, rather disparagingly, a "fluking iron," referring to the seemingly accidental way in which touches were arrived at.

To be fair, however, the game of épée, when approached in a sensible manner, is a balanced union of both strategy and feeling. It is a game with ever shifting possibilities, making it an ideal complement to its conventional cousin, the foil.

Today, the épée is recognized for the beneficial influences it exerts on your fencing, especially its ability to sharpen both timing and point control.

We will now dicuss some of the particulars of the épée in detail.

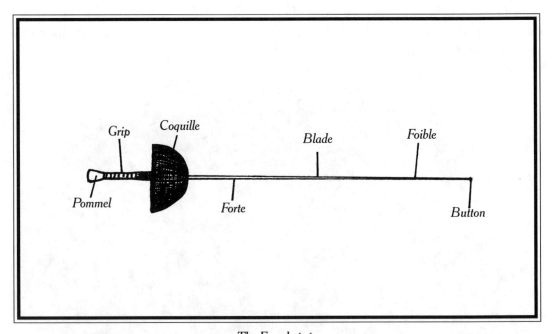

The French épée

THE FRENCH ÉPÉE

To keep things uncomplicated, when we talk of épées from now on, we will be referring only to the French animal. The Italian épée, like the Italian foil, does not fall within the purview of this book.

Someone once remarked to me that the épée looked like a pregnant foil. In a way, I guess, this is a fairly accurate description. The overall shape of the épée is, indeed, the same as the foil — only bigger.

The blade of the épée, like a foil blade, is tapered for flexibility. It has a button, a foible and a forte. But it is much stouter than a foil blade and triangular in shape. It is also fluted, or grooved, length-wise, which adds strength to the metal while decreasing its weight.

The épée's hand guard is much larger than that of the foil's. Noticeably so. This affords the épéeist's sword hand as much protection as possible, since it may, by the rules of épée fencing, be attacked. Offsetting the épée blade slightly from the center of the hand guard also helps in this task.

The French grip for the épée is exactly the same as it is for the foil. Same length — everything.

The pommel employed by the épée, however, is larger — and, hence, heavier — than the pommel attached to the foil. This effectively offsets the greater weight of the épée's imposing blade.

HOLDING THE ÉPÉE

It should be noted that the épée of the French variety is grasped in exactly the same manner as you hold the French foil. No difference. The design of the grip, of course, promotes the same agile finger control one strives for with the conventional weapon.

Holding the épée (Photo taken by Anita Evangelista)

THE ÉPÉE ON GUARD

The épée on guard looks similar to the foil on guard stance, but because the emphasis is now on an entire body target, there are some very important differences that, if ignored, will lead you into trouble.

THE ÉPÉE

The standard on guard position for épée places the weapon slightly into sixte (the high-outside line). This protects the sword arm from the straight thrust. The tip of the épée should be dropped slightly below hand level.

THE FEET AND LEGS

The stance should be somewhat shorter than the one used in foil. Extending the front foot too far forward exposes both it and the front leg to sudden attacks. For this same reason, the knees should not be overly bent.

THE FREE ARM

The free arm should be raised in the same manner as you would hold it in foil fencing. It is there, of course, to help maintain balance and to facilitate lunging.

THE SWORD HAND

The sword hand is kept primarily in a partially supinated position.

THE SWORD ARM

The sword arm should be nearly straight. To employ the bent arm guard used in foil would subject the under part of the forearm to an opponent's probing thrusts.

Care should also be exercised to avoid sticking your elbow out. Such an error in form presents a splendid angle for an incoming épée point to make contact.

THE TORSO

Finally, the torso should be kept fairly upright. Leaning only presses your target area forward, shortening the distance your opponent has to travel to score a touch.

The épée fencer should constantly remind himself that the stance he assumes, thanks to an enlarged target area, will either promote his safety or lead him continually into painful collision with his opponent's weapon. Often a booming touch to the kneecap or wrist will underscore this fact and stimulate even the most faulty memory.

GENERAL PRINCIPLES OF ÉPÉE FENCING

We build our whole épée technique around the fact that we may hit or be hit anywhere on the body. Forget this and you will be hit everywhere on the body.

Distance becomes an essential factor in the épée bout. To maintain your safety — that is, keeping your forward body parts out of reach — a greater separation between yourself and your opponent should be sought while looking for openings.

With the full body as a target, you may find increased opportunities to hit your adversary; however, you must remember that your opponent, likewise, has more chances to score against you.

Finally, to be an effective épée fencer, it is best to put yourself into the mind-set that you are actually fighting a duel. If this is done, every action you contemplate — both offensive and defensive — will be weighed as to its effect on your theoretical survival in the encounter taking place. Certainly never allow yourself to be so shallow as to weigh your successes only in touches given and received, but consider the manner in which you manage to both protect vital body parts and place potentially lethal thrusts.

Sober reflection combined with conservative movement is the key to being effective with the épée.

The target area of épée fencing

ÉPÉE OFFENSE

OFFENSE

The main principle of the épée offense can be summed up in the term "defensive offense." This means, no matter what attack move you use, it must be performed in such a way that you are also protected by your actions.

You are never fully and freely offensive, as you are with foil. There are no conventions to safeguard your forward plunge from immediate counterattack. Therefore, always frame your attacks so that they also take into account those body parts once placed off limit by foil rules. Your sword hand and arm, your front foot, your front leg and your mask are now fair game.

FOOTWORK

Use your footwork extensively, advancing and retreating constantly to ease yourself in the proper distance for attacking. Remember, in épée, your distance is measured from hand guard to hand guard rather than from body to body, as it is with the foil.

SIMPLICITY

For the most part, keep your attacks as simple as possible. The straight thrust and the dégage are the best choices, since, taking little time to accomplish, they are less likely to be countered.

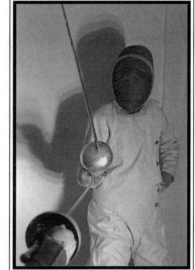

An attack to the exposed sword arm

THE UNLIMITED TARGET AREA

There is an irony awaiting the novice épéeist. When you first pick up the dueling sword, you look at the area you can touch — the entire body — and think, "Man, this is great! No more limitations. I can hit any place I want." Possibilities for attacking seem endless. Then, with experience, your scope begins to narrow. Guided by thoughts of practicality, you suddenly zero in on those few spots that are most easily and safely touched. And, in the end, you find the focus of your attacks is even more specialized and restricted than it was in foil fencing.

To be able to attack everything is to find that not everything should be attacked.

THE BEST TARGETS

Attack your opponent's sword arm, especially the hand and wrist, more than any other spot on his body. This is his closest point to you. It is the one that also puts you at the least amount of risk. Keep this in mind: if you attack to the hand, and your opponent attacks at the same moment to your body, you will hit first.

Here, the point control you have diligently honed in foil fencing will allow you to confidently place your point onto these narrowest of target areas.

The front leg and foot should also be considered excellent targets when attacking.

THE BLADE POINT

Keep your blade point in line, menacing your opponent at all times. If you remove it, for whatever reason, you will certainly give up opportunities to deliver touches.

LUNGING

Employ half lunges (short lunges) as much as possible. These will not overextend you — and, hence, open you up to counterattacks — when you attack.

BODY ATTACKS

While many fencers attack to the body —as a matter of course over and over and over and over again — this strategy should, in fact, be considered secondary to attacks to the sword arm. To do otherwise is to ignore the self-preserving concepts of dueling. The body is the furthest thing away from your blade point and so will be the most difficult spot to hit. Pursuing difficulty may be good for the soul, but in épée fencing it will just invite a big, thick blade to come crashing into your mask.

Attack to the body only when the action has been preceded by careful preparations. A sound feint of straight hit to the sword hand, employing the advance or the half lunge, may be used in this way.

To launch yourself into an unplanned body attack often leads to being hit as you hit, which, of course, is poor épée technique. In the old days, it would have been called "dead."

A full lunge or a fleche should be executed when attacking to the body.

PREPARATIONS

Make use of the beat and bind to displace your opponent's blade point . With his weapon thus dominated, he cannot hit you.

PRONATION

When attacking the hand, or the underside of the forearm, of your opponent, it is acceptable to turn your sword hand into a pronated position. Indeed, to create the correct angle of approach for executing this action, pronation actually facilitates your delivery.

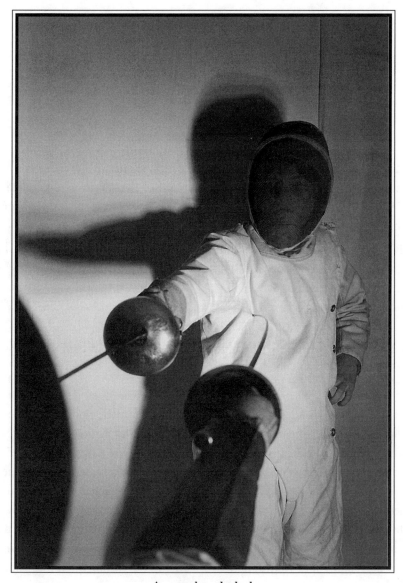

An attack to the body

COUNTERATTACKS

Counterattacks are vital to effective épée fencing: the coup de temps, the coup d'arrêt and tension. Timing and blocking actions neutralize the attacking force of even the most aggressive fencer.

ÉPÉE DEFENSE

DEFENSE

In the same way that the offense of épée possesses a distinctively defensive nature, its defensive methodology, likewise, contains an element of the offensive. "Offensive defense," as it might be called, demands that whenever a fencer is defending himself, he must frame his actions to include an offensive perspective.

To go fully defensive in épée implies that a fencer has, for the moment, lost his cool. He's been spooked into a reaction and that can be taken advantage of. On the other hand, remaining offensively defensive suggests that he has retained his wits and is in total control of his actions.

Offensive defense is, then, more than anything else, a mind-set — a mind-set whose presence, or lack thereof, will either turn your defense into an impenetrable wall or a Swiss cheese.

DEFENSIVE DEFENSE

There are some distinct disadvantages to falling into a defensive mode that neglects offensive possibilities. Invariably, a reactive fencer will bend his sword arm too much when defending, which is a killer for the épéeist. To make a standard foil type parry with an épée — a parry that has just one firm objective — to stop an attacking blade from striking, period — will always displace your blade point from where it should be directed, right at your opponent. At the very least, potential touches may be sacrificed in the maneuver. If your blade point has been raised to eye level in a desperate attempt to parry, it certainly cannot pick off a momentarily exposed wrist. At worst, a sword arm bent means a sword arm exposed means a sword arm hit; so you'll probably find your opponent's blade tip burrowing often into your wrist.

Also, to go 100 percent defensive means to focus your attention on a single area, which will certainly leave the rest of your body exposed. Even for a moment, this can be disastrous. I'm parrying heavily into quinte, and, oops, there goes a touch to my foot!

Lastly, because reactive parries tend to slow down a fencer's ability to counterattack effectively, your opponent will certainly be encouraged to execute repeated remises against you.

I should say here that given the choice of going fully defensive with a parry and being hit, I would most definitely choose to parry. But the point is to not settle for working from the lowest common denominator, but rather to control the situation you find yourself in, and avoid the circumstances that force a fencer down the reactive road.

OFFENSIVE DEFENSE

By defending yourself in such a way that your blade point is nearly always directed at your opponent, the opportunity to counterattack is always within your reach.

The épée parry should be framed in such a way that your blade point moves as little as possible from its on guard position. This means, with sword arm nearly straight, you will end up crossing your opponent's blade at a much less pronounced angle than when parrying with the foil.

The épée parry may be expressed as either a parry of opposition or a beat parry. But if the beat parry is used, the sword arm, rather than the fingers (as French foil technique dictates), should manage the action. The sturdiness of the épée blade demands that considerable energy be channeled into your defensive response.

You may further enhance your position by parrying with the hand guard of your weapon. This creative maneuver is carried out by a simple raising, lowering or sideways flexing of the sword hand and wrist. It both aids in point control and keeps your blade free for immediate counteroffensive maneuvers.

WHICH PARRY?

The parry of prime, much favored by modern fencers, should, in fact, be avoided entirely as it uncovers the entire forearm. Quinte, producing a inadequate blade displacement, should, likewise, be set aside.

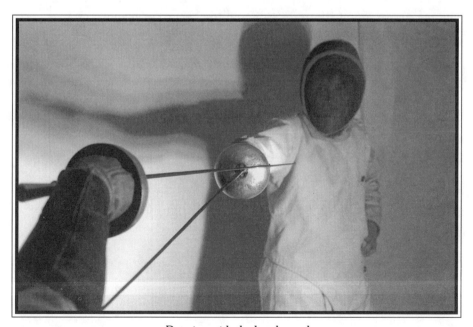

Parrying with the hand guard

Seconde is a strong parry and is, therefore, much recommended in the French school. Quarte and sixte are good. Likewise, the counterparries of contre de seconde, contre de quarte and contre de sixte may be employed successfully.

DISTANCE

Keeping proper distance is a great defensive enhancement. If, when your opponent attacks aggressively, you are too far away for him to land a touch, his action has been wasted, and you are safe.

COUNTERATTACKS

Certainly, by hitting with counterattacks (coup de temps, coup d'arrêt and tension) that either out-time or block an opponent's advancing attack, you are, in effect, performing a defensive action.

THE RIPOSTE

The riposte coming off the épée parry should block the line in which the parry was made to prevent a successful counterattack. This is easier if the parry has been made with opposition. Continued blade contact, in this case, may be naturally maintained, producing a response that seems almost one action. If a beat parry has been employed, fortify your riposte by moving your hand guard over slightly in the direction in which the parry was made.

Futhermore, riposte to your opponent's sword arm as much as possible — the closer to the forearm the better. These ripostes are less likely to be countered than those to the body. But, of course, point control is essential to effective arm shots.

In épée, we have seen that the line between defense and offense is a fine one. That is because the line separating hitting and being hit is also relatively narrow. But, if you diligently keep in mind the true character of the épée encounter, and what it represents, it becomes relatively simple to maintain a balance of thought and action that will generate a satisfying outcome.

THE ÉPÉE BOUT

The épée bout differs considerably from the foil encounter, mainly because of the lack of conventions. Straight arm first means nothing — only who hits first.

In the electrical bout, a successful touch must land at least $1/25$ of a second ahead of its counterpart. Anything less is considered a double touch.

Unlike foil, where double touches without established right of way are discarded, the double touches of épée count as a touch against each fencer, as would be the case in an actual duel — two hits, two wounds.

It's interesting to note that épée bouts were once one touch affairs, again reflecting the grim, abrupt consequences of fighting with sharp swords. Today, however, embodying more of a sport outlook, épée is fenced for five touches, in the same manner as the foil and sabre (except in the modern pentathlon, where the one touch épée bout has been retained for symbolic military reasons).

REMINDERS AND FINAL THOUGHTS

Use your footwork, not just as random movement, but as true enhancements to both your offensive and defensive games.

Study your opponent's responses on the fencing strip thoroughly before committing yourself to any attack.

To defend the front leg, carry it straight back (away from an advancing blade), and counterattack to your opponent's mask.

Attack the forearm often.

Vary the rhythm — the tempo — of your actions.

Make point control a priority of your épée education.

An attack to the foot from a bind in seconde works extremely well.

Approach each touch with caution, as you would in a real encounter.

Cultivate your ability to counterattack at a moment's notice.

Composed attacks work best in épée against the reactive fencer who falls into a completely defensive mode and parries heavily.

The tall épéeist will attempt to use his height and reach to his advantage, both physically and psychologically. To counter this, you must press in on him relentlessly, attacking his hand. Remember this fact: no matter his actual size, the distance from the tip of your épée to your sword hand is exactly the same as his. This, then, makes him no tougher to touch than anyone else.

On the other hand, keep the shorter fencer out of distance by retreating often, causing his actions to forever fall short. This will both frustrate him and tire him out. Then, counterattack quickly.

Above all, make your épée game a mixed bag. To be predictable is to be hit often.

Finally, I think, ultimately, épée is best learned on the fencing strip. While basic moves can be acquired from the fencing master, épée technique itself can only be solidified under fire. Foil's rite of passage has already given you the building blocks of fencing: timing, distance, point control, a strategy-oriented thought process. You need only mold these to épée's particular point of view to become a credible practitioner of the dueling sword.

Nedo Nadi, one of the finest fencers of all time, was forbidden by his fencing master father to fence épée, which the elder Nadi considered an undisciplined weapon. Nedo, wishing to learn the weapon anyway, convinced a friend to practice with him out behind their fencing school. In the end, he figured out the workings of the weapon by critiquing what went on in these practice sessions. Nedo Nadi went on to win two Olympic gold medals in épée.

PART VII
THE SABRE

THE SABRE

The sabre is a "military" weapon. Its origins are to be found in cavalry use — that is, fighting on horseback. It is also, by far, the flashiest weapon of fencing. There's a saying in fencing, "Foil fencers talk about the techniques of fencing. Épée fencers talk about the esoterics of fencing. And sabre fencers talk about themselves." The weapon, then, lends itself to the broad, the loud, the boisterous and the flamboyant. That is its personality.

The sabre should be the third weapon to be added to a student's repertoire, because it is fundamentally the most different of all three weapons of fencing. Of course, if you are to become a well-rounded fencer, eventually learning sabre is essential.

The modern sabre can be traced back to the sleek, curved Arabian scimitar. It was introduced to Europe as a result of contact between Hungarian tribesmen and Turkish invaders during the 16th century. The sabre was then spread throughout the western world by the Hungarians, who, by the 18th century, had adopted it as their national sword.

During the 18th and early 19th centuries, the sabre was much practiced among the armies of Europe. By the mid-18th century, more than 80 percent of all European swords were of the sabre design.

The sabre of this time period was a broad, heavy weapon and did not lend itself to intricate usage. It was basically a hacking tool, although the point could, if necessary, be brought into play. Even the stout hand guard might be employed across an adversary's face in the heat of battle.

The strongest significance of the sabre, with its cutting edge, was that it could be utilized more readily on horseback than a point weapon. In a melee, where distance was at a premium — with soldiers often finding themselves packed in horse against horse — the cut was definitely far superior to the thrust.

Just the same, 18th century duelists scorned the sabre as a rather crude implement unfit for gentlemen, preferring instead the sleek, deadly small sword. Traditionally-minded fencers refused to even consider the sabre as a weapon of artful combat.

But the sabre couldn't be denied. It simply presented itself too many possibilities as a weapon of skill. In the 19th century it was finally accepted into the sporting world. The early sport sabre closely resembled its ponderous military counterpart. The game produced was rather slow, especially when compared to foil; and, because of the sturdiness of the blade, a certain amount of discomfort could be produced whenever contact to the body was made. Still, this brutality lent a certain macho quality to the encounters. Among its proponents, the sabre was considered "a real man's weapon."

In 1868, the Italians founded their first sabre school, run by the famous Milanese maestro Giuseppi Radaelli, whose book on sabre set down the basics of the Italian style for the first time. His method stressed fast, swift cuts delivered by the hand and forearm, with the elbow acting as a pivot point. The forearm, wrist and blade created a single rigid line. Luigi Barbasetti and Euginio Pini were two highly successful sabre masters who worked with Radaelli.

In the latter part of the 19th century it was the Italians, led by Radaelli, who championed a streamlined version of the sabre for sport purposes. Many traditional sabre users of the time looked upon the cut down weapon with scorn. Alfred Hutton, one of England's leading fencers, called it "a silly, little toy." Still, it produced a game that was both energetic and stylish and did much to popularize sabre among students of the sword.

While fast becoming a weapon of sport, as late as 1908, the French, among others, were still touting the sabre as a weapon of war and taught it with that thought in mind. In the opening days of World War I soldiers still carried sabres into battle; however, against machine guns, swords proved to be of little use and were quickly discarded as excess baggage of another age.

It was left to the Hungarians to take up the sabre and truly develop it to its greatest potential.

The Hungarians organized their first school of sabre fencing in 1851, when Joseph Keresztessy, known as "the father of Hungarian sabre fencing," began teaching a style that involved simple, short cuts and parries that emanated from circular wrist motions.

In 1896, Italo Santelli, an Italian fencing champion of great renown, was invited by the Hungarian government to come to Hungary to teach sabre. He adapted his Italian learning to the Hungarian method to create a new approach to sabre play that made the Hungarians nearly invincible for decades.

Today, the Hungarian school has supplanted all other approaches to the sabre. Blade control comes from the fingers and a flexible wrist. Wide arm movements are discouraged. Much importance is also placed on footwork, timing, mobility and tactics.

While once considered the prerogative of male fencers alone, the sabre is now fenced widely by women. Although it has yet to be added to women's Olympic or World Championship fencing events, this condition is expected to change in the near future.

THE NATURE OF SABRE FENCING

The sabre is both a cutting weapon and a point weapon. This means that touches can be scored with either the tip or the edge of the blade, although sabre technique definitely stresses the former over the latter.

The sabre, like the foil, is a conventional weapon, meaning that it has rules of right-of-way and a limited target area that must be observed. It is, then, a weapon of governed behavior. Therefore, I believe, to have learned foil previous to picking up the sabre is fundamental to establishing an initial control over it.

Also, since the sabre tip may be used offensively, first mastering both the foil and épée will generally enhance point work in your sabre game.

The target area for sabre is all body parts from the waist up, including the arms and mask. It has been said that this reflects the attacking area of someone sitting on horse-back. It has a certain logic behind it. Certainly, even though you could strike an adversary on the leg if you were fighting on horseback, it would be rather stupid to try to whittle on his foot while he was chopping you on the head. Therefore, you would want to keep your mental focus considerably up above the toes, wouldn't you? Furthermore, if you throw in the sabre's cavalry origins, you would say, "Makes sense to me."

There are some members of the fencing community who deny this explanation, calling it a major myth of fencing. They say that modern sport sabre has absolutely no connection to cavalry. They further state that the conventions of modern sabre argue against the traditional explanations for sabre fencing's target area, since real fighting on horseback didn't deny attacks to the lower part of the body. So, what's their explanation for the sabre target area? Well, the target area is from the waist up simply because you can do more damage with a cutting weapon to that area.

Anyway, you can make up your own mind on this one. I personally think modern sabre fencing, being a conventional weapon, reflects a symbolic connection to both a cavalry origin and a practicality of use. It teaches self-control with a cutting sword, the same way the foil teaches control with a point weapon.

THE CONVENTIONS OF SABRE FENCING

While the sabre differs from the foil in techniques employed, they are similar in the demand for the adherence to specific behavior. An attacker is established by performing a properly defined attack with either the point or cutting edge; a defender is established with regard to this attack. A proper attack must be parried before a counterattack may be instituted. A delineated attack area — the body above the waist — must be conformed to in order to maintain blade control.

For these reasons, learning to fence with the foil is more than a good idea before tackling the sabre. The self-control gained in adhering to foil conventions is ideal preparation for a weapon which — because of the arm movement involved in instituting attacks — can easily lead to a wild, undisciplined approach to fencing.

I have fenced, over the years, with fencers who took up the sabre before they developed a strong hold on the other two weapons. Their entire game fell apart because of it. I once had my free hand laid open in a foil bout by a fencer who, taking a few premature sabre lessons, began fencing like Conan the Barbarian.

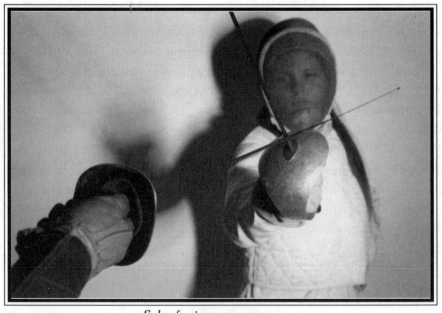

Sabre fencing (photo by Anita Evangelista)

To learn sabre well, it must be approached with caution. Learn the conventions, practice them, apply them to your basic technique, drill them into your very being.

Too many fencers employ the sabre like a cutlass or a weapon without conventions. You see way too many double touches out on the fencing strip these days. Learn to attack with your thoughts directed toward timing, distance and proper form. Learn to parry and riposte when you should be parrying and riposting. Control your responses so that you will not only avoid initiating double touches but you will be able to avoid them when they are directed at you. That's why we have conventions.

Then you will be a sabre fencer.

THE BODY OF THE SABRE

The sabre looks nothing like either the foil or the épée except, of course, in a general way. It does have portions common to all swords: a blade, a hand guard, and a pommel. Specifically speaking, its shape is entirely unique to its usage.

The sabre blade is lighter and more flexible than either the épée or foil blade. It is triangular at its forte, while tapering to a flat rectangularity at the foible. The tip, rather than being flat, ends by being rounded over.

The edge of the blade is made up of the cutting edge and the back. A cut may be delivered with the entire portion of the cutting edge. The upper third of the back of the blade is called the back edge or sometimes the false edge. A cut may also be delivered with this portion of the blade. The tip may be employed in the same manner as the tip of any point weapon.

The sabre hand guard, almost as large as an épée guard, possesses a feature missing from foil and épée coquilles: a curved knuckle guard (sometimes called a finger guard or knuckle bow), which stretches all the way to the pommel. This protects the sword hand from cuts.

The sabre grip, slightly curved to fit into the fold of the sword hand, is rounded on all sides except the top (where the thumb is placed), which is flat.

The sabre pommel, like the pommels of all swords, acts as a counterweight. But, rather than being a perceptible weight — as in the case of foil and épée pommels, which must offset sturdier blades — it is simply an oversized nut. The lightness of the sabre blade does not warrant an extreme counterweight to neutralize it.

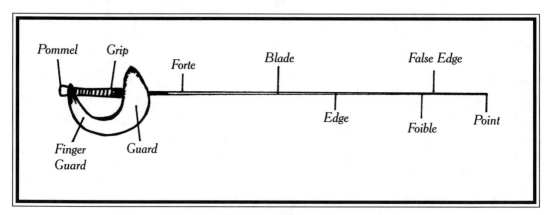

The body of the sabre

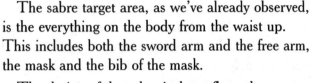

THE SABRE TARGET AREA

The sabre target area

The sabre target area, as we've already observed, is the everything on the body from the waist up. This includes both the sword arm and the free arm, the mask and the bib of the mask.

The design of the sabre jacket reflects the weapon's target area by being cut off sharply at the waist, rather than possessing the extending crotch strap of foil and épée jackets. Moreover, it may contain additional padding in the chest area to counteract vigorous cuts to that portion of the body.

The sabre glove, reflecting the fact that the sword hand may also occasionally encounter cuts delivered with a bit of force, includes extra padding across the back of the hand.

The sabre mask, bending to the certainty that it will be attacked constantly, generally has a thick strip of leather stretched across its top and sides to cushion the fencer's head from uncomfortable concussions.

All in all, the sabre fencer's uniform is greatly molded to the needs generated by his unique form of swordplay.

SABRE LINES

Another difference from foil and épée fencing is the way in which the sabre target area is divided up. Where foil and épée have eight distinct lines (four in supination, four in pronation), the sabre has five, all in pronation. This, of course, is because the sabre is employed only in pronation.

PRIME

Prime (1) is the first position in sabre's line grouping. It covers the left side of the body, with the sword hand thumb pointing downward, and the blade point lower than the hand.

SECONDE

Seconde (2) is next line. It covers the right side of the body, with the sword hand thumb pointing downward, and the blade point lower than the hand.

TIERCE

Tierce (3) follows seconde. It covers the right side of the body. It is taken with the sword hand thumb pointing upward, the blade point higher than the hand, and the blade cutting edge turned toward the outside.

QUARTE

Then comes quarte (4). It covers the left side of the body. It is taken with the sword hand thumb turned upward, the blade point higher than the hand, and the blade cutting edge turned toward the inside. (The sabre "quarte" should not be confused with the "quarte" of foil and épée, which covers the high-inside line with the sword hand held in supination.)

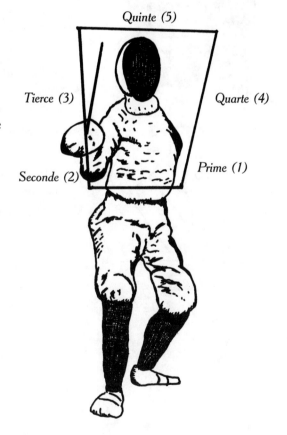

Quinte (5)

Tierce (3)

Quarte (4)

Seconde (2)

Prime (1)

QUINTE

Finally, we arrive at quinte (5). It is the position that covers the head and shoulders. The sword hand moves to the right, the thumb of the hand points to the left, the palm of the hand faces forward. The cutting edge of the blade is up; the blade itself is almost completely horizontal to the ground. (The sabre "quinte" should not be confused with the "quinte" of foil and épée, which covers the high-inside line with the sword hand in pronation.)

Many modern fencing teachers simply call the sabre lines by their prosaic English names: one, two, three, four, and of course, five.

HOLDING THE SABRE

Learning to grip the sabre properly will do much in determining how well you manage your weapon. To grasp it like a prehistoric club will definitely inhibit your progress. Finding that light, but firm, hold that cushions the handle in the hand is the key to the process.

HAND CONTACT POINTS

There are five points of hand contact on the sabre grip: 1) the thumb, 2) the index finger, 3) the little finger, 4) the palm where it meets the little finger, and 5) the two middle fingers.

THE CORRECT GRIP

The ball of the extended thumb rests on upper (flat) portion of the grip, which places the tip of the thumb at the top of the grip. The first joint of the index finger is wrapped around the underside of the grip directly opposite the thumb. The last three fingers curve nimbly around the side of the grip, making contact at the second joints. The grip is then pressed against the heel of the hand.

MAINTAINING AN EFFECTIVE GRIP

To be an effective sabre fencer, the grip must be held with ease. For this reason, it should always be carried in the fingers — not the palm of the hand. A tight grasp, caused by forcing the handle into the palm — will both tire the sword hand and draw the whole arm into your sabre maneuvering. The secret here is to always maintain a space between the palm of the hand and the sabre handle. This will insure that the fingers will not be subverted in their mission.

Photo by Anita Evangelista

THE SABRE ON GUARD POSITION

The sabre on guard position differs considerably from the on guard positions in either foil or épée.

THE FREE ARM

Most noticeably, the free arm is lowered to a position that places the hand on the rear hip (this is to remove it from the line of fire, since it is part of the valid target area). It remains on the hip, by the way, even in the lunge.

THE SWORD HAND

The sabre, by its very construction, demands that the sword hand be held and employed in pronation (palm down). In the on guard position, the sword hand is turned slightly outward, placing the cutting edge and hand guard of the sabre in direct opposition to any cut emanating from the outside line.

THE SABRE

Where the foil is held at chest level and the épée slightly lower, the sabre is held just above hip level. The sword hand is held in tierce (the high-outside line), with the point of your weapon maintained at eye level. Also, by angling the point inward slightly, rather than placing it straight out from the sword hand, the upper body is bisected by a blade placement that is generally speaking diagonal to the target area.

THE LINE OF TIERCE

In sabre fencing, all blade movements should flow from the line of tierce.

THE FEET

The feet are lined up in the same manner as in foil fencing. However, to increase mobility, the distance between them is often recommended to be slightly shorter than in foil.

THE TORSO

The torso should be held upright to maintain balance. Moreover, leaning will only present a more attractive target to the sabre cut.

FOOTWORK AND DISTANCE IN SABRE

ADVANCING AND RETREATING

Mobility is a key word in sabre fencing. Therefore, forward and backward steps should be executed quickly and evenly. Advancing and retreating may be produced with the standard advance/retreat employed in foil or by crossing one foot in front of the other (called either "stepping" or "passing"). This constant movement is demanding physically and requires much practice to build adequate endurance.

ATTACKING

Attacks may be delivered with a standard lunge, with a running attack or with a fleche.

DISTANCE

Distance in sabre is measured from hand guard to hand guard — just as it is in épée fencing. This means attacks to the body can be met with counteractions to the sword arm. This is further complicated by the fact that either action may be executed with a cut or a thrust. For this reason, your footwork in establishing safe distance and proper attacking distance can be nothing less than correct. (Is it any wonder that I've suggested perfecting both foil and épée technique, before tackling the sabre?)

Without a mastery of distance in sabre, the classical precept of fencing — to hit and not be hit — is a virtual impossibility.

CUT AND THRUST: SABRE OFFENSE

As has already been noted, the sabre may strike a touch with either its tip, its cutting edge or its false edge. It has been proven historically that the thrust is more efficient than the cut, yet the sabre of sport is not fenced as a practical dueling weapon, but a conventional weapon bent on effectively integrating the cut and thrust into a single fighting form. Its aim, like the foil, is to develop personal control. Since we already have the foil and épée to develop point play, the sabre focuses principally on the cut, with the point tossed in as a supplementary feature.

CUT VERSUS THRUST

Anyone watching a sabre bout these days would definitely see more cuts attempted than thrusts (point work is almost nonexistent among many modern sabre fencers). The sabre is, to be sure, a weapon that promotes the former. However, it stands to reason that a fencer who can integrate the tip of his blade into any encounter with a fencer who doesn't has a distinct advantage.

The exact amount of point work woven into your sabre game should always be determined by individual situations.

THE CUT

A cut can be accomplished with the cutting edge, flat or upper third of the back edge of the sabre blade.

To make a proper cut, the sword hand and blade are extended toward your opponent. At the moment of contact, the cut is completed with a downward dip of the thumb and wrist, creating a nice, crisp, snapping action, an action that is both firm and decisive without being heavy.

BRUTALITY

Brutal cuts should be avoided at all cost. Not only does it display an obvious lack of personal control, labeling you forever as a "ferailleur" (a clumsy, unpleasant fencer), but it is physically painful for your opponents. Such heavy actions will further get in the way of moving easily into extended exchanges.

VALID/INVALID?

A cut is pronounced valid if it arrives on target before a parry can be successfully instituted. Even a cut arriving on target at the exact same instant that it is met by a parry is considered good. However, a cut which first strikes an opponent's hand guard or blade, and subsequently whips around to make contact with a valid target area, is not considered a touch.

TYPES OF CUTS

There are several types of cuts that might be made with the sabre: the cut to the head, the cut to the cheek (right or left),the cut to the chest, the cut to the flank (right only) and the cut to the sword arm.

THE HEAD CUT

1) From the on guard position, the sword hand turns the cutting edge of the blade directly toward your opponent. 2) The sword arm extends forward. 3) The fencer lunges. 4) The cut is completed on the top (center and forward) of the mask.

This is an especially useful attack because it is difficult for so many fencers to bring the quinte parry — the only parry that will protect the top of the head — into play.

Care should be made not to elevate the sword hand when making the cut, as this will expose the arm to counterattack.

THE CHEEK CUT

Cuts may be made to either the right or left cheek.

1) The sword arm extends forward at chest level. 2) The sword hand rotates so that the fingers are down (left cheek cut); the sword hand rotates so that the fingers are up (right cheek cut). 3) Lunge. 4) The cut, delivered laterally, is made with the fingers.

The cheek cut (photo by Anita Evangelista)

THE FLANK CUT

The flank, or flanc, is the target area situated under the fencer's sword arm. To make a flank cut, the opposing fencer must raise his sword arm sufficiently, so that the attack may pass beneath it.

1) Extend the sword arm at chest level. 2) Rotate the sword hand palm down. 3) Lunge. 4) The cut is delivered laterally (sometimes even slightly upward — this to facilitate passing easily beneath the sword arm).

You must be careful not to drop the sword hand when attacking. This would be a direct invitation for an opponent to perform a stop cut.

THE CHEST CUT

The chest cut is self-explanatory. 1) Straighten the sword arm, extending the blade forward horizontally toward the chest area of the opposing fencer. 2) Just before making the cut, angle the blade point sharply to the right. 3) Lunge. 4) Moving to the left, the cut is executed across the chest with the flat of the blade rather than the cutting edge.

THE ARM CUT

Arm cuts are directed to the wrist and forearm of the sword arm. Cuts are made, of course, with an extended arm. 1) Cuts to the outside of the forearm are made with a lateral action. 2) Cuts to the inside of the arm are made with a vertical action. 3) Cuts to the top of the arm are also made with a vertical action.

A beat may be employed to expose an adversary's sword arm to the cut. (Experienced sabre fencers have remarked that the beat/cut to the forearm action is extremely difficult to defend against and is, therefore, a highly desirable action to add to your sabre repertoire.)

POINT ATTACKS

If I were to suggest a single difference in the sabre technique I was taught over 20 years ago from what is being widely disseminated today, I would look back in time to the vigorous use of the point in offensive and counteroffensive work.

My fencing teacher, Ralph Faulkner, who was essentially a sabreman and fenced as a sabreman for the 1928 and 1932 U.S. Olympic teams — looked upon the point as the proverbial fly in the ointment for the average sabre fencer. Finding that the vast majority of opponents he met on the fencing strip were totally confounded when they ran up against the point, he cultivated this aspect of his sabre game until it became a distinctive part of his style.

He once said to me that a sabre fencer who could use his point effectively against a fencer who couldn't was like a two-armed man fighting against a one-armed man. This seems rather obvious and logical. If you have a tool at your disposal that someone else is lacking, you will be better off when it gets down to the nitty-gritty.

Still, if you watch the average sabre bout these days, you will almost never see the point employed. In part, this is because so many young fencers jump into sabre before they ever get a chance to develop their point control with a foil or épée. It's hard enough learning to guide the tips of these weapons effectively (and they're exclusively point weapons!). Think how

Attacking with the point of the blade (photo by Anita Evangelista)

much more difficult it is with a weapon where almost no one stresses the value of the point game. It would be easier to organize a swim team in the Sahara Desert.

In truth, your point training in sabre should begin the day you first pick up the foil. You enhance it when you move on to épée. When you do get to sabre, you're only polishing that which already exists. Is this approach really that important? I'll tell you this: my teacher thought so. I wasn't allowed to pick up a sabre until I'd been fencing for five years. But, when I finally did, I could place the point where I wanted it to go without too much trouble.

Anyway, let's talk a bit now about how you might use the point in sabre play.

THE STRAIGHT THRUST

The straight thrust (the most common point attack), is made by extending the sword arm straight, lowering the sabre point so that your blade is parallel to the floor, and lunging. The sword hand is kept in pronation. To be sure, because of its simplicity, it must be delivered without hesitation.

ATTACKING THE SWORD ARM

You might also occasionally attack with the point to an opponent's forearm or hand, as with the épée. Because this will most likely be unexpected, it has a real chance of being performed successfully. Of course, such actions do take an extreme amount of point control, so all those years of foil and épeé training (hint, hint!) will certainly prove valuable at this juncture.

CUTS AND THRUSTS

It's also important to remember that you should never think solely in terms of making a cut or a thrust. It shouldn't be an either/or kind of thing. Rather, offensive actions may be framed to incorporate both responses. In the same manner that you mix lateral parries and counterparries to confound an opponent's offensive position, mixing the thrust with the cut will make it tough for any defending sabre fencer to generate the proper parry to block your attack.

FEINTS

A simple idea: you might employ the point in a feinting action, and follow it up with a cut; or the cut as the feint, with the attack being delivered by the point.

It is important to remember that the game of sabre was designed to integrate the thrust and the cut into a single approach to sword fighting. Remember the military origins of the weapon, for this can be a guiding mind-set for you. There is a wealth of opportunity in the sabre match that is just waiting to be tapped into. Develop all aspects of your game; and, because there are those who do not, you will win.

THE SABRE DEFENSE

The sabre defense has gone through many transitions. Guard positions have come and gone: the hanging guard, St. George's guard, the half-circle guard, the spadron guard, the medium guard. Various parry systems have clashed, mingled and then dissolved. Italian? French? Hungarian? Some teachers of the sabre advocated limiting the parries to just a few (Alfred Hutton had two primary parries: tierce and quarte; he also had six auxiliary parries to be used only sparingly). Others found it necessary to complicate things to the extreme by designing both high and low versions of the same parry (created by raising or lowering the sword hand).

THE BLADE

We should note here that all parries must be accomplished with the cutting edge of the sabre blade. The flat of the blade, more often than not, produces a weak parry.

THE PARRIES

Today, we have five parries: prime, seconde, tierce, quarte and quinte. Each one corresponds to the lines already mentioned earlier. More often than not, however, the three most often used will be those of tierce, quarte and quinte.

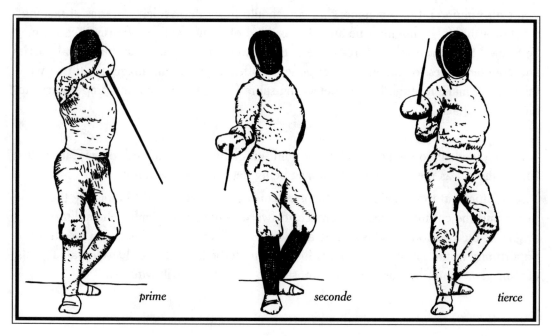

prime   seconde   tierce

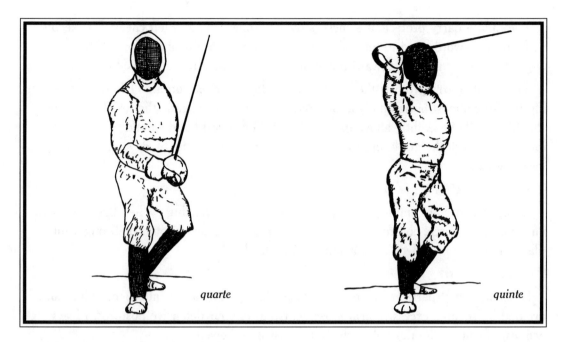

quarte   *quinte*

PARRY CLASSIFICATIONS

The parries of sabre fencing fall into three distinct categories: those that parry lateral or horizontal cuts, those that parry vertical cuts and those that parry point attacks.

Vertical cuts may be parried by prime, seconde and quinte. Lateral or horizontal cuts are parried by tierce and quarte. Point attacks are stopped by tierce, quarte and occasionally prime.

THE INDIVIDUAL PARRIES

The prime parry protects the inside line from any vertical or diagonal cut aimed at the chest or left shoulder. To execute it: 1) The sword arm is straightened (parallel to the floor). 2) The sword hand, raised to shoulder level, moves to the left and away from the body. 3) The fingers of the hand are turned downward. 4) The point of the blade, angled out, is well below the level of the sword hand.

The seconde parry protects the flank and the outside of the sword arm. To execute it: 1) The sword arm is extended about at chest level. 2) The sword hand moves slightly to the right, rotating so that the fingers point downward. 3) The tip of the blade drops to about thigh level. 4) The cutting edge of the blade faces away, toward the direction of the incoming cut.

The tierce parry protects the right flank and the right cheek. To execute it: 1) Pull back the sword arm so that the elbow nearly touches the torso. 2) The cutting edge of the blade is turned to the right. 3) The tip of the blade is at eye level. 4) The wrist of the sword hand is also turned to the right.

The quarte parry protects the chest, stomach, inner arm and left cheek. To execute it: 1) Move the sword hand to the right, about at the level of the abdomen. 2) Turn the edge of the blade inward, toward the attack. 3) The blade tip remains about at eye level.

The quinte parry protects the head and shoulders. To execute it: 1) In one movement, lift the sabre almost horizontally above and in front of your head (the tip of the blade should actually be slightly above the hand). 2) The sword hand should be about 10 inches in front of the mask and to the right. 3) The edge of the blade should be up to meet the cut.

COUNTERPARRIES

Counterparries are employed very irregularly in sabre fencing. When they are used, only contre de tierce, contre de seconde and contre de quarte should be brought into play. They are used specifically against point attacks.

PARRY STRENGTH

Remember that parries should meet attacks firmly, not smash into them. This can be avoided by keeping excessive arm movements out of your defensive postures. Heavy actions, of course, are not only ugly, but are easily deceived.

DISTANCE

Finally, we can't forget that defense may also be measured in your ability to maintain a safe distance. That is, when you are attacked, you retreat.

THE RIPOSTE

As in foil fencing, the riposte must be made immediately following a successful parry. It can be executed as either a cut or a thrust.

DIRECT RIPOSTE

Direct ripostes move in the nearest open target. Examples of these include:

Prime parry/riposte to the flank or head

Seconde parry/riposte to the right cheek

Tierce parry/riposte to the head or chest

Quarte parry/riposte to the right cheek

Quinte parry/riposte to the flank or head

INDIRECT RIPOSTE

Indirect ripostes pass into a line other than where you would riposte directly, because a heavy parry has closed off that normally accessible line.

THE FLYING PARRY/RIPOSTE

This parry/riposte action both catches the attack and, at the same time, passes over the top of the blade into the opposite line. The riposte will then be executed in the line passed into.

THE MOULINET

The moulinet, which is a circular, windmill-like movement of the blade made with the forearm — by moving it first toward and then away from the body — is used in conjunction with the prime parry to create a riposte-type action. The counterattack, with the moulinet, is most often directed to the head.

RIPOSTE POINT

When reposting point, you most often attack to the chest.

COMPOSITE RIPOSTE

The composite riposte is made up of a feint of a riposte to attract a parry, followed by the deception of that parry and a true riposte. These actions can be made as either cuts or thrusts. For instance, following your parry, you might feint a cutting riposte to the right cheek (drawing a tierce parry), and then actually cut to the flank. Or, you might feint a cutting riposte to the flank (drawing a seconde parry), another to the head (drawing a quinte parry), and then riposte point to the chest. You might even feint a cut to the chest (drawing a prime parry), and then cut to the head.

THE REMISE AND REDOUBLEMENT

Because the sabre is a conventional weapon, like the foil (with its well-defined rules of right-of-way), hesitating to riposte after a parry may draw either the remise or redoublement.

COMPOSED ATTACKS

Many modern sabre fencers depend heavily on straight cuts as the foundation of their offensive tack. But, as with foil, it is more sensible to employ a well-practiced repertoire of composed attacks (that is, making a feint followed by the deception of a parry).

We might combine: 1) a feint to the head with an attack to the flank; 2) a feint of straight hit with a cut to the flank; 3) a feint to the flank with a cut to the head; 4) a feint to the right cheek with a cut to the left cheek; 5) a feint to the head with a cut to the chest; 6) a feint to the head, feint to the flank with a cut to the head; or 7) a feint to the right cheek with a cut to the arm.

SABRE COUNTERATTACKS

The stop cut (or stop point) and time cut (or time thrust) are the counterattacks — attacks launched against attacks — of sabre. They are employed for the same reasons the stop and time thrusts are employed in foil fencing. You see a break in the timing, or the validity of an opponent's attack...and attempt to claim right-of-way and land a touch first.

To be considered successful, these counteractions must be timed to land a full beat ahead of the final movement of the initial attack.

STOP CUT

A stop cut is a cut made (without lunging) against an already attacking opponent. It is most often directed at his sword arm or hand. It is useful against a slow fencer or one who executes his attacks with exaggerated motions. The fencer who lifts his sword arm high when attacking is asking for a stop cut to be launched against him.

STOP POINT

A stop point is an extension of your sabre blade point into an opponent's attack (without lunging). Because of its reach, it may be directed against any valid target area. Used in épée fashion against the sword hand or forearm, it can be quite devastating (this, of course, demands precise point control). The stop point may be used successfully against a hesitant fencer or one with wide, careless movements.

TIME CUT

A time cut is made to the sword arm of an attacking opponent, followed by a step backward, a parry of the attacker's riposte and a counterriposte.

TIME THRUST

A time thrust, a thrust that both blocks an attack and hits at the same moment (tension), is very difficult to accomplish in sabre fencing, as this often entails thrusting against a cut. However, if attempted, it should only be done in the lines of seconde and tierce.

When the time thrust is performed in the line of seconde, the sword hand should be raised slightly as the action is accomplished. When done in tierce, the sword hand should be extended from chest level.

The time thrust is also useful as a thrust executed between two ineffective feints. This action is to be delivered with a passata soto (a ducking action — pass — into the low line), especially against a straight cut being directed against your head.

THE SABRE BOUT

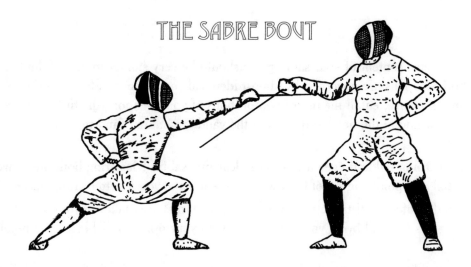

The sabre bout is governed by conventions, or rules of behavior. Without conventions, we would need sharp weapons to let us know when we were in error.

For a touch to be scored, we must have an obvious attacker and an obvious defender. Without this, double touches are generated and discarded.

Valid touches must land somewhere on the prescribed target area, that is, any part of the body from the waist up. Touches may be scored with both the cut and the thrust.

Body contact — the corps-a-corps — is discouraged by the rules.

A bout lasts for five touches, the same as in both foil and épée bouts.

SOME FINAL THOUGHTS ON THE SABRE

The strategic content of your sabre game should be very similar to that of the foil, since both weapons are governed by almost identical conventions. The main differences for sabre, of course, entail the use of two portions of your weapon (the tip and edge) and the inclusion of the head and arms in the valid target area (and the exclusion of the groin).

Make learning foil and épée a priority to learning sabre. Mastering both the conventions of foil and point control of both weapons will make you a better sabre fencer.

Be mindful of your distance in sabre, since your target area takes in your sword arm. Forgetting this fact will bring you into contact with your opponent's blade on a regular basis.

Vary your distance constantly. This will both protect you and enhance your ability to attack.

Take care not to expose your sword arm when attacking.

Mix the thrust with the cut to confound your opponent.

Be prepared to attack both the sword arm and the body.

Your attacks may be delivered with either the lunge on the advance, a running attack or a fleche. Alternate your approach to keep the tempo of your attacks unpredictable.

With the lunge on the advance or the fleche, either the cutting edge or point may be used. With the running attack, employ only the cut.

Use feints continually, but keep them clean and tight. Wide feints will expose you to counterattacks.

Study your opponent. Find out if he depends chiefly on his feet or his hand for his attacks. Notice how much arm he employs in his parries. Does he expose his sword arm when he makes his cuts? Is he especially vulnerable to point attacks? Does he lean forward, exposing his head to cuts? Is he timid? Does he forget to riposte? All these things will help you formulate your strategy.

As in foil fencing, the secondary intent may be useful in breaking down an opponent's strong defense.

Master the counterattack. With the sword arm as part of the target, and the potential for wide, overblown actions made with the cut, these can be useful.

Always parry with the edge of the sabre blade. Parrying with the flat creates a weak parry that may let an otherwise blocked attack force its way in for a touch.

Finally, it is important when attacking to always return to the on guard position as quickly as possible, whether or not you've hit. This will improve your ability to be ready for counterattacks. It will also lessen the chances of you being hit needlessly by mistakenly lowering your guard after a supposed touch that wasn't.

PART VIII
ASSORTED ASPECTS
OF FENCING

CONVENTIONAL EXERCISES

At the end of my first year in fencing, I was doing okay, it seemed; but, to me, something was missing. I felt like I was just walking through my lessons and my fencing encounters, as though I was only scratching the surface of something I knew was as deep as the sea. I was frustrated.

I finally decided to go back to my roots, to pick apart everything I'd learned so far, to discover the underlying elements of the art, the science and the sport of fencing.

I began my task by working on conventional exercises.

Conventional exercises are the halfway point between the lesson and the bout. They are a way of academically experiencing the bout without the pressure of the win/lose aspect that competition on the fencing strip always generates. And they work. In various guises, they've been used as an educational aid in fencing at least since the 17th century.

Such training sessions can be framed into two ways.

The first, merely mechanical, sets the fencer to practicing a particular action against an opponent over and over and over again. Let's say you want to get the feeling for a

A conventional exercise from the 18th century

224

doublé. So, focusing in on all those physical elements that make up a doublé — the finger control, the extended arm on the feint, the direction of the deception's course, the correct lunge — you repeat it until it becomes second nature to you. This can also be done for the coulé, the coupé, the dégage, the doublé-dégage or any other attack you may wish to smooth out.

The formula approach can even be set up, with the help of an obliging attacker, to secure a properly executed parry-riposte sequence.

On the other hand, to really understand how any action is applied in fencing, you must first encounter the one element missing in all actions produced by rote: intent — that explosive mingling of meaning and desire. When your purpose is to hit, and your opponent's purpose is to stop you cold, that is the essence of bouting. The irresistible force meeting the immovable object. The lesson can't usually give you this. Superficially reproducing any action, even a zillion times, can't do it.

Of course, the bout is the best way to discover intent. Unfortunately — and here's the catch! — if intent is present in such a learning experience, you are likely to be overwhelmed by it at the expense of all other input. At this point, learning comes to an abrupt standstill.

What can we do, then, to circumvent this? Enter the second personality of conventional exercises: intentional training. Here, we take a limited set of related attacks — two, actually — and pit them against a specific parry. The most common form of this lesson includes, on the offensive side, the implementation of the dégage and the one-two; and on the defensive side, the lateral parry. Nothing else.

We begin with one fencer attacking five times, setting up his movements carefully, establishing his proper lunging distance, weighing all the possibilities of his offense, making feints, getting the sword arm extended, deceiving parries and lunging forcefully. But it should be understood that a fencer isn't really trying to perfect either a dégage or a one-two, per se; instead, he is attempting to bring together all those elements common to every attack — distance, timing and form. Moreover, for the sake of simplicity and uniformity, he is forbidden to add to his offensive tack; nor can he attack on the advance. He is limited by strict precepts. If you get too complicated in your conventionals, the point of them is lost. You might as well be bouting.

The trick in all this is that each attack must be executed against an opposing fencer who really and truly wants to stop you. But the good news is that, as the attacking fencer, you can carry out all your maneuverings without worrying about what your opponent is going to do. You know you have five attacks to set up as you wish, in your own good time; and you know what your opponent is going to basically do defensively. Of course, with limited attacks at your disposal, everything must be performed with quality in mind, or it will have little chance to succeed.

On the other side of the coin, the defending fencer has an opportunity to practice parries against a fencer who really wishes to stick him. His plus is that, knowing he is defending, he can set himself mentally and prepare for the onslaught. But, like the attacker, he is restricted in his responses: he can't add counterparries to his defense; nor can he retreat, or even lean back. It's do it right, or be hit. No excuses.

Both fencers, then, have the time and space to blend mind and body without the major distractions of the fencing strip. Better still, there's no competition. The goal is to simply perform correctly. Arriving at one good hit or parry is better than blundering through a dozen sloppy actions. There is no winner, no loser, only unlimited opportunities to learn.

This is what conventional exercises are all about.

THE LEFT-HANDED FENCER

Fencing master Domenico Angelo, the author of the much celebrated *The School of Fencing*, observed in 1763, "It often happens that the right-handed fencer is much embarrassed in defending himself against a left-handed one...."

As long as fencing has been in existence, the left-handed fencer has been the bane of the right-handers. Some of the greatest fencing champions of our time have been left-handed. The French foilist Lucien Gaudin, considered one of the three greatest fencers of all time, was a lefty.

Part of the left-hander's distinct advantage is the awkward position he imposes on a right-handed fencer. A right-handed fencer against a right-hander creates a kind of balanced symmetry on the fencing strip. They both occupy the same lines at the same time. In form, they are mirror images. This makes the right-handed fencing experience both physically accessible and psychologically comfortable.

A left-hander against a right-hander, however, produces an anomaly on the fencing strip. Suddenly, the right-hander sees a foreign body in front of him. Everything he knows is suddenly turned backward. His opponent's stance appears awkward. His lines are somehow distorted. A slight twist of the left-hander's body causes his inside line to melt away in an instant. These things are very disconcerting to a right-handed fencer who has little experience with such abnormalities.

The whole problem is further compounded by the fact that since there are far fewer left-handed fencers than right-handed ones, the right-hander is always at a loss experience-wise when compared to his alien nemesis. The left-handed fencer naturally has most of his contact with right-handers and so is trained from the start to adopt to this singular pairing. Of course, the most difficult opponent a left-hander ever encounters is another left-hander.

FACING THE LEFT-HANDER

Early fencing masters suggested that the best way to counter a left-handed fencer's advantage was to learn to fence left-handed. This was supposed to instill the southpaw's experience into your psyche, and thereby expose all his tricks and mental quirks. Not a bad idea in general terms, and even now to learn to fence with the opposite hand tends to produce a more balanced fencing experience.

But there are some obvious principles regarding left-handed fencers that have been gleaned from countless sword crossings over the years.

The most oft echoed idea regarding encounters with left-handed fencers is a simple one: stay out of his inside line as much as possible. In part, this translates into avoiding his parries of quarte and contre de quarte, because for him, these defensive responses are usually strong and decisive.

Furthermore, the outside line is the closer line for a right-hander to attack. Obviously, the shorter the distance a lunge has to travel, the less time it takes to drive it home. Not a bad thing. So, it will be advantageous for the right-hander to feint much into the inside line, but attack with purpose mainly to the outside. The one-two feinted into quarte, and the doublé feinted in sixte are two offensive actions that will keep a right-handed fencer on track. Also, the coulé-dégage and the double coupé, both feinted into the inside line, will prove useful.

But if a right-handed fencer does end up finding himself being parried in the left-hander's quarte line, he may formulate a defensive maneuver that will allow him to exit this trap as soon as possible. As he recovers, he can perform a contre de quarte parry, which will immediately shift him to the left-hander's outside. Or, parrying sixte, he might follow with a riposte by dégage or coupé, or any composed riposte that will allow him to avoid that dreaded inside position.

Dealing with left-handed fencers is indeed a unique fencing experience. It can be, in its worst case scenario, both mind-numbing and humbling, a reminder that you aren't as good as you think you are. But, in the end, rather than sidestepping opportunities to fence against left-handers — which is easy to do with those things we find uncomfortable or threatening — seek them out, and bask in their difficulty. As disconcerting as these moments might be, they have much to teach you.

Learn as much as you can about left-handed fencers. Then, the next time you come up against one who relies chiefly on being left-handed to win the day for him, pick him apart.

FOR THE LEFT-HANDER FACING THE RIGHT-HANDER

As for specific strategies, all the concerns of line previously mentioned also apply for the left-handed fencer. Basically, keep your right-handed opponent on your inside as much as possible. Moreover, attack mostly to the right-hander's outside (but don't completely avoid the inside line; to become too regular in your actions is to be stopped).

If forced toward your opponent's inside line by a closed outside line, feint to the open line to draw him inward, and then direct your attack to sixte. To do this, you might use either a one-two, a dégage-coupé, or a double coupé.

If your right-handed opponent isn't buying your feints into his quarte line, and his blade isn't too far removed, you might employ a firm beat to force him into parrying.

Riposte by dégage to the right-hander's line of sixte.

If the right-hander attacks strongly in the inside line, employ the croisé in quarte. To do this, move your sword hand slightly to the right, drop your point down as your hand fully supinates, and extend your arm.

As a left-hander, you have a distinct advantage over the right-handed fencers. But don't rely simply on being left-handed to win. Be a left-handed fencer who fences well.

FENCING FOR KIDS

I think fencing is one of the greatest skills a child can acquire. Fencing helps develop self-confidence, poise, a sense of uniqueness, balance, flexibility and physical endurance; and so it is ideal for young bodies and psyches.

But I have a problem with children being allowed to bout too early. Numerous studies have shown that youngsters do not begin employing abstract thought until they are about 12 years old; and this, beyond any doubt, is a quality absolutely vital to fencing. It is the problem-solving mechanism of our brain. With it we may formulate complex strategies based on previous input. Without it, we might as well be blind and deaf.

Fencing, real fencing, takes place between the head and the sword hand. If abstract thought is absent, the child competitor will be little more than a hopping, poking, jabbing bundle of energy. There's no way around it.

Moreover, in younger fencers, it is usually the early physical developers who do best, like the six foot tall, 13 year old, for instance. The muscular, aggressive boy and girl will generally mow their tiny opponents down. Puberty, at this point, is a kid's greatest competitive asset. But what are these kids actually accomplishing? They may have foils in their hands, but if the old brain isn't in the game — even if they manage to become "winners" — they still aren't fencers. Six year olds shouldn't be bouting. Eight year olds shouldn't be bouting. Even 10 year olds shouldn't be bouting.

Junior fencers should be progressed slowly and deliberately, encouraged constantly, and kept away from the fencing strip, especially the tournament fencing strip, until they can tell you specifically why they are doing what they are doing. After watching count-less young fencers flounder through competitions during my competitive years — kids lost to any significant improvement simply because they were allowed to plunge into bouting before they were ready for it — I promised myself when I began teaching that I would do what I knew was best for the kids who came to me, even if they thought I was being mean for holding them back.

That's the bottom line on that.

Lastly, the parents of young fencers should be more or less kept far away from the teaching process. When parents come to watch their kids work with me, they may ask questions; but they are never allowed to make observations. That is the law. It's my opinion that if parents believe they're knowledgeable enough to interject themselves into

A young fencer being put through her paces

lessons, maybe they should open their own fencing establishments. There's nothing as damaging to a child's rapport with his fencing instructor than a meddling parent.

Obviously, this subject of children fencing always ends up being a tough subject to discuss calmly and rationally. Just like every adult who comes to fencing, kids want to get in there and mix it up. And it's difficult saying no to them when you see them so eager to participate. If you hold them back too long, they get bored. But let them jump in too soon, and they end up a mass of bad fencing habits. If they do manage to win a few tournaments, they may even turn into insufferable, little brats. That happens, too. I've seen 14 year olds act as though they knew everything there was to know about fencing. I'm nearly 50 years old, and I'm still learning.

In the end, there isn't much room for compromise. When a child's future in fencing is on the line, it's better to err on the side of discretion. If a kid is serious about fencing, he'll stick with it no matter what.

WARMING UP

Warming up before fencing should be an integral part of every fencer's game plan. It is the single most important physical preparation to bouting you can engage in. Not only does it stretch the muscles, making it easier to move, but it gets the fencing juices flowing. I have taken it for granted for years that all fencers do this. It's so ingrained in my thought process — *fencers warm up before they fence* — I almost overlooked including this subject in these pages.

My mistake!

In more ways than one.

When I recently came across an article in an old issue of *American Fencing Magazine* dealing with fencing injuries, I was informed that at least 13% of such misfortunes today are caused by warm-up procedures deemed inadequate. It suddenly became apparent to me that something I thought was self-evident isn't all that self-evident to some fencers.

So, here we are.

ATTITUDE

In my years of training to become a fencer, I often arrived at my school an hour or two early just to stretch out, practice my footwork, lunge in front of the full-length mirror and work on my point control with a target. This warm-up was a ritual for me. Some fencers I knew looked on this as boring as heck and wondered how I could keep it up day after day, week after week, year after year. I suppose, in a way, practicing by yourself is a bit tedious. I simply focused my thoughts on what I was doing at that moment and did it. It was just part of my education.

Today, I still warm up before fencing. It is a habit I've never outgrown. And, in over 25 odd years of fencing, I've never had a serious physical injury.

MODUS OPERANDI

As for the warming up process itself, I think there are some definite points that should be addessed:

Besides an overall limbering routine employing sit-ups, toe touches, knee-bends and the like, center in on stretching the leg muscles specifically — especially the front thigh muscles, those on the inside of the thighs and the calves. Giving the hamstrings a good stretch is also vital. All these guys take the brunt from bouncing around on the fencing

strip, I think, and so should receive your thorough attention before bouting. If you do this, you will not only most likely save yourself from painful injury, but it will also make your fencing movement more effective.

FOOTWORK

Once you have brought those cold muscles to life, you can practice your footwork and lunging. Over and over and over again. This will further warm you up and get your body primed fully for fencing movement.

WARMING UP FOR TOURNAMENTS

Along with the aforementioned exercising, before competing in a tournament, a little warm-up bouting can also prove useful. This will help prepare you, both physically and mentally, for the competitive challenge that you are about to undertake. The alternative is revving yourself in your opening bouts, but sometimes the blood doesn't start pumping until you've lost a bout or two.

A CAUTION

Learn to gauge your capabilities. As with too little preparation, over-warming can also lead to problems, pooping you out before you ever get on the fencing strip.

With regard to this dilemna, use your brain.

CARING FOR YOUR FENCING EQUIPMENT

It's a truism that when you go to a fencing tournament that the most impressive looking fencer is the one sporting the cleanest, neatest uniform and the shiniest weapons. And he has, more than likely, been fencing for two weeks. It's the fencer with the rumpled, stitched up jacket, the droopy socks, and the foils that look like they were on the losing side of World War II, you have to watch out for. He's been hacking around in the fencing world for 30 years, and he's more concerned with fencing well than looking snappy.

Still, there's no point in actively competing for the "Slob Fencer of the Year" award. And, certainly, equipment will last longer if it's maintained in a thoughtful manner.

Here are a few tips, then, on the care of your fencing gear. I've learned them over the years through my own experience. And I've made all the mistakes.

BLADES

Keep the blades of your weapons from getting wet. Setting them in a damp place, or carrying them through the rain, will rust them up something awful. This won't exactly cause them to instantly crumble away to nothing, but over the long haul rust and metal never go well together.

If a blade does get rusty — you might, after all, live in a humid environment you have no control over — it can be cleaned with a piece of steel wool or metal sandpaper. Be careful, though, if you attack an electric weapon in this manner; you don't want to damage the wire running the length of the blade.

A coating of WD-40™, or some light oil, like 3-in-One™, will further enhance your weapons. But keep away from heavy lubricants like motor oil. The thick stuff is way too messy! I once had a student who coated his foil blade in lard, thinking that no moisture could possibly get through something that thick and greasy. He was right; but when he took his weapon out of his fencing bag a few weeks later, it looked as if he'd been using it for a dip stick in his car.

You can further protect the blades of all your weapons by keeping them housed in scabbards made from an old hose or black, pliable PVC pipe. This will both deter moisture and prevent you from snagging innocent bystanders.

COQUILLES

The hand guard on a foil can take a real beating; and, in time, the hole through which the blade passes may enlarge, causing the coquille to wobble badly. This can be fixed with a couple metal washers — one on top of the guard and one on the bottom. I have hand guards that I would have had to junk years ago without washers.

GRIPS

The covering on the grip of your foil, sabre or épée may wear out if it's made from twine or leather; or, through constant use, it might become glazed and slippery. These problems can be remedied by wrapping any handle with baseball bat tape. I've tried every kind of tape from duct to electrician's; but I've found baseball bat tape provides the very best surface for gripping. It's cheap, too.

UNIFORMS

Be warned! Don't keep your sweaty fencing outfit overly long in any confined place where it has no opportunity to dry out. You'll start to develop a splendid medium for mildew. I once had a fencing jacket that ended up looking like a leopard after about two months of being constantly stuffed damp into an equipment bag. The mold was awful, and the jacket didn't smell very nice, either. Even spraying it with a disinfectant didn't help much.

So, hang up your jacket and pants, and let them dry out before you tuck them away until the next time you fence.

And when you wash your clothing, take it easy on the bleach. I had another jacket that needed to be cleaned real bad, so I soaked it overnight in water heavy with bleach. The thing definitely came out white, but the next time I fenced, my first opponent punched an inch wide hole in the bleach-rotted material.

MASKS

Your fencing mask, since it protects a pretty important area of the body — your face — should always be kept in good repair and free of rust. Never, then, wad up a damp jacket and cram it into a mask. Even a damp glove can encourage rust.

The bib of the fencing mask, which protects your neck, should always be kept free of rips. With permanently attached bibs, this can be accomplished with a little sewing. Snap-in bibs can be easily replaced.

GLOVES

Leather fencing gloves — like all fencing gear — wear out. They will last longer, though, if they can occasionally be allowed to dry. Otherwise, they will rot fairly quickly.

EQUIPMENT BAGS

While equipment bags tend to be rather expensive, having one will make your fencing life a lot easier. If not losing pieces of equipment can be considered part of your equipment care, then having a place where your collection of weapons and clothing can be safely rounded up and housed is definitely a worthwhile purchase.

PART IX
ELECTRICAL
FENCING

SOME THOUGHTS ON ELECTRICAL FENCING

The point of electrical fencing is to make the scoring of touches a more simple task. There is no other reason for it to exist. If you understand this, you will not be overawed by the nature of the electrical game.

The first touch recording apparatus was introduced in 1896. It operated on similar principles to our modern electric scoring systems. However, it was prone to frequent breakdowns, and there was no way to differentiate on-target hits from off-target ones.

All modern competition fencing is carried out with electrical weapons. For foil, épée and sabre, this is simply a fact of the game. Fencing with electric weapons in form and theory, of course, is just the same as fencing with standard weapons. The moves are the same. The tactics are the same. The objectives are the same. The rules are the same. There are some noticeable physical differences, however, worth mentioning.

For instance, a fencer in an electric match is hooked up to a machine — via cords and cables — that scores touches. Moreover, for foil and sabre, your entire valid target area

An electrical fencing bout (photo appears courtesy of the Southern California USFA/photographer: Marc Walch)

is enveloped in a tight fitting jacket (lamé) of metallic material that helps to generate the recognition of valid touches. Also, due to the special tip and electric socket attached to them, electric épées and foils possess a singular balance and weight quite unlike their standard cousins. These elements are, in themselves, neither good nor bad. They are simply ingredients of another level in your fencing experience, something to be integrated into your overall game. They just take some getting used to.

The épée was the first fencing weapon to be officially accepted for electrical use in tournaments. This took place in Europe in the 1930s. The foil was electrified in the 1950s.

Both electric foil and épée blade tips are fitted with a small spring-loaded cylinder. The button on the very end of this arrangement depresses when pressure is applied, which triggers the "touch" sensor on the electric scoring box.

Electrical fencing can be a bit disconcerting, at least in the beginning. Attached to a cable that moves in and out of a reel as you advance or retreat, you always feel a bit like you're on a leash. This connection tugs insistently at your backside, where it is attached, and you are somewhat daunted by the contact. In time, though, this distraction fades away. Hopefully, it will, anyway. You have more important things to think about on the fencing strip.

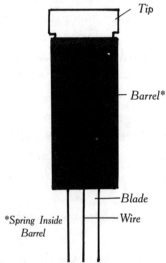

The tip of an electrical foil

Touches are acknowledged on a scoring machine through the use of blinking lights and buzzers. Green and red lights signify on-target touches. White lights stand for off-target touches.

Some beginners start off fencing with electrical weapons, thinking that since they will one day be fencing in competition, anyway, they might as well get used to them from the start. But, for the sake of the learning process, I believe every fencer should begin with standard weapons. Standard weapons will give the beginner a better feel for what they are trying to accomplish.

Take everything in its proper turn. There's plenty of time to adapt to electric weapons. First, learn to fence.

Foil and épée electric tips are connected to an electric socket stationed beneath the hand guard of each weapon by a thin copper wire. For protection, this wire is indented into a narrow groove on the surface of the blade.

Electrical weapons are ideal when you wish to engage in some decisive play with a fencer who is known to be less than truthful in the acknowledgement of touches with standard blades. When that light flashes on the scoring machine, even the worst offender of fencing etiquette can't deny he's been hit. No matter how much you may dislike your opponent, it beats using sharp weapons.

Some fencers employ "dummy" electric blades when they're not competing. A dummy is a standard foil or épée fitted with an electric tip so that it simulates the feel of your electric weapons. This serves basically two purposes. First, it saves on the wear of true electrical weapons, weapons that are both expensive and prone to stop functioning at a moment's notice (the more they are used, the sooner they will break). And second, rather than requiring the fencer to switch back and forth between the disparate weights of standard and electrical weapons, the dummy allows the fencer to be continually in touch with one specific weapon balance and weight.

An electric cord — called a "body" cord — runs from the fencer's blade into his glove, down the inside of his sword arm sleeve and out through the backside of his jacket. Here, it connects with a cable issuing from a reel at the far end of the fencing strip. This retractable cord allows the fencer to move freely without danger of becoming entangled in his line. The reel is then attached to the scoring machine via long floor cables.

This completes the electrical connection for the fencer. He is hooked up and ready to fence.

Electrical épée is fenced on a metallic strip that negates any point contact made with the floor.

In the 1980s, the sabre — the final holdout to 20th century technology — was added to the electrical weapon family. It took the longest to electrify because of problems arising from its being both a cutting and point weapon.

The problem of touch recording was eventually overcome by the implementation of space age motion sensors, rather than relying on any blade portions that depress, as is the case with the foil and épée. These sensors, which detect both motion and the pressure of contact with your target, are fitted on the underside of the sabre hand guard.

In the end, electrical fencing is just another avenue of expression, another piece of the learning process — just like lessons, just like conventional exercises, just like bouting, just like competition. For that reason, embrace it when it comes time for you to add it to your experience. It will offer you interesting challenges; but if you weren't ready for challenges, you wouldn't be fencing, now would you?

PITFALLS OF ELECTRICAL FENCING

There are psychological quirks generated and expressed in the electrical game of fencing that represent something that is quite divergent from standard fencing thought, something that can be highly destructive to the unwary competitor.

Some believe that the implementation of a scoring machine that "knows all" has short-circuited the notion that personal form — operating with grace and artistry — has any value whatsoever. The process no longer matters, only the outcome. "Well, it may not be right, but it worked!" is a phrase you hear with alarming frequency these days. Making a touch is all that counts. And, when there's a "magic" box in front of you letting everyone know what you've done, what difference does it make how it looked? Come beautiful fencing or ugly fencing, if you hit, your touch will be acknowledged with cold, impersonal certainty.

Unfortunately, this attitude emphasizes only those attributes, all physical, that allow you to activate electric circuits — speed, strength, aggression, forceful impact — and nothing else. That good form very often translates into dependable skill is forgotten in a flurry of jabbing blades and screaming buzzers.

Once, of course, in the pre-electric fencing world, the need for reproducing recognizable actions on the fencing strip — actions that left no doubt in anyone's mind as to what had happened — was an unquestioned critical ingredient of personal combat. There was the pride of mastery, a sense that, while one was an athlete, one was also an artist interpreting an age-old art. True winning meant winning well.

On a more practical level, when fencing bouts were monitored only by the eyes of human beings, a fencer had to make his touches good enough for all those watching to see them. Sloppy fencing translated into hard to follow actions and missed calls. A missed call might occasionally be visited on even the best of fencers — just because; but the worst fencers were virtually assured of them in spades. Bad fencers simply went on being bad. The good ones worked harder to overcome the ambushes.

This, then, was fencing as it once was — a carefully defined activity. And it was obvious when anyone violated its boundaries. Sword handling styles might alter, but that inner quality of fencing, that driving spark, that dependency on your own mettle, was inviolate.

Or so it seemed.

But the unreliability of human judges had been a thorn in the side of fencers for too many years. The interjection of some kind of mechanical device for detecting touches into the people equation was an inevitability. The electrical approach was the final outcome of numerous experiments in automatic scoring.

From the start, this new technology was looked on as a boon by the fencing world. A touch would finally be a touch in everybody's eyes. Nothing would be missed; nothing would be misinterpreted. Few people foresaw that a simple tool for accurate judging might herald the downfall of fencing form, of self-reliance on the fencing strip.

Certainly, having a reliable method of insuring the acknowledgment of touches is not, in itself, a bad thing. I merely suggest that the emphasis in the electrical game be shifted back to real fencing. It can be done — if the scoring machine is, once and for all, put in its proper place — not as that of a minor fencing god, but as a simple signpost of successful fencing.

There is one other rather insidious psychological element attached to electrical fencing. There is the danger of what is sometimes called "fencing to the box." That is, whenever any offensive maneuver is performed, a fencer may compulsively look over to see if his action has registered a touch on the scoring machine. This is not so much even for the touch, but for what the touch produces. The touch, accompanied by a loud buzzer and flashing lights, may be viewed as a subconscious psychological perk, a reward, so to speak, for performing an attack or counterattack successfully. (The same sort of audio/visual hook is used overtly in video games to signify victory.)

The buzzers and lights of the scoring machine ultimately become a soughtafter psychologically pleasing public acknowledgment of accomplishment. (Think of what Pavlov did with his dogs, training them to drool hungrily at the sound of a ringing bell.) The unwary fencer ends up spending more and more time looking for an artificially-induced emotional gratification than he does trying to relate to his opponents. Exchanges may be halted in midstream as he turns to see if the machine has given him its approval. Meanwhile, his attention focused elsewhere, he is hit with a counterattack by his still fencing opponent.

Basically, this fencer has conditioned himself into one heck of a bad habit, and only through the most drastic of measures will he break free of it.

Ultimately, I think the best approach to take with electrical fencing is, when you go out on the fencing strip and hook yourself up to all those specialized attachments of modern swordplay, act as if none of it exists. Forget it. Wipe it from your mind. See yourself free in body, mind and spirit, depending on your own resources for success.

Leave the technology to the director of your bout, and just fence. That's the way it was meant to be.

PART X
FENCING LIVES

THE MAN WHO MADE SPORT OF FENCING

Domenico Angelo was a man of destiny. Acknowledged as the greatest horseman in Europe, teacher of the manly graces, and expert swordsman, he was, more than any other figure of his time, responsible for turning the deadly art of sword fighting into the sport of fencing.

Angelo, the son of a wealthy Italian merchant, was born in Leghorn, Italy, in 1716. In his youth, he traveled all over Europe, gaining knowledge and personal skills that were soon to launch him on his life's path. Finally settling in Paris, Angelo began studying fencing under the great master Teillagory; and, because of his natural physical ability, quickly became a master of the art.

In one celebrated fencing match, Angelo was persuaded by a friend to try his luck against some of the most successful teachers and amateurs in France. As he was about to fence his first bout, a famous English beauty, Margaret Woffington, stepped forward and presented Domenico with a small bouquet of roses. With a grand flourish, the Italian pinned the flowers to the chest of his shirt, announcing to one and all, "This will I protect against all opposers!" Angelo crossed blades that day with a number of able fencers, but not one of them managed to touch a single leaf of the bouquet.

Soon after this incident, Angelo, convinced that his fortunes lay across the English Channel, moved to London, where his charm, grace and accomplishments made him the toast of English society. Such gifted men as the actor David Garrick and the artist Thomas Gainsborough, not to mention numerous politicians and noblemen, eagerly cultivated his friendship.

The man who turned a killing art into a sport, Domenico Angelo

At this time, despite his popularity, Angelo remained an amateur fencer, content merely to display his prodigious talents in the occasional tournament.

This situation, however, changed. Challenged to a public demonstration of fencing skill by a Dr. Keys, said to be the strongest fencer in Ireland, the Italian found himself in a situation that would test his fencing prowess to the utmost and elevate him to the position of the most illustrious swordsman in England. Keys, a large, muscular man, began the encounter with much force and violent movement. Angelo, versed in the science of fencing, immediately sized up his opponent and adjusted his own approach to fit the situation. Allowing his opponent to exhaust himself in useless assaults by calmly maintaining a safe distance, and parrying all attacks with a minimum of energy and motion, Domenico then proceeded to, "plant ten palpable hits on the breast of his enraged antagonist," as his son, Harry, later noted in his book, *Reminiscences of Henry Angelo* (1828).

Following this masterful display of fencing skill, Angelo's friends urged him to take up the sword professionally. And this, tempted finally by the fame and fortune that most certainly lay before him, he did. Immediately, Domenico was the most sought after teacher in England. In time, he was forced to open a second school to handle the growing number of fencing students clamoring for his tutelage.

Angelo's establishment became "a school of refinement," where wealthy and noble families sent their sons to be versed in the gentlemanly arts. Domenico's pupils included King George III of England.

In 1763, Angelo wrote one of the greatest and most popular studies of fencing technique of the 18th century, *Ecole des Armes (The School of Fencing)*, a book that had a profound influence on the future of fencing. Angelo infused his work with his own strong notions concerning fighting technique, but he also emphasized the idea that fencing could be employed, not merely as a killing activity, but as a competitive exercise to be practiced to improve one's health, poise and grace. It is from this point in time that we see fencing settling into its present status as a sport.

Angleo's success continued for the remainder of his life. Moreover, he founded a dynasty of fencing masters that dominated fencing thought and practice for 150 years.

Domenico Angelo died in 1802, at the age of 86. In keeping with his amazing life, he taught fencing right up to a few days before his death.

THE GREATEST SWORDSMAN IN THE WORLD

In his own estimation, Aldo Nadi was the greatest fencer of the 20th century. This might not have meant too much — except that his opinion was also shared by most of the notable fencers and masters of his time. But then, why not? He had beaten all of them in matches at one time or another over the years.

European fencing champion Georges Buchard said simply of Nadi, "Aldo Nadi is the most powerful fencer in the world." Professional champion of France René Haussy observed, "If God had desired to create a prototype of a fencer, He would certainly have chosen Aldo Nadi as a model." Famed U. S. fencing master Giorgio Santelli added, "I have been fencing for four and a half decades and the only person I have seen who approaches perfection in form, technique and execution is Aldo Nadi."

Born in Livorno, Italy, in 1899, Aldo Nadi was the son of a successful fencing master, Beppe Nadi, and the brother of Olympic champion Nedo Nadi. If ever there was a human being destined for a fencer's life, it was him.

Nadi began his fencing career at the age of three or four, won his first tournament at the age of 11, captured the amateur foil championship of Italy at the age of 20 and was

The world's greatest fencer, Aldo Nadi (photo appears courtesy of Laurette Press)

246

an Olympic medalist at the age of 21. At the advanced age of 22, he became a professional fencer.

At six feet in height and a mere 130 pounds, Aldo Nadi may not have looked the robust fencing champion, but on the fencing strip he could hardly be touched. It was once remarked that it was his footwork that was his strongest asset. He competed in — and won — some of the most celebrated international professional matches of his day, and he did it with an ease that was the envy of fencers everywhere.

Nadi's fencing experience was vast and varied. In his twenties, he even fought a duel. Sparked by a chance compliment he'd paid to French fencing champion Lucien Gaudin, the encounter placed young Nadi opposite an Italian newspaperman who took exception to his praise of non-Italian fencers. In a fight that lasted for almost seven minutes, Nadi inflicted enough damage on his adversary to curb the latter's inflated sense of nationalism. Hostilities ended with the two men drinking wine together.

When Nadi had beaten everyone there was to beat in the competitive arena, he turned to teaching. His methods favored simplicity, which he saw as the cornerstone of fencing methodology.

A lifetime of martial experience formed his precise sense of how fencing should be carried out. "Curb your adversary's aggressiveness by attacking every time he comes too near during the preparation of his own offensive. The best strategy is to keep holding the initiative, upsetting with threats, early parries and effective mobility any and all attempts of your opponent to gain ground. Your aim is to compel him to attack under the worst possible conditions, not upon his own choice of timing."

In 1935, Aldo Nadi emigrated to the United States, opening the successful Nadi Fencing Academy in New York City. He remained there until 1943, when he moved to Los Angeles to ply his trade in the movies.

Having already starred and fenced in a successful French historical film, *The Tournament*, in 1928, Aldo Nadi was no stranger to the movie camera. Although he ended up working on only a handful of films, the fencing he produced was always clean and lively. His credits include *Frenchman's Creek* (1944), *Captain From Castile* (1947) and *Mississippi Gambler* (1953). Later in life, feeling somewhat disillusioned with Hollywood, Maestro Nadi simply referred to the entire movie process as "nonsense."

Still, he continued with a flourishing teaching career in Los Angeles. The name of Nadi could be counted on to attract serious students of the fencing art. One of his students, Janice Romery, went on to win numerous U.S. national titles. Another, William Gaugler, founded the first successful fencing master training program in the United States.

Despite failing health brought on by a bad heart, the greatest fencer in the world taught right up to the time of his death in 1965. And, to the very end, he maintained within his approach, his art, that there was no more important thing a man could do with his life.

Aldo Nadi wrote two books dealing with fencing: *On Fencing* (1943) and *The Living Sword* (1995).

On Fencing, Nadi's "how-to fence" book, was reissued in 1994 by Laureate Press (1-800-946-2727), a Florida-based publishing house specializing in fencing-related books. The autobiographical *The Living Sword*, published for the first time in 1995 (30 years after the author's death), again by Laureate, saw the light of day thanks to the dedicated efforts of the maestro's long time friend and student Dr. William Gaugler.

Both volumes, full to overflowing with Nadi's astute observations on fencing, are well worth reading.

SWORDSWOMAN, UNEXCELLED

To the world, she was the greatest female athlete of the first half of the 20th century. A tall, willowy blonde, she was the kind of woman who showed her abiding sense of assurance in a calm, steady gaze and in her dynamic physical prowess. She was world-renowned, loved and hated, fighting her personal and public battles during some of the most explosive moments of our age. She was the center of an international Olympic controversy that rocked the Western nations with its overt racism. Today, a scant 42 years after her death, she has nearly been forgotten by the public that once adored her.

Her name was Helene Mayer.

Her career was in the male-dominated sport of fencing. She possessed, in abundance, all the requirements of a successful fencer: a quick mind, physical endurance, grace. With a prodigious talent that far surpassed the majority of most female and male competitors she encountered, she almost effortlessly amassed an array of championships that has never been equaled. But the events that clouded the most productive years of her life colored that reputation and cast a shadow over her memory.

"She had perfect form," recalled the late fencing master Ralph Faulkner, himself an Olympic competitor. "She was solid. When you came up against her, it was like running into a brick wall."

Born in Offenbach, Germany, in 1910, Helene was the daughter of a Jewish father and a Christian mother. She began showing an interest — and a surprising aptitude — for the art of the sword as a child. With her parents' encouragement, she took lessons and went on to competitive fencing, winning the women's fencing championship of Germany when she was barely 13 years old. With a genius for the foil, as refined and brilliant as Mozart's was at music, she captured her first Olympic gold medal at the 1928 meeting in Amsterdam, Holland. Out of 20 bouts, she lost only two. She was 17 years old.

A year after that, she competed in the most important international women's fencing meet in Europe, the European (World) Championship, and easily took first place. In 1931, she fought for and held that title. She was destined to lose and regain this title, but in her last World Championship, in 1937, she breezed through, undefeated in her bouts.

By the time of the 1932 Olympics in Los Angeles, antiSemitic sentiments were brewing in Helene's homeland that would affect and color the rest of the fencer's life. She fought for Germany, distressed and distracted by the events affecting her family, yet still managed to corner fifth place. When the games ended, she struggled with the prospect of returning to the country which despised her for her ancestry and chose to stay in the United States and attend college. She eventually became a German language teacher at Mills College in Oakland, California.

In 1933, Helene's hometown fencing school — the Offenbach Fencing Club — publicly expelled her as a member. With a Jewish father, she was deemed, no matter her excellent fencing record, racially incorrect.

Higher level officials in the German government, however, were already eyeing the 1936 Olympics, which were to be held in Berlin. Who could they find to compete in women's fencing to ensure victories for the fatherland? Helene's name was known throughout fencing and athletic circles. So was her father's ethnic background. Would she be allowed to fence for Germany, the only country, due to Olympic rules, that she could represent? Would she want to? Already Jews were being weeded out of Germany's athletic ranks.

The almost unbeatable Helene Mayer (photo appears courtesy USFA)

The U.S. Olympic Committee met with Helene, urged her to forget German policies and fence for Germany if the Nazis would let her, simply as the great athlete she was. Jewish groups in the U.S. opposed the suggestion after all, because of Nazi actions against Jews under their jurisdiction. Germany, itself, remained, for the moment, non-committal on the subject of the Jewish fencer Helene Mayer.

Helene vacillated. She knew of fellow Jewish athletes being shunned in Germany. It was becoming plain that Hitler would not let them compete in the Nazi Olympics and embarrass the mythmakers by winning over Aryan superiority. Was it even worth her while to offer her services?

Suddenly, out of seemingly nowhere, the German government did a radical about-face on Helene. They asserted that she was clearly of proper Aryan stock — since her Jewish blood was canceled out by two "German" grandparents on her mother's side. They wanted her to fence for them, to win for Nazi Germany. They insisted.

Helene stalled. She wrote to her family back in Germany, expressing her concerns about her loyalties and their safety. Dark stories began to surface: someone was threatening Helene Mayer's parents. "If she doesn't fence for her country, who knows what may happen?" the rumor ran. There was also a possibility that the U.S. government was exerting a certain amount of political influence, both on Germany and Mayer, to get Helene included in the games.

As abruptly as the Nazis had declared her "pure" enough for their purposes, Helene did her own counterpoint. In 1935, she issued a public statement announcing that she would be pleased to go back to Germany and fence as a German in the Olympics. She included in the statement that she also intended to visit her family, an attempt, perhaps, to draw attention to them, making them safe, by putting them in the light of public scrutiny. The fencer refused to discuss the matter with anyone.

Helene journeyed from her adopted California home to Berlin for the Olympic Games in 1936. There, she was pleasantly surprised to find, she was being portrayed as a national hero. "Helene Mayer" souvenir figurines were selling at shops throughout the city. When she fenced at last, her bouts were the most keenly watched. While America's black Jesse Owens outran his Aryan competitors, the half-Jewish girl racked up win after win. In her last encounter in the tournament, a bout called "the most dramatic fencing match of the age," she was barely defeated — 5 touches to 4 — by European fencing champion Ilona Schacher-Elek of Hungary.

Finally, when the points were tallied, Schacher-Elek was declared the winner of the tournament. Helene was in second place. The defending Olympic champion, Austrian fencer Ellen Preis, took third.

While speculating on sports contest outcomes is, at best, no more than "armchair quarterbacking," one wonders, minus the many distractions and worries of the previous months, what the outcome of this contest might have been for Helene Mayer.

Whatever the case, Helene took the situation as a personal defeat. She went home from Germany determined to come back on top. A year later, using virtually all her savings, she entered the World Championships in Paris, France. Now, in top form, she defeated all opponents, including the 1936 Olympic winner Ilona Schacher-Elek. Satisfied with her performance as a proven champion, Helene issued a statement that she was permanently retiring from international competition. She would not fence for Germany ever again.

Yet, Helene Mayer was not to give up the sword. In the U.S.A., she was virtually an unstoppable force. Between 1934 and 1947, she entered the Nationals nine times. She took home eight championship titles. Her only loss came in 1947. She was edged out of first place in her last bout of the tournament, losing, according to *American Fencing Magazine*, "to an inspired Helene Dow."

It was time, Helene decided, to give up competitive fencing all together. She was 37 years old, an antique in the sports world. Better to leave on top, with dignity.

She fenced on a casual basis for a number of years at the San Francisco school of her longtime friend Hans Halberstadt. With characteristic enthusiasm, and an eye for excellence, she helped guide the skills and careers of young fencers. Those who met her in the school marveled at her still great talent.

In 1951, now in her early 40s, Helene was diagnosed as having breast cancer. The following year, she returned to her homeland for treatment and to be near her family. She married for the first time, to a Stuttgart engineer. A year later, in 1953, she died.

In 1954, a new annual international fencing event was begun, the Helene Mayer Memorial Women's Foil Tournament. It has been held regularly ever since. And, in 1968, with its past indiscretions forgotten, West Germany honored its most brilliant fencing star by issuing a "Helene Mayer" postage stamp to commemorate the Mexico Olympics.

Still, in spite of her raging talent and her uncompromising spirit, the questions remain. Did Helene fence for Nazi Germany of her own free will and thereby turn against her ancestry? Was she, in fact, coerced by a corrupt German government that was shortly to go into the business of wholesale slaughter? Or did she compete at the behest of the American government, functioning as a propaganda tool against Nazi superiority?

The questions will remain unanswered forever. Helene Mayer, the best woman fencer of her time, never told anyone.

AMERICA'S FENCING MASTER

Giorgio Santelli will always be remembered as America's premier fencing coach. He was both loved and respected by everyone who knew him. His legacy — in the form of countless champion fencers and teachers personally trained by him — continues to influence the sport, even a decade after his death.

Son of the illustrious master Italo Santelli, one of the principle shapers of the Hungarian style of sabre technique, Giorgio Santelli was born in 1897. He began studying fencing six years later. He once pointed out that when he was a young man, people learned to fence not for the sake of sport, but because they might have to one day fight a duel.

By the time he was 25, Giorgio had won the Hungarian sabre championship; also, the Austrian foil and sabre championships. By the time he was 27, he had fought one duel. Following in his father's footsteps, he started teaching at the age of 28.

In 1924, Giorgio came to the United States at the invitation of the New York Athletic Club, then the center of fencing in the United States, to take the post of their number one fencing master. Much later, he established his own school, Salle Santelli.

Over the years, Santelli also found time to coach five U.S. Olympic fencing teams (1928, 1932, 1936, 1948 and 1952), three of which produced medals. He

Five time U.S. Olympic fencing team coach
Giorgio Santelli

also trained numerous U.S. nationally-ranked competitors, including Albert Alexrod and Dean Cetrulo.

Santelli was less a teacher of theories than of simple practical skills. He admitted that he must have frustrated some of his more analytical students, but that he nevertheless managed to create enough champions along the way to bear out the validity of his system.

His philosophy of fencing was basic and to the point. To his way of thinking, in competition, a fencer should simply fence to his best ability, with the same mental calmness he might employ in friendly bouts at his fencing school. "After all," he observed, "victory should not mean too much. It is when you measure up to what you have got and have the ability to bring it out in yourself which should give you the real inner satisfaction."

Santelli, like most dedicated masters of fencing, never came close to retiring. While age slowed him down somewhat, to give up the focus of his long life would have been an impossibility.

In 1984, he noted with humor, "Being my age, I cannot move very fast. But the moment I put a foil in my hand, I start to move. I get a kick seeing myself hopping around."

Giorgio Santelli died in November, 1985.

THE FRENCH CONNECTION

Lucien Gaudin (1886-1934) has been called the greatest practitioner of the classical French School of fencing who ever lived. He was, in the words of British master Felix Bertrand, "poetry in motion."

Gaudin had a long and illustrious fencing career in both France and internationally. And he was much loved as a national hero by his countrymen.

In 1911, Gaudin crossed swords with Italy's most talented fencer Nedo Nadi and handed him his first international defeat. The Frenchman was at his height as a fencer from the years 1910 to 1914.

Some years later, Gaudin fought a much publicized match with Nedo Nadi's younger brother Aldo in what was once described as "the greatest fencing match of modern times." In a contest that lasted 1 hour, 20 minutes, Gaudin won 20 touches to 11. Nadi later complained about the judging, and some experts agreed that Gaudin should have had an advantage in touches by no more than two. Three at most. Yet, the fact remains that these two giants of fencing — the most talented interpreters of their respective schools — had certainly given the world its money's worth in their pairing on the fencing strip that day.

Gaudin became the only other fencer besides Cuban Ramon Fonst to win both the individual foil and épée events in a single Olympics (1928). He was 41 years old at the time of these wins. This, of course, was, and is, an advanced age for any internationally competitive fencer.

The masterful French fencing champion Lucien Gaudin (photo courtesy of the collection of Ralph Faulkner)

Other Gaudin Olympic efforts include: Team Foil (1920), second place; Team Foil (1924), first place; Team Foil (1928), second place; and Team Épée (1924), first place.

In addition to these achievements, Gaudin was the European (World) Épée champion in 1921. He was also a many time fencing champion of France.

The Frenchman's premature death in 1934, at the age of 48, was mourned by the entire fencing world.

KING OF THE SWASHBUCKLERS

From his earliest days in film, Errol Flynn was recognized as the best swashbuckling actor in Hollywood. While he was rarely praised by the critics for his dramatic work, it was said of Flynn that no one could handle a sword, wear a costume or woo a lady like he did.

Film fencing master Ralph Faulkner worked twice with Errol Flynn. They first met in 1935. "I doubled for Errol in *Captain Blood*, the movie that made him a star. Later, we crossed blades in *The Sea Hawk*, which was done in 1940. It's one of his best films."

Added Faulkner, "Most people underrated Flynn. But he never failed to impress me. In those days, he had a memory like an elephant's. He could remember duels, move for move, even after we'd laid off of them for days at a time. That's not an easy thing to do. I never tried to remember them. I always wrote everything down."

While never a real fencer in the competitive sense, Errol Flynn was a natural athlete who was able to look good with a weapon in his hand. Other films in which he wielded a sword include *The Prince and the Pauper* (1937), *The Adventures of Robin Hood* (1938), *The Adventures of Don Juan* (1949), *Against All Flags* (1952), *Master of Ballantrae* (1953), *Crossed Swords* (1953) and *The Warriors* (1955).

A man without much personal discipline, Errol Flynn died in 1959, at the age of 50, from a life of extreme dissipation. Yet, the legacy of his greatest swashbuckler films continue to impose their magical influence on the public's recognition of fencing even to this day.

Movie swordsman Errol Flynn
(from the collection of Ralph Faulkner)

Confident, aggressive and contentious, Sewell Shurtz was the greatest of fencing master Ralph Faulkner's male fencers. A winner of numerous championships over the years, he, more than any other student, was the embodiment of the clean, dynamic Faulkner style of fencing.

Sewell Shurtz began fencing at the age of five, in 1938. He took up the sport for reasons of health. He says, "I was round shouldered, pot-bellied, and doctors believed I had some degree of rickets." His fencing training began at Falcon Studios with Ralph Faulkner, and before long, he was a premiere student.

Shurtz started competing at the age of 14 and was soon firmly demonstrating his fencing skill, capturing many fencing honors. In the Pacific Coast Championships, he was the first fencer to win all three open events — foil, épée and sabre — in the same year. In 1954, he became the first West Coast-based fencer to win the National Épée title in 67 years. He won other prestigious tournaments as well, including the Cathcart Men's Épée Tournament and the Bowen Handicap Foil Tournament.

Sewell Shurtz in a classic pose (Courtesy of Sewell Shurtz — Official U.S. Navy Photo)

On a national level, he made a number of impressive showings. In 1954, he placed first in Individual Épée at the U.S. Nationals. At the 1956 Nationals, he placed first in Foil and third in Épée.

Shurtz was also a strong international competitor. In 1955, at the Mexico City Pan-American Games, he placed second in the Individual Épée event and second in Team Épeé. That same year, he placed llth in Foil at the World Championships, in Rome, Italy. In 1956, he placed first in both Individual Foil and Épée in the Canada/U.S. Championships. He also competed in the 1956 Olympic Games in Melbourne, Australia, his team taking fourth in the Team Foil competition.

In describing his life in fencing, Sewell Shurtz cannot separate the sport from his love and admiration for his teacher. "Mr. Faulkner was my surrogate father," he confesses. "He basically raised me. All my success in life is due to his training. Without the Boss, there would have been nothing." He credits Faulkner with developing his sense of integrity and honesty, and molding his love of competition.

Of fencing, Sewell Shurtz says simply, "God, I love this sport!"

A.K.A. SPEEDY

At the height of her fencing career, it was said of Polly Craus that she had the fastest footwork of any woman fencer in the world.

Polly Craus began fencing in 1940, at the age of 16. She came to Ralph Faulkner's Falcon Studios as an assistant to a little theatre group and stayed on for the swordplay. She paid for her lessons by doing work around the school, and as Maestro Faulkner recalled, "doing it on the double."

In less than two years, Polly was a member of Faulkner's Junior Pacific Coast fencing team. Before long, she also took the Pacific Coast Junior and Intermediate Individual Women's Fencing Championships.

In 1946, Polly placed fourth in the U.S. Nationals, her first such major tournament. As Faulkner later noted, "She created a sensation by her tremendous speed, unlimited vitality and wonderful sportsmanship."

U.S. fencing champion and Olympian Polly Craus
(courtesy of Polly Craus August)

In the coming years Polly Craus became the leading woman member of a number of Falcon fencing teams that competed in the U.S. Nationals. In 1947, her team missed winning the championship of the United States by one touch. The following year, however, her team came away with the National title. This was repeated in 1949, 1950 and 1951.

The year of 1948 was a landmark year for Polly. She tied for third place in the National's Individual Foil event. Furthermore, she was chosen to compete as a member of the United States fencing team at the World Team Championships in The Hague, Holland. In these matches, she performed better than any of her six teammates, winning a total of

20 bouts (her nearest teammate won 13). During her bouts, she met and decisively defeated Ilona Schacher-Elek, one of the greatest Olympic fencing champions of all time. She also traveled to London, England, as a member of the U.S. Olympic team.

In 1949, Polly capped her national fencing career by finally winning the U.S. Individual Women's Fencing title.

Other fencing achievements included winning the right to represent the U.S. at the 1951 Pan-American Games, an honor she eventually was forced to decline due to work commitments. She also won a spot on the 1952 Helsinki, Finland-bound U.S. Olympic Team and the 1952 U.S. World Team, which competed in Copenhagen, Denmark.

After a dynamic fencing career spanning 13 years, Polly retired from organized fencing to devote herself full-time to husband and family.

Said Polly Craus of her fencing, "Fencing was a great benefit to my life. Through Mr. Faulkner's constant encouragement and great coaching, it helped me build a strong sense of self-confidence. This was very important for me because I suffered from dyslexia. Fencing also helped give me an identity and earned me respect. In my professional life — I was a script supervisor for MGM and other movie studios — fencing provided me with the mental tools of observation and planning, which aided me immensely on the job. My life would have been much different, I'm sure, had I not become a fencer."

MAESTRO AND SCHOLAR

William Gaugler is a professor of classical archaeology and a fencing master. While this might seem rather incongruous to the casual observer — the man of the mind versus the man of action (a kind of Indiana Jones duality of identity) — for Dr. Gaugler, the two seem a rather natural combination. The classical quality of fencing's artful methodology and its scientific search for truth appeal greatly to his sense of scholarly order.

The seed of fencing was planted in William Gaugler as a child by his German father, who told him stories of his own fencing experiences in the Bavarian army before World War I. His interest was further stimulated by regular visits to a fencing school located near his home in Detroit. The clash of blades and the blur of white garbed fencers was a siren's call to his young mind. He also read books on fencing, as many as he could locate.

Fencing master and university professor William Gaugler
(courtesy William M. Gaugler, La scienza della scherma {Bologna: Zanichelli, 1992})

All the while, his father continued to encourage his fencing interests. "He first taught me to execute a circular parry," Gaugler says, "and to elude this with a feint direct and deceive." But it was Aldo Nadi's impressive fencing book, *On Fencing* (1943), that finally tipped the scales, prompting him once and for all to take up the sword.

Still, it was some time before he actually took the plunge. As Gaugler explains, "Despite my great interest in swordplay, I had to wait until I was 24 before I could receive professional instruction. After finishing my undergraduate studies in Chicago, I moved to Los Angeles, where I was accepted by Maestro Aldo Nadi as a student. This was in 1956. Between 1956 and 1958, I took lessons regularly from the Maestro and participated in the weekly controlled fencing encounters he organized for purposes of observation and criticism."

In time, Gaugler became a close personal friend of the great teacher and fencer.

A move to Europe with his wife and daughter in 1956 to pursue his archaeological studies took Gaugler away from his lessons with Nadi, but this in no way interfered with the advancement of his fencing education.

"In Cannes, I studied fencing with faculty members of the French Military Fencing Masters School at Antibes. Then, I spent some time working with Maitre Edmond Durrieu in Monaco. After that, when I was in Florence, I trained for six years with Maestro Ettore Spezza."

Finally, Gaugler became a teaching assistant of Maestro Amilcare Angelini, in Frankfort, Germany.

On returning to the United States, Gaugler taught fencing privately for some time.

A few years later, however, the scholar was back in Rome, where he completed his preparation to become an accredited professional fencing master. Under the tutelage of two great Italian masters, Giorgio Pessina (president of the Italian Fencing Masters Association) and Umberto Di Paola (director of the Fencing Masters Preparatory Course at the National Institute of Physical Education), he immersed himself in the pedagogy of the Italian school of fencing.

In 1976, he took and passed the fencing master's examination at the Accademia Nazionale di Scherma of Naples. Then, from 1976 to 1979, he taught privately again.

Perhaps William Gaugler's greatest achievement in fencing came in 1979, when he initiated the Military Fencing Masters Program at San Jose State University in California, where aspiring fencers could come to earn legitimate degrees as teachers of the art of fencing. This internationally recognized course — which covers all aspects of fencing — has produced more than a few accomplished masters since its inception. It is, to date, the only successful long-term program of its kind in the United States.

Gaugler explains his specific fascination for fencing, "It is the science of swordplay that interests me the most. As far as I am concerned, there is only one kind of fencing — classical swordplay based on dueling practices."

"Science" and "classical" are the key words of his approach. To the inquiring mind of the scholar, it is the time-tested methods of fencing that bear the greatest potential for study, for it is through this avenue that the secrets of fencing might be unlocked, exposing the treasure beneath.

Of fencing in general Gaugler notes, "Since 1956, when I first became a student of Maestro Aldo Nadi, fencing has played an important role in my life. It has been both a source of personal satisfaction and a challenge to my technical mind. It also serves admirably as a counterbalance to the sedentary existence I lead as a scholar and university professor."

He has written one book on fencing, *Fechten*, published in Germany in 1983. Since then it has been translated into both English, *Fencing Everyone* (1987), and Italian, *La scienza della scherma* (1992). He has also written a fencing dictionary, *Fencing Terminology* (1995), plus numerous scholarly articles on fencing history and methodology.

William Gaugler has proven that fencing is much more than a mere sport. He has shown, through his dedication and diligence, how a scholarly interest can form a basis for an understanding of fencing that is both thorough and practical. He is living proof that the science of fencing, that calculated mingling of mind and sword, is something that can bring stimulation and enlightenment to last a lifetime.

THE MODERN MUSKETEER

Peter Westbrook is perhaps the best sabre fencer the United States has ever produced, which seems a remarkable outcome for someone who was initially steered into fencing by his mother merely to keep him off the streets and away from the seamier elements he was encountering daily in his neighborhood.

To begin with, to encourage his interest in fencing, his mother offered him five dollars for every fencing lesson he took. But, before long, bribes were unnecessary. A highly competitive teenager, Westbrook took to fencing immediately. In time he became one of the leading members of the powerhouse New York Fencer's Club.

By the time he was 22, in 1974, Peter was the National sabre champion of the United States. Since then, he has won 11 more such titles (1975, 1979, 1980, 1981,1982, 1983, 1984, 1985, 1986, 1988 and 1989), a record.

Westbrook has been a member of five U. S. Olympic fencing teams: 1976 (Montreal), 1980 (Moscow), 1984 (Los Angeles), 1988 (Seoul) and 1992 (Barcelona). At the 1984 games in Los Angeles, he performed an almost unthinkable feat for a modern American fencer, winning a bronze medal in the individual sabre event against stiff competition from Italy, France and Germany. He was the first U.S. fencer to garner an Olympic fencing medal in 24 years.

Peter Westbrook continues to fence for the United States as a member of its elite international team. Moreover, on a personal note, he has founded the Peter Westbrook Foundation to teach fencing to inner-city youth in New York City.

United States fencing champion and Oympic medal winner Peter Westbrook (courtesy of the USFA)

PART XI
THE SECRET OF
SUCCESS

THE FIRE

There once was a young, aspiring fencer who had an opportunity to bout before a renowned maestro. Giving his fencing his most heartfelt effort for over an hour, the young man paused at last for the master's hoped-for approval.

"Well, how was I?" he implored. "Was I good?"

If the young man was given the encouragement he desired, he would dedicate his life to fencing. In time, he hoped to become a national champion, maybe even an Olympic competitor. After that, he would strive to become a fencing master.

The old man, who had sat quietly and impassively during the fencing, looked squarely at the young swordsman and said, "You lack the fire."

The young man was crestfallen. He rushed away, sold his equipment and immediately found employment with a large corporation. He forgot about fencing.

Years later, the would-be champion, now the president of his own successful company, ran into the old master at a society function.

"You changed my life," the businessman told him. "I was crushed when you told me I'd never make it as a fencer, but I finally accepted it. Today, because of what you said to me, I'm a man of business instead of a man of the sword. But tell me, how could you tell so easily that I lacked the fire?"

"Oh, I hardly watched your fencing," the old master explained. "That's what I say to everyone who fences for me — that they lack the fire."

The businessman staggered back, barely able to comprehend what he'd just heard. "What? How could you do that to me! Perhaps I could have been a great champion, a master, another Santelli or Faulkner or Elthes."

The old man shook his head.

"You don't understand. If you had the fire, really had it, so that it burned inside you with an unquenchable passion, you would have paid no attention to what I said to you. You'd have stuck with fencing, no matter what. You gave up the first time your dream was challenged. You, young man, answered your own question."

"Oh," said the former fencer.

The secret of success is now before you.

A FINAL THOUGHT

Every day, people find ways to indulge their fantasies with instant gratification — movies, dice-tossing adventure games, computer programs, role-playing societies, video games and even novels. Be what you want to be instantly. All you have to do is think it.

Fast-food world.

To me, the hard-won reality of mastery in one of life's difficult pursuits is the ultimate high. To take on a task, accept what it dishes out, and make it yours is what existence is about.

The doing.

The experience.

To put yourself on the line, to go beyond simple knee-jerk reactions of the everyday hum-drum, to rise to the occasion, to dredge up the best you have to offer and to look back on what you've done and say, "I did that."

Fencing is one path to this end.

APPENDIX I
FENCING TERMS

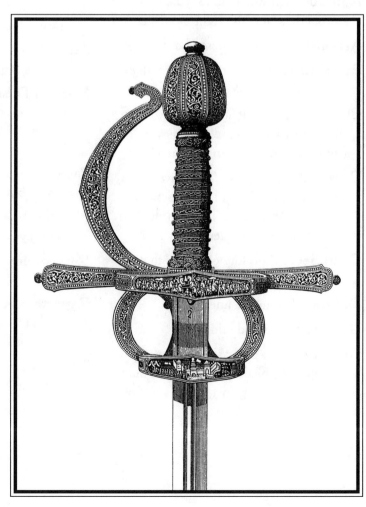

ASSORTED FENCING TERMS

Angulation: An arm and blade movement that incorporates an exaggerated angle in its presentation. It may be employed in an attack, a parry or counterattack.

Appel: A stamp of the front foot.

Apropos: The ability to execute an action properly at just the right moment.

Assault: A friendly fencing bout.

Balestra: An attack comprising a slight forward jump followed by a lunge.

Body Evasion: Attempting to avoid an incoming attack simply by moving out of its way rather than parrying.

Caver: Meaning "cave," the caver is an attack angled around an opponent's blade. The space in between the two blades is the aforementioned cave.

Coup Sec: A meeting of blades that is both crisp and firm.

Dedans: The inside line.

Dehors: The outside line.

Derobement: An evasive slide off an opponent's blade. Such a move may be performed against either an offensive action or a parry.

Dessous: The low line.

Dessus: The high line.

Finalé: The last portion of an offensive action.

Flick: A forceful whipping of the foil blade employed offensively.

Invalid Parry: A parry that does not sufficiently divert an incoming blade away from your target area.

Jour: An opening into which an attack may be launched.

Parry of Despair: Any parry made out of a sense of panic. Because it is reactive in the extreme, it will always be of a muscular nature.

Passé: Where the point of a blade slides along, but never hits directly.

Plaqué: Where the point of a blade hits sideways and flat.

Rassemblement: Bringing your feet together.

Reparteé: Repeated jabbing motions made by extending and withdrawing the sword arm.

Tac: A parry that immediately detaches from the blade it has stopped.

Tempo: Timing.

Touché: A touch.

PRONUNCIATIONS

Appel (a-pel)

Apropos (ap-ro-po)

Attaque (at-ac)

Battement (bat-ma)

Caver (cav-ay)

Contre (con-tra)

Corps-a-Corps (kor-a-kor)

Coulé (ku-lay)

Coup (ku)

Coup d'arrêt (ku dar-ay)

Coupé (ku-pay)

Croisé (qwah-zeh)

Dedans (deh-dah)

Dégage (deg-a-zheh)

Dehors (de-or)

Dessous (deh-soo)

Dessus (deh-see)

Doublé (du-blay)

Derobement (de-robe-ma)

Développment (de-vel-op-ma)

Enveloppement (en-vel-op-ma)

Épée (epp-ay)

Fer (fair)

Fleche (flesh)

Foil (foy-el)

Froissement (f roys-ma)

Garde (gard)

Liement (lee-a-ma)

Octave (ock-tav)

Passé (pass-ay)

Plaqué (pla-kay)

Prime (preem)

Quarte (kart)

Quinte (kant)

Rassemblement (ras-em-bleh-ma)

Redoublement (re-du-bleh-ma)

Remise (rem-ees)

Reprise (re-pre-z)

Riposte (rip-ost)

Sabre (sab-er)

Seconde (sec-own)

Septime (sep-teem)

Sixte (see-s)

Tierce (tier-s)

Touché (too-shay)

APPENDIX II
RESOURCES

THE UNITED STATES FENCING ASSOCIATION

Founded in 1891 as the Amateur Fencers League of America to develop and promote the sport of fencing in the United States, the U.S. Fencing Association has proven itself worthy to its task.

For over 100 years, the USFA has held fencing tournaments, disseminated fencing information to the public, sponsored fencing camps and clinics and supported international U.S. fencing efforts.

Moreover, since the late 1940s, the USFA has produced a magazine, *American Fencing*. Once little more than a dry, technical journal, this publication has lately evolved in to a slick, stylish collection of articles, photos and drawings highlighting not just the sport of fencing, but also history, movies and occasionally, literature. The reading of *American Fencing* should be a must for every budding fencer.

For more information concerning the United States Fencing Association, write to:

The United States Fencing Association
1 Olympic Plaza
Colorado Springs, CO 80909

FENCING EQUIPMENT SUPPLY COMPANIES

Not every fencer is lucky enough to live in a city where he can simply run down to the local fencing equipment emporium and pick up that extra foil, mask or jacket. The vast majority of fencers, in fact, live nowhere near such businesses and must, therefore, purchase their gear through mail order outlets. This, of course, is a highly acceptable method of obtaining the necessities of fencing. And, because of the knowledgeable individuals these places usually employ, one is fairly assured of satisfaction in these transactions.

All fencing equipment supply houses have detailed catalogues from which to order. To be safe, I think it is best to have two or three separate sources to draw upon. That way you can be sure of obtaining not only the best equipment for your needs, but the best prices.

I have purchased equipment this way for most of my fencing career — especially since I moved to the middle of the Missouri Ozark Mountains. Talk about remote!

The following is a current list of fencing equipment suppliers:

American Fencers Supply
1180 Folsom Street
San Francisco, CA 94103

Blade Fencing Equipment
212 W. 15th Street
New York, NY 10011

Blue Gauntlet Fencing Gear, Inc.
246 Ross Ave.
Hackensack, NJ 07601

Colonial Distributing Fencing Equipment
N77 W7287 Oak Street
P.O. Box 636
Cedarburg, WI 53012

George Santelli, Inc.
465 South Dean St.
Englewood, NJ 07631

Herb Obst Agency
CP 788 NDG Station
Montreal, QC., H4A 3S2, Canada

Physical Chess, Inc.
622 Route 10, Unit #6
Wippany, NJ 07981

Southern California Fencers Equipment Co.
16131 Balerio
Van Nuys, CA 91406

Triplette Competition Arms
162 West Pine Street
Mt. Airy, NC 27030

Vintage Sporting Equipment
P.O. Box 364
Sheboygan, WI 53082

THE SWASHBUCKLER FILM: FENCING IN THE MOVIES

Movies have always been fencing's most visible form of advertising. From the jaunty silent films of Douglas Fairbanks to the most recent epic staring Hollywood's latest "heroic" hunk, the swashbuckler film has kept sword fighting in front of the public, without pause, since its inception.

The best films, stimulating our fantasies and feeding our sense of daring, have inspired many of us to take up the sword for real. The worst films, laughable at best and boring at worst, are, like most mediocrities, quickly forgotten. There are always more of these clunkers, unfortunately, than classics; but the awful productions do serve to remind us how great the latter really are.

Movie fencing is not, of course, a representation of real fencing. Nor should it necessarily be. It merely suggests at that reality. It is there, after all, to thrill, not to educate.

The following is a short list of some of the more noted films in which fencing plays a significant part:

The Mark of Zorro (1920), Douglas Fairbanks

The Three Musketeers (1921), Douglas Fairbanks

The Black Pirate (1926), Douglas Fairbanks

Don Juan (1926), John Barrymore

The Iron Mask (1929), Douglas Fairbanks

Captain Blood (1935), Errol Flynn

The Three Musketeers (1935), Water Abel

The Prince and the Pauper (1937), Errol Flynn

The Prisoner of Zenda (1937), Ronald Colman

The Adventures of Robin Hood (1938), Errol Flynn

The Mark of Zorro (1940), Tyrone Power

The Sea Hawk (1940), Errol Flynn

The Corsican Brothers (1941), Douglas Fairbanks, Jr.

The Black Swan (1942), Tyrone Power

Frenchman's Creek (1944)

The Bandit of Sherwood Forest (1946), Cornell Wilde

The Exile (1946), Douglas Fairbanks, Jr.

The Three Musketeers (1948), Gene Kelly

Black Magic (1949), Orson Welles

The Adventures of Don Juan (1949), Errol Flynn

Cyrano de Bergerac (1950), Jose Ferrer

Anne of the Indies (1951), Jean Peters

At Sword's Point (1952), Cornel Wilde

Scaramouche (1952), Stewart Granger

The Prisoner of Zenda (1952), Stewart Granger

The Court Jester (1956), Danny Kaye

El Cid (1961), Charleton Heston

Jason and the Argonauts (1963), Todd Armstrong

The Great Race (1965), Tony Curtis

The Three Musketeers (1974), Michael York

Royal Flash (1975), Malcolm McDowell

The Four Musketeers (1975), Michael York

The Duellists (1977), Keith Carradine

My Favorite Year (1982), Peter O'Toole

Conan the Barbarian (1982), Arnold Schwarzenegger

The Highlander (1985), Christopher Lambert

The Princess Bride (1987), Mandy Patinkin

Robin Hood Prince of Thieves (1991), Kevin Costner

Hook (1991), Robin Williams

Robin Hood: Men in Tights (1993), Cary Elwes

By the Sword (1993), Eric Roberts

Braveheart (1995), Mel Gibson

Cutthroat Island (1995), Geena Davis

The best books dealing with fencing in the movies include: *The Films of Errol Flynn*, by Tony Thomas, Rudy Behlmer and Clifford McCarty (Citadel Press: New York, 1969); *Swordsmen of the Screen*, by Jeffrey Richards (Routledge & Kegan Paul: Boston, 1977); *Cads and Cavaliers*, by Tony Thomas (A. S. Barnes: New Jersey, 1979); and *The Encyclopedia of the Sword*, by Nick Evangelista (Greenwood Press: Connecticut, 1995).

Ronald Colman in The Prisoner of Zenda *(from the collection of Ralph Faulkner)*

LITERATURE OF THE SWORD

Over the years, there have been countless novels in which fencing, in one form or another, has played an important role. The sword has proven itself an integral literary plot device to stimulate change, conflict and resolution.

Novels in which the sword has played an important role include:

Don Quixote (1605), Miguel de Cervantes

Tom Jones (1749), Henry Fielding

Ivanhoe (1822), Sir Walter Scott

The Three Musketeers (1844), Alexandre Dumas

An illustration from a nineteeth century edition of The Three Musketeers *by Alexandre Dumas*

Lorna Doone (1869), R. D. Blackmore

Kidnapped (1886), Robert Louis Stevenson

Men of Iron (1892), Howard Pyle

The Prisoner of Zenda (1894), Anthony Hope

Princess of Mars (1917), Edgar Rice Burroughs

Captain Blood (1922), Rafael Sabatini

Conan the Conqueror (1935), Robert E. Howard

Master-At-Arms (1940), Rafael Sabatini

Frenchman's Creek (1941), Daphne du Maurier

The Adventurer (1950), Mika Waltari

The Glory Road (1963), Robert Heinlein

The Hobbit (1965), J.R.R. Tolkien

Royal Flash (1970), George MacDonald Fraser

The Princess Bride (1973), William Goldman

The Seven-Per-Cent Solution (1974), Nicholas Meyer

The Miko (1984), Eric Van Lustbader

The Bastard Prince (1994), Katherine Kurtz

The literature of the sword is discussed in detail in my book *The Encyclopedia of the Sword* (Greenwood Press: Connecticut, 1995).

BOOKS ABOUT FENCING: A SELECTED READING LIST

There are a number of fine books dealing with the subject of fencing that, as companions to your lessons and bouting, can shed much light on the process at hand. Gleaning from the minds of those who have gone before you is always a useful thing.

Some of the books mentioned here are more advanced than others. Some are easy reading. Some lean more to the historical. Some focus primarily on sport. Yet, in building a sense of what fencing truly is, no aspect should be ignored.

The following is a short list of some of the more interesting and useful fencing-related books I've encountered over the years. A few are long out of print and will be almost impossible to find, but will be well worth the search if you do manage to dig them up. Others may be found more easily. Some are being sold at this very moment.

Aylward, J. D., *The House of Angelo*. London: The Batchworth Press, 1953.

Aylward, J. D., *The English Master of Armes from the Twelfth to the Twentieth Century*. London: Routledge and Kegan Paul, 1956.

Angelo, Domenico, *The School of Fencing*. London: H. Angelo, 1787 edition. Reprinted: New York: Land's End Press, 1971.

Baldick, Robert, *The Duel*. New York: Spring Books, 1965.

Barbasetti, Luigi, *The Art of the Foil*, with a Short History of Fencing. New York: E. P. Dutton, 1933.

Beaumont, Charles de, *Fencing Technique in Pictures*. London: Hulton Press, 1955.

Bertrand, Leon, *The Fencer's Companion*. London: Gale and Polden, 1939.

Burton, Richard F., *The Book of the Sword*. London: Chatto and Windus, 1884. Reprinted: New York: Dover Publications, 1987.

Castle, Egerton, *Schools and Masters of Fence*. London: George Bell, 1885. Reprinted: Pennsylvania: George Shumway, 1969.

Castello, Julio, *Theory of Fencing*. Boston: Bruce Humphries, 1931.

Evangelista, Nick, *The Encyclopedia of the Sword*. Connecticut: Greenwood Press, 1995.

Garret, Maxwell, Emmanuel Kaidanov, and Gil Pezza, *Foil, Sabre, and Épée Fencing.* Pennsylvania: Penn State Press, 1994.

Gaugler, William, *Fencing Everyone.* North Carolina: Hunter Textbooks, 1987.

Gaugler, William, *A Dictionary of Universally Used Fencing Terminology.* Sunrise, Florida: Laureate Press, 1995

Hobbs, William, *Techniques of the Stage Fight.* London: Studio Vista, 1967.

Hutton, Alfred, *The Sword and the Centuries.* London: Grant Richards, 1901. Reprinted: New York: Barnes and Noble, 1995.

Kogler, Aladar, *Preparing the Mind.* Lake Zurich, Illinois: CounterParry Press, 1993.

Morton, E. D., *The Martini A-Z of Fencing.* London: Queen Anne Press, 1992.

Musashi, Miyamoto (Translated by Victor Harris), *A Book of Five Rings.* Reprinted: New York: The Overlook Press 1974.

Nadi, Aldo, *On Fencing.* New York: G. P. Putnam, 1943. Reprinted: Sunrise, Florida: Laureate Press, 1994.

Nadi, Aldo, *The Living Sword.* Sunrise, Florida: Laureate Press, 1995.

Palffy-Alpar, Julius, *Sword and Masque.* Philadelphia: F. A. Davis, 1967.

Selberg, Charles, *The Revised Foil.* Ashland, Oregon: Spotted Dog Press, 1993.

Stone, George Cameron, *A Glossary of the Construction, Decoration, and Use of Arms and Armor.* New York: Jack Brussel, 1961.

Szabo, Laszlo, *Fencing and the Master.* Hungary: Franklin House, 1982.

Thimm, Carl, *A Complete Bibliography of Fencing and Duelling.* London: John Lane, 1896. Reprinted: New York: James A. Cummings Booksellers, 1992.

Vebell, Edward, *The Sports Illustrated Book of Fencing.* Philadelphia: J. B. Lippincott, 1962.

Wise, Arthur, *Weapons in the Theatre.* New York: Barnes and Noble, 1968.

Wise, Arthur, *The Art and History of Personal Combat.* New York: Arma Press, 1971.

Fencer J. Christoph Amberger publishes a magazine devoted to the literature and history of fencing, *Hammerterz Forum.* This interesting, insightful and highly readable publication highlights, in essay form, the lore of fencing and dueling. It is a must for anyone who is fascinated by the multifaceted world of the sword. For more information, write to: Hammerterz Verlag, P.O. Box 13448, Baltimore, MD 21202.

APPENDIX III
THEATRICAL
FENCING

THEATRICAL FENCING

Fencing on stage or in the movies is nothing like real fencing. Most actions, to be dramatic, must be overstated in the extreme. Film fencing master Fred Cavens, who directed the swordplay in such classic movies as *The Adventures of Robin Hood* (1938) and *The Mark of Zorro* (1940), once observed, "For the screen, in order to be well photographed and also grasped by the audience, all swordplay should be so telegraphed with emphases that the audience will see what is coming. All movements — instead of being as small as possible, as in competitive fencing — must be large..."

This is the nature of theatrics.

Nevertheless, I suggest to any actor in need of sword-related skills — whether for stage or film — that he begin his education in standard fencing training. The more an actor understands the whys and wherefores of fencing, the better he will be able to translate his theatrical chores into meaningful, effective action. Interjecting a sense of purpose, of intent, into his movement, he will create swordplay that is both credible and fun to watch.

Furthermore, true fencing skill breeds self-confidence, which, of course, always translates into safe behavior. When actors know where their blades should be at all times, no one gets hurt.

In the end, an ability to handle a sword should be a skill every actor automatically brings to his trade. Rather than being a last minute acquisition, an afterthought, fencing should be an ingrained and polished attribute. When there is plenty of time to really digest it, it will always enhance, never detract. That, after all, is the nature of fencing the art.

Over my years of teaching fencing in Southern California, I taught a number of actors. Some of them, without any fencing training whatsoever, came to me after they had already been hired for an acting role that required them to use a sword with expert skill. I did my best to help them, but such a situation was always traumatic.

Once an actor came to me on a Thursday, saying that he needed to learn to fence for a movie role. "When does the film begin shooting?" I asked him. "This coming Monday, " he told me. I sighed (I sighed a lot when I worked in Hollywood). "Well," I said, "that's not much time, but we'll see what we can do." I never turned anybody down, no matter how hopeless they seemed. Then I added, "When you start work on the film, maybe you can get the film's fencing instructor to give you some extra practice time." The actor stared at me. "I'm going to be in charge of the fencing," he announced flatly. "Oh," I replied.

Said 'Fencing Master to the Stars' Ralph Faulkner of theatrical fencing, "To produce a decent film duel, you must have a thorough knowledge of swordplay and how to translate it to the stage or screen. It's vital. But in many fights staged these days, this knowledge seems to have been overlooked or thought unimportant. So you end up with nothing more than an exhibition of body movement and noise. Example — you put your blade here, and I'll put my blade there. Then we'll scream and yell and knock over some furniture. I don't think displaying an understanding of swordplay in a sword fight is too much to ask for."

When the whole thing is done right, both the actor and his audience will come out winners.

Fencing master Ralph Faulkner training actor Douglas Fairbanks, Jr. (from the collection of Ralph Faulkner)

ABOUT THE AUTHOR

Nick Evangelista has been teaching the art of fencing since 1973. Beginning his training in Hollywood with famed fencing master Ralph Faulkner, he evenually broadened his scope with an extended period of study in Europe. Opening his own school in Los Angeles in 1980, he taught both sport and theatrical fencing and acted as a consultant to the film and television industries. In 1985 he moved to the Missouri Ozark Mountains,where he started a new fencing school from scratch. Over the years, he has written numerous articles on fencing. He has also produced a 720 page reference volume covering all aspects of the sword, *The Encyclopedia of the Sword* (Greenwood Press, 1995).

Anthony De Longis (the author of the foreword) has spent over 20 years as a professional actor, combat action choreographer and teacher. He has appeared on television series such as *Star Trek Voyager*, *The Highlander* and *Kung Fu*. His film credits include *Circle of Iron* (1978), *Sword and Sorcerer* (1983), *Warrior and the Sorceress* (1985), *Masters of the Universe* (1987) and *Batman Returns* (1992). He has trained actors like David Carradine, Richard Chamberlain, Dolph Lundgren and Angelica Huston. He has held the position of staff fight choreographer for the Los Angeles Music Center Opera since 1985 and taught Fencing, Stage Combat and Character Movement in the UCLA Theater Arts Department from 1974 to 1993.